T0312571

THE GEORGE GUND FOUNDATION
IMPRINT IN AFRICAN AMERICAN STUDIES

The George Gund Foundation has endowed
this imprint to advance understanding of
the history, culture, and current issues
of African Americans.

Named in remembrance of

the onetime *Antioch Review* editor

and longtime Bay Area resident,

the Lawrence Grauman, Jr. Fund

supports books that address

a wide range of human rights,

free speech, and social justice issues.

*Shirley Chisholm in
Her Own Words*

The publisher and the University of California Press Foundation gratefully acknowledge the generous support of the George Gund Foundation Imprint in African American Studies.

The publisher and the University of California Press Foundation also gratefully acknowledge the generous support of the Lawrence Grauman, Jr. Fund.

Shirley Chisholm in Her Own Words

SPEECHES AND WRITINGS

Edited with an Introduction by
Zinga A. Fraser

UNIVERSITY OF CALIFORNIA PRESS

University of California Press
Oakland, California

© 2024 by Zinga Fraser

Library of Congress Cataloging-in-Publication Data

Names: Chisholm, Shirley, 1924-2005, author. | Fraser, Zinga A.,
    1976- editor.
Title: Shirley Chisholm in her own words : speeches and writings /
    edited with an introduction by Zinga A. Fraser.
Description: Oakland, California : University of California Press, [2024] |
    Includes bibliographical references and index.
Identifiers: LCCN 2024007623 (print) | LCCN 2024007624 (ebook) |
    ISBN 9780520386983 (cloth) | ISBN 9780520387003 (ebook)
Subjects: LCSH: Chisholm, Shirley, 1924-2005. | African American women
    politicians. | African American women—Intellectual life. | United
    States—Politics and government—20th century.
Classification: LCC E840.8.C48 A5 2024 (print) | LCC E840.8.C48
    (ebook) | DDC 305.48/896073—dc23/eng/20240314
LC record available at https://lccn.loc.gov/2024007623
LC ebook record available at https://lccn.loc.gov/2024007624

Manufactured in the United States of America

33 32 31 30 29 28 27 26 25 24
10 9 8 7 6 5 4 3 2 1

For

SHIRLEY ANN DAWSON FRASER

LEONARD D. FRASER

RUWANDA FRASER

ANNETTE P. WASHINGTON

DERIDA BRADLEY

JIM HARRISON

Contents

Photos follow page 150

Introduction

In 2019, I was interviewed for a *New York Times* article that proclaimed, "2019 Belongs to Shirley Chisholm."[1] As the first Black woman elected to Congress, who had successfully completed twenty years in elected office and public service, Shirley Chisholm had reached iconic status, albeit posthumously. The article speaks to the popular memory of Chisholm and a resurgence of interest in her life and career as evidenced in children's books, documentaries, films, upcoming biographies, and even body art. Yet she is primarily evoked as a way to discursively measure women's and Black political achievements, or lack thereof, rather than viewed as a substantive political figure in her own right.

On the cusp of another presidential campaign season and at the dawn of Chisholm's centennial birthday, we face the question of what she means in this current moment and how her legacy will be reconstructed for future generations. Chisholm's "living history" extends beyond symbolic gestures and monuments to highlight memories of her, both real and imagined.[2] In March of 2024, Participant Films and Netflix released the first feature film dedicated to Shirley Chisholm and her historic 1972 presidential run. In summer of 2024, she is being memorialized in an exhibition I am co-curating at the Museum of the City of New York titled *Changing the Face of Democracy: Shirley Chisholm at 100*. As the first exhibit dedicated solely to Shirley Chisholm, it will speak to both her substance and the symbolism that has accrued around her. Years ago I imagined that Chisholm's centennial commemoration would be an optimistic occasion as we celebrated the political progress the nation had made by continuing Chisholm's efforts to build coalitions that were antiracist, anti-imperialist, antisexist, and antiwar. I never thought that we would be in a political retrenchment. Yet the 2024 presidential campaign will undeniably be an election of two old white men dueling for their second turn at political power.

During 2020 there was short-lived jubilation over the widespread protests in response to the killings of George Floyd and Breonna Taylor and over the historic election of Vice President Kamala Harris. Harris, and more importantly the Black women who advocated for her selection, enhanced the visibility of Black women and girls who had been either ignored or vilified during the previous administration. Marking the historical moment, the first African American and South Asian woman VP candidate connected her run to her Black political foremothers like Chisholm. Simultaneously, we also saw a national racial reckoning around the Black Lives Matter movement that drove both individuals and corporations to address race, diversity, and equity. Corporations in particular tried to ensure that their brands would exhibit "social corporate responsibility" around the Black Lives Matter movement. Even Chisholm's voice and likeness emerged in media ads as a way to represent Black political independence and aspirations for the achievement of Black women globally. Corporations' attempt to connect with Black women's political and consumer power, whether or not they also sought to grapple with their own transgressions, suggests the conflicts between social justice activism and consumerism.

The state violence against Black men and women and the public support for Black Lives Matter during the spring of 2020 brought together an unprecedented multiracial and intergenerational global coalition of people who protested against the state and imperial project on everything from defunding the police to climate change, affordable housing, and workers' rights. At the height of the Black Lives Matter movement, the emergence of book clubs, workshops, reading lists, and podcasts reflected a renewed interest in an untold national history as well as how to reckon with racism and white supremacy. Academic institutions, political organizations, and corporate boards were forced to review themselves internally and externally around diversity. Very quickly, discourses around race, African American history, and critical race theory, along with public efforts to unlearn white supremacy and become "antiracist," were met with opposition by those on the right.

Yet these efforts would be short-lived because of the failed insurrection that occurred on January 6, 2021. In an effort to pivot from their losses, the GOP executed a previous playbook tactic to both distract and capitalize on their followers' angst. They began rallying against a "woke" campaign and fabricated culture wars that sought power over PTAs, school boards, and state administrations. Books and materials that had once been accessible were now being banned across the country. In this moment, despite Chisholm's historical significance, her critique of white supremacy, sexism, and colonialism and her support of Black studies would firmly place her and the books she wrote on the banned list in states like Florida, where she resided until her death. Additionally, the current attacks on Black studies by the right would have been opposed by Chisholm, who advocated for Black studies' inclusion in elementary and secondary education. She wrote extensively about the importance of Black studies as both an intellectual enterprise and a prescriptive responsibility for Black students to utilize the knowledge gained from the field that was beneficial to Black communities.

When I first began to work on Chisholm seventeen years ago, I did so using an approach to Black women's history that Deborah Gray White identifies as "mining the forgotten."[3] It quickly became evident that significant silences in the scholarship had minimized her role and that of other Black women within American political history. The frequent mining, excavating, and recycling of various accounts of Chisholm's life, rather than allowing her and her archive to establish what she said and believed, have resulted in the creation of an alternative narrative that is far from her own making. Yet the most salient engagement with Chisholm and her politics is through her own writings, speeches, and position papers. I found it essential and valuable that Chisholm speak in her own words and possibly on her own terms. This book, *Shirley Chisholm in Her Own Words*, allows her profound words to provide insight into America's conservative policies, the all-pervasive sexism in politics and society, and the siege on Black and Brown people in the U.S. and around the globe. It also holds up a model for a new cadre of political leaders, illuminating the ways Chisholm dared to be herself through words and actions.

Shirley Chisholm in Her Own Words is the first collection of Chisholm's intellectual works. Her writings, speeches, and position papers illuminate the historical moment in which she operated, capturing both her critical worldview and her urgent framing of democracy. Her words continue to be as relevant today as they were when she crafted them. This work addresses a wide audience interested in learning about the depth and breadth of Chisholm's political legacy rather than accepting superficial sketches of her life and likeness. Unlike so many of the Black women activists of her time, Chisholm left a treasure trove of records that illuminate developments beyond the time span of her own political career. By prioritizing these records, this edited volume poses two important questions: What can Chisholm tell us about the current moment in which we find ourselves? And how does her work help contribute to the Black feminist tradition, which has long been built on intellectual production and political action? To be sure, the speeches and writings collected in this volume provide only a snapshot of the larger collage that is Black women's intellectual history. As director of the Shirley Chisholm Project, it is my hope that this book sparks more questions and fosters new scholarship that engages Chisholm and her works.

In the sections that follow, Chisholm's speeches and writings are divided thematically. The eight themes are meant to identify the breadth of the subject areas that Chisholm addressed during her political career. The thematic divisions allow the reader to engage her speeches separately. Beyond the obvious themes of women's leadership and U.S. politics, the sections on criminal justice, colonialism, and youth and student revolution situate Chisholm outside her typical framing, while also providing lasting lessons. The remainder of this introduction offers historical context to Chisholm's entrance into political power, provides an analysis of Chisholm as an orator and intellectual, and rightfully situates her work within a Black feminist intellectual tradition.

Shirley Chisholm and Early Intellectual Influences

Shirley Chisholm was born on November 30, 1924, to West Indian parents from Barbados who migrated to the United States in the early 1920s. Her origin story begins with her and her sisters moving from Brooklyn to Barbados because of the economic hardship her parents faced during the Great Depression. This reverse migration and separation from her parents during her early adolescent years had a significant impact on Chisholm's worldview and would later shape her policies and writings around poverty and working-class issues. Living in Barbados with her maternal grandmother on her farm and attending British-run schools allowed Chisholm to see the influence British colonial power had on every aspect of Barbadian life. Chisholm's mother believed that her daughters would excel with a foundation in Barbados schools. In Barbados and later in Brooklyn, Chisholm was surrounded by a close-knit Black community that embraced racial pride and Black self-determination. Chisholm would attribute much of her resilience to her grandmother and the women in her family. Her father, Charles St. Hill, a laborer, followed and admired Marcus Garvey and the Universal Negro Improvement Association. Described by Chisholm as an avid reader of newspapers who engaged in kitchen table debates on international news and followed local politics, he showed by example that intellectual acts are not confined to traditional academic spaces or educated people. Excelling academically and attaining a premier education was a requirement for all the girls in the St. Hill family. Chisholm would receive honors in elementary and high school and would later receive a bachelor's degree from Brooklyn College in 1946 and a master's degree in education from Columbia University in 1952.

Collegiate life would serve as Chisholm's entryway into politics. She advocated for "Negro History" at Brooklyn College and created a Black sorority-like organization because Black women were excluded from the college's social clubs. When she entered a gendered workforce as a teacher's aide and day care administrator, she would also join local Democratic politics, which was dominated by white men. Though the North lacked the South's overt Jim Crow laws, the Brooklyn machine, like other Northern cities' political institutions, operated by what scholars Jeanne Theoharis, Brian Purnell, and Kristopher Burell describe as "Jim Crow North," a system that hid the equivalent of "de jure segregation in plain sight."[4] At the Democratic Club meetings in the Seventeenth Assembly District, Chisholm noted, "The blacks sat on one side, the whites on the other. There was not a sign that said, 'Colored Side.' It was an unwritten law. In many clubs, even in the 1940s, blacks were not welcome unless they were brought in by a white member. In the 17th A.D. club they came but they stayed in their place."[5] These political conditions were what radicalized and motivated Chisholm to participate in an insurgent politics against Kings County Democrats in the 1960s.

Having been involved in Black political clubs, Chisholm ran for her first political office by 1964. Not dissuaded by those reluctant to endorse a woman, she won a seat in the state assembly. Her legislative platform focused on implementing antipoverty measures, increasing educational aid and opportunities to low-income and minority students, and expanding day care and maternity leave. By 1968 she would run for Congress as the nation's first Black woman to sit in the House of Representatives. In her political life she was both an activist and a public intellectual.

Chisholm as Orator

Chisholm's oratorical style is as important as the content of her speeches and writings. Her oratory and delivery signaled an authenticity and compassion that connected her to broad audiences across racial, economic, gender, and class lines. As a recipient and participant in a militant political movement in New York, she embodied a younger generation's demand for a political maverick whose tone and ideas demanded political transformation. Chisholm's fiery speeches and off-the-cuff commentaries revealed a bold and unapologetic politician who did not shy away from the spotlight or confrontation. While the cultural norm for Black women, especially those in political organizations, was to operate behind the scenes, Chisholm reveled in the spotlight.[6]

This compilation of Chisholm's writings and speeches also locates her activism and intellectual work within a larger context of an African American oral tradition that challenges white supremacist rhetoric of racial inferiority and gender norms. Public oratory is at the center of the Black freedom struggle, serving as one of its most valuable weapons. Complementing judicial and legal efforts against legalized discrimination, Black American orators held up a mirror that reflected both their optimism and their skepticism about American democracy. From various sites such as the pulpits, street corners, and statehouses, Black orators inspired, motivated, and educated masses of Black people on how to fight for social, economic, and political change. Traditionally, the Black church has served as one of the few safe places for African American speech. The flamboyant preaching and rhetoric of New York politicians and activists like Adam Clayton Powell and Milton Galamison are embedded in what Black theologian James Cone identifies as the oral tradition of the Black church.[7] What is also seen in Chisholm's oratorical style is the influence of Harlem soapbox orators like Malcolm X, and other religious and secular speakers that emerged in the twentieth century. First- and second-generation Caribbean radical intellectuals who became known for their political soapbox speeches contributed to Harlem's radical intellectual scene.[8] While these influences connect to both regional and cultural distinctions, Chisholm crafted her own style that was unique to her and her experiences.

One cannot view Chisholm's speeches solely as static prose compositions. To understand the breadth of her rhetoric, one must also view her speeches as performances where she connects to her audiences through nonverbal messages, emotions, and rhythmic stylings. Chisholm understood how to use both her voice and her physicality in her public talks. Under the gaze of both patriarchy and whiteness, her fiery speeches would be heard in different ways, depending on the audience. For Black audiences, her presence would also be viewed against a traditional representation of Black womanhood. Her broad-rimmed black spectacles, perfectly coiffed wig, and colorful tailored suits reflected her respectable and fashionable presentation. Yet her presentation did not neatly correspond with her irreverent and bold speeches, which often expressed anger and radicalism. Chisholm's rhythmic cadence and faint and singsong Barbadian accent (which got louder during her most passionate moments) held an endearing quality for many listeners, especially marginalized ones. While her speeches may have been unconventional for Black leadership, she would inevitably connect to the masses and cause them to rethink mainstream political norms.

Whether in massive crowds or one-on-one, Chisholm was a master communicator who spoke about more than policies and legislation and found ways to connect to both adversaries and supporters. That attraction stemmed from their admiration of her sincerity, despite their agreements or disagreements with her on the issues. Whatever the political cost, Chisholm did not change her political stance, no matter who her audience was. During her presidential campaign she did not switch her position on hot-button issues like busing, while a majority of her liberal competitors did.[9] In her congressional speech on the topic, Chisholm condemned her congressional colleagues on the House floor, asserting,

> The fact of the matter is racism is so inherent in the bloodstream of this country that you cannot see beyond a particular limit. You are only concerned when whites are affected. If you were indeed concerned about the busing of young children for the sake of getting educational equality, your voices would have been raised years ago in terms of the fact that black and Chicano, Spanish-speaking children were getting an inferior education by being bused right past the white schools in their neighborhoods in which they lived to the dilapidated schools in the outlying districts.[10]

Young people, especially those located on college campuses, were often the audiences for her greatest enthusiasm and optimism about the possibilities of American democracy. Many of Chisholm's speeches were delivered on the campuses that she visited throughout her career. As Kansas State University president James A. McCain once proclaimed, "Behind a microphone, Mrs. Chisholm comes alive and delivers her ideas with unprepared force and emotion that shocks her listeners into realization. Her personal manner and well-chosen dialect are backed by rationalization and wit that prompts belief."[11]

Chisholm found ways to both enlighten individuals and inspire them to assert their own agency, while placing the responsibility for their political engagement squarely on their shoulders. Congresswoman Barbara Lee recalled that after hearing Chisholm speak at Mills College, she felt the need to become politically active for the first time. She remembered Chisholm being the first person to speak to her specific needs as a single mother. After the speech, Chisholm challenged Lee to register to vote as the first step in engaging in a political process and then encouraged her to join her presidential campaign. Chisholm's rhetoric empowered Lee and a host of others to connect their actions with her words.

The Power of Chisholm's Rhetoric

A significant portion of Chisholm's speeches and writings are for mal and took place during ceremonial occasions like conventions and graduations or on the House of Representatives floor. Viewing these addresses as merely ceremonial, however, only reinforces the absence of critical analysis of her oratory and rhetoric. Chisholm understood that her words mattered. Her mastery of language and rhetoric was an essential part of her creation of a successful political persona. Chisholm received invitations to give talks long after her political life ended because she was a gifted speaker and a political powerhouse. Central themes in her speeches identified the importance and strategic use of coalition building, unity, and social and political revolution within institutions of power. Chisholm pointed to the importance of self-awareness and self-knowledge for marginalized peoples. She believed that the lack of truth telling about American history played a significant role in maintaining the political servitude of the oppressed. She declared, "Oppressed people cannot remain oppressed forever. Freedom is never given by the oppressor. It must be demanded by the oppressed."[12] For Chisholm, movement building required oppressed people to understand history and their place in it. Her speeches included Black and women's history and utilized the scholarship within a newly configured Black studies discipline that sought to confront the nation's historical amnesia around slavery, suffrage, and social movements. Chisholm utilized such scholarship to challenge racist public policies stemming from Black children's academic achievement gap and the myth of Black women's maternal pathology. Her speech to students at Howard University issues this charge:

> Black teachers and scholars have lived in their own special kind of ivory tower. They must come down from it. A Black university has no room at this time for mere "academicians." It needs scholars, but they must be men of action, who are able to apply their knowledge of the world around them in which their brothers and sisters suffer, starve and die. They must hear what their community is saying, and go into it and work.[13]

Her discussion of Black studies and Black colleges was linked to cultivating black communities.

Chisholm offered a critical perspective that colonization also existed for Black people within the United States. Her speech "The Black as a Colonized Man" draws on Frantz Fanon and his essential framing of colonization as a lens to understand Black life in America. Chisholm declared, "When we talk about the Black American as a 'colonized man,' it is important to remember that he has always lived in a capitalistic democracy that has not hesitated to use violence as well."[14] Observing poverty in both Barbados and Bedford-Stuyvesant, she identified the system of capitalism as central to the exploitation of labor. Drawing on Black scholar-activists like E. Franklin Frazier, W. E. B. Du Bois, Horace Mann, and Malcolm X, Chisholm's speech pointed to what she viewed as a singular factor in the maintenance of the Black American as a colonized man: the manipulation of the educational system, which she referred to as "cultural implantation." As she writes, "But it must be said that the type of education available on the one hand and the lack of education for many on the other produced a break between the classes of Black people that made it easy to maintain control or colonization, if you will, of all Black people."[15]

Chisholm had significant ideas about the role of colleges and universities, especially historically Black colleges and universities. She reminded Atlanta University students of the history of the establishment of schools within Black communities and the influence of white-controlled boards and philanthropists. Drawing their attention to the past and the opportunities of the present, she stated, "You no longer have good reason to perpetuate or succumb to innocuous mind-deadening education designed to control you."[16] While some of Chisholm's speeches required her audience to reimagine their social and political possibilities, her rhetoric was pragmatic and placed the responsibility for education in the hands of Black students. Speaking to the survival of Black colleges and universities, Chisholm lambasted historically Black colleges and universities (HBCUs) and their alums for benefiting from their geographic expansion and the economic opportunities associated with their growth yet choosing to be disconnected from the communities they inhabited. She believed that if HBCUs were to remain relevant, their administrators and institutions had to take on the responsibility to work and mobilize within their Black communities. While most of her policy efforts focused on the U.S., Chisholm rhetorically constructed the important role of Black self-determination within education as a key force for the liberation of Black people around the globe.

Although Chisholm is known for her catchphrases like "unbought and unbossed" and "catalyst for change," she is not associated with a singular defining speech, like Martin Luther King's "I Have a Dream" speech, Malcolm X's "Bullet or Ballot," or even Barbara Jordan's 1972 Watergate speech. Yet she remains one of the nation's most inspiring orators and a figure who made a generation revise their dreams and rethink possibilities that they believed were out of reach. *Shirley Chisholm in Her Own Words* illustrates the historical significance of her ideas about how to address the inequities that existed for disadvantaged and marginalized people throughout the U.S. and abroad. This book provides insight into the complexities that exist at the intersection of race, gender, class, and American democracy, especially for Black women in electoral politics. Chisholm's speeches, articles, position papers, and poems engaged a broad spectrum of issues and reflected her fundamental belief that "people's power" was central to transformational politics. While the speeches in this collection do not follow a chronological biography of her life, they represent the fervor and vitality of the era from which Chisholm emerged.

Despite her commanding presence and her charisma, Chisholm guarded her privacy. In fact, much of her personal life remains a mystery. Yet in her speeches she did reveal particular snapshots of her life, especially her adolescent years, when the everyday economic struggles of the St. Hill family connected to those of Black,

Brown, and immigrant families more generally and highlighted the dire needs of the oppressed people for whom she advocated. Through her personal reflections in her memoirs and speeches she revealed the contradictions of a nation whose abundant resources and wealth expanded while her family and many Black communities in the U.S. faced a constant struggle to survive.

Chisholm the Intellectual

The names and writings of Black women intellectuals such as Anna Julia Cooper, Maria Stewart, Frances M. Beal, Toni Morrison, and many others enjoy a robust presence within African American intellectual discourse because of the corrective work of Black scholars, especially Black women historians. Beyond merely comparing Black women intellectuals to their male counterparts, the work on Black women's intellectualism has helped to illuminate the gendered, racial, and class terrain on which such women exist.[17] While the work within African American intellectual history, especially Black women's intellectual history, has grown exponentially, a portion of Black women intellectuals still exist outside of the larger historiography or appear mainly in biographies. Anthologies like Beverly Guy-Sheftall's *Words of Fire: An Anthology of African American Thought* both recover and situate Black women firmly within the Black intellectual tradition.[18] Beyond the important work of recovery, engaging such outliers, especially those that existed during the civil rights and Black Power movements, provides transformative understanding of concepts around freedom, liberation, citizenship, and radicalism.

Although she gave hundreds of speeches and wrote numerous articles, Chisholm did not claim to be an "intellectual," nor is she remembered or examined for her intellectual contributions. Indeed, her maverick persona, her bold oratorical style, and her unconventional politics work to obscure her role as a public intellectual. Although she was engaged in an intellectual project by speaking publicly and writing in scholarly publications like the *New York Amsterdam News*, *The Black Scholar*, and *Issue: A Journal of Opinion*, few colleagues and scholars recognized her as an intellectual. In fact, Chisholm belongs to a long list of Black women intellectuals who lacked recognition for their contributions to shaping Black social and political life in the 1960s and 1970s. This exclusion, as sociologist Patricia Hill Collins argues, reflects a concerted effort to suppress Black women's thought. Collins suggests that "obscuring . . . this complex Black women's intellectual tradition is neither accidental nor benign."[19]

In both her public activism and legislative policies, Chisholm's speeches and writings confront America's contradictions and its broken contract with its citizens. In alignment with her Black foremothers and other Black women activists during the civil rights and Black Power movements, her intellectual work did not occur in the abstract but represented the daily lives of marginalized people. Moreover, its intersectional nature provided a tangible dynamism of thought and action beyond the U.S. Chisholm was operating as a legislator during a time of intense Black radicalism in the U.S. and across the globe. In her own Brooklyn district, activists and intellectuals were advocating for community control and political autonomy over various entities like schools, businesses, and affordable housing. While she did not self-identify as a Black cultural nationalist, Chisholm aligned with those who advocated for community control of public schools in her district. As an educator, she understood the important psychological and intellectual benefits of increasing the numbers of Black and Brown teachers, seeking community input in creating a racially diverse curriculum, and cultivating support for Black independent schools. Her speeches and writings on education reflect her understanding that schools operated as bastions of inequity that allowed white administrators, teachers, and others to instruct without accountability to Black and Brown parents, and that this phenomenon extended white control over Black and Brown majorities.

Focusing on wage and gender disparities, poverty initiatives around food insecurity, and trickle-down economics, Chisholm attacked the tendency of Black middle-class intellectuals to disconnect themselves from working-class Blacks and embrace goals and strategies that did not include them.[20] In part, her willingness to deliver speeches and talks on street corners, in the back of loud trucks, and in front of low-income housing projects showed her rejection of the gender and class boundaries that usually confined intellectual production to middle-class, elite, and male exercises that occurred only behind podiums or in statehouses. Her spatial negotiations would turn such assumptions on their head. Beyond her intellectual contributions, Chisholm's praxis affirms political theorist Antonio Gramsci's belief that "we are all intellectuals" and that "intellectual work occurs everywhere."[21] As a member of Congress, with an education from an elite institution like Columbia University, Chisholm represents the kind of person Gramsci identifies as a "refugee from the bourgeois class," who provides "theory and ideology (and often leadership) for a mass base of non-intellectuals, i.e. workers . . . rather than using that knowledge to protect the state."[22] At first glance, Chisholm's status and social location situate her as an elite. Yet she fits Gramsci's description of an organic intellectual who strategically seeks ways to reform and transform social forces and institutions like Congress and the U.S. presidency. Chisholm's 1972 presidential campaign, albeit extremely optimistic, attempted to unify and build a coalition of voters around a policy agenda that spoke to Black, Hispanic, Native American, working-class, and poor people along with women and youth voters.

Chisholm and the Black Feminist Intellectual Tradition

Collecting, transcribing, and organizing Chisholm's speeches, writings, and position papers is part of the process that acknowledges how her activism and rhetoric, which would usually be placed outside an academic intellectual tradition, should be situated within Black women's intellectual history. *Toward an Intellectual History of Black Women*, edited by Mia Bay, Farrah J. Griffin, Martha Jones, and Barbara Savage, provides groundbreaking and field-defining work on Black women intellectuals that explores how Black women are "producers of knowledge" instead of "objects of intellectual activity."[23] This book aims to focus on Chisholm's knowledge production and her political ideas. Patricia Hill Collins asserts, "Black women intellectuals have laid a vital analytical foundation for a distinctive standpoint on self, community, and society and, in doing so, created a multifaceted, African-American women's intellectual tradition."[24] While Chisholm is acknowledged for her political leadership, her intersectional analyses of gender, race, and colonialism have often gone unacknowledged and understudied because they mainly originated from her lived experiences instead of emerging from research or academic institutions.[25] Hattie Williams, in her work on Black women intellectuals, suggests, "African American women and their ideas about empowerment are integral to understanding the history of the United States."[26] I would suggest that the political engagement and critiques of government articulated by congressional Black women like Shirley Chisholm, Barbara Jordan, Maxine Waters, Barbara Lee, and Cori Bush provide a fundamental analysis of American democracy.

In the 1960s and 1970s, Chisholm found herself being influenced by and participating in a burgeoning intellectual community of Black women who revised the historical, cultural, and social narratives of the Black Power movement. We see this in the activist-intellectual work of women such as June Jordan, Sonia Sanchez, Johnnie Tillmon, Barbara Smith, Flo Kennedy, and Frances Beal. Like many such Black women intellectuals and artists, Chisholm posed questions about women's role in social/political movement building as well as their influence on Black struggles with economic disenfranchisement and public education. Although the work of Black women artists within the Black Arts movement is not often paired with that of Black feminists operating within electoral politics, both are articulating their issues and visions within a public political sphere in hopes of transforming it and their conditions.[27]

Chisholm's speeches and writings, like those of her political foremothers Maria Stewart and Ida B. Wells and her contemporaries Ella Baker and Fannie Lou Hamer, which are often placed at the political and social margins, are actually fundamental to a broad understanding around freedom and human rights within modern American history. These Black women activist intellectuals expressed a radical humanism that places them at the center of intellectual theory and praxis.

Chisholm achieved political power at an electrifying moment for Black feminist culture and politics. Using poetry, position papers, manifestos, plays, dance productions, and political speeches, Black women writers, artists, and organizers documented a generation of Black women's triumphs and failures that served as a living testament to their resilience. Members of this intellectual community did not disconnect their lives as artists and scholars from their activism. In part, their creative works and activism operated as extensions of one another. As Cheryl Clarke explains in *After Mecca: Women Poets and the Black Arts Movement*, "We dreamed a different world and imagined a different black community . . . and challenged [a] . . . hegemonic and racist White Anglo Saxon Protestant culture."[28] That challenge was articulated within the pages of literary magazines, newspapers, and anthologies and across Black feminist organizations like the Third World Women's Alliance and the Combahee River Collective. Newly formed Black political clubs like those Chisholm participated in challenged the usual operations of traditional political spaces. Chisholm's political club, the Unity Democratic Club (UDC) in Brooklyn, which she helped form and which then supported her run for political office, shook up the gender dynamics within political clubs by having Black women in leadership positions both as strategists and as potential candidates. Moreover, the UDC was a departure from the masculinist and hierarchical structure of Brooklyn machine politics. Chisholm's run for political office against all-white and all-male political machines tangibly reimagined electoral politics by directly confronting the racist patriarchy in local and national politics. Throughout the late 1950s and the early 1960s, her participation in political organizing in Brooklyn's Black political clubs disrupted the intraracial restrictions on Black women organizers for civil rights that kept many of them "behind the scenes" rather than placing them in formal leadership positions.[29] Breaking with her political foremothers and colleagues during the civil rights movement, Chisholm's ambition allowed her to reach for political heights that were unprecedented for Black women then and now.

Chisholm released her political memoir *Unbought and Unbossed* in 1970, the same year as Toni Cade Bambara's groundbreaking anthology *The Black Woman* and Frances Beal's transformative article "Double Jeopardy: To Be Black and Female." *Unbought and Unbossed* provides a personal account of Chisholm's life and an in-depth description of Caribbean immigrant strivings and contentious Brooklyn machine politics.[30] It also documents her transition from political volunteer and New York State assemblywoman to congresswoman. The memoir would be the first of its kind to provide a personal and political narrative of a Black woman politician. In it, Chisholm explains that while she faced racism daily, the roadblocks thrown up by gender discrimination were the hardest to navigate politically. Her description of what it felt like to be both raced and gendered aligns with Beal's concept of "double jeopardy," which expresses the interlocking and simultaneous nature of racial and sexual discrimination. In a speech "The Black Woman in Contemporary America" that Chisholm gave in 1974 at a conference on Black women, she said, "The black woman lives in a society that discriminates against her on two counts. The black woman cannot be discussed in the same context as her Caucasian counterpart because of the twin jeopardy of race and sex which operates against her. . . . To date neither the black movement nor women's liberation succinctly addresses itself to the dilemma confronting the black who is female."[31] She speaks to the inadequacies within these movements that do not grasp how divisive a "race versus gender dichotomy" is for everyone.[32]

Central to Beal's argument in "Double Jeopardy" is a critique of capitalism. Although she acknowledges capitalism's role in exploiting Black men and women, she refutes claims that Black women operating outside the confines of patriarchy are "oppressing black men."[33] She writes, "It must be pointed out at this time that black women are not resentful of the rise to power of black men. . . . This kind of thinking is a product of miseducation; that it's either X or it's Y. It is fallacious reasoning that in order for the black man to be strong, the black woman has to be weak."[34] Chisholm directly quoted from Beal's manifesto in her 1974 speech to develop her point that Black women are not Black men's competitors.[35] Here we see Chisholm the politician in conversation with Beal the leftist feminist activist and other Black women writers in the 1970s, not only identifying race, class, and gender oppressions but also courageously calling out Black male sexism. Like Beal in "Double Jeopardy," Chisholm also criticizes white feminists' performativity of feminist solidarity that was tone-deaf to Black women's needs. This would be a constant theme in her critique of white feminists.

Though many contemporary Black women did not identify with or align themselves with the mainstream women's movement, Chisholm proclaimed herself a feminist. *Unbought and Unbossed* reveals the trauma of patriarchal and sexist treatment experienced by Black women who dared to see themselves as political leaders. Both of Chisholm's books, in documenting encounters and disagreements with her white and Black male colleagues, make public what had once been communicated only in whispers and private conversations between Black women: the vitriol directed against Black women who refused to accept a secondary citizenship status.

If we draw on historian Darlene Clark Hine's conception of Black women's creation of and participation in a "culture of dissemblance," we are able to understand why Chisholm wrote two books that trace her personal and political life.[36] Hine describes how Black women, in an act of both resistance and self-protection, create an appearance of "openness" while in reality they conceal their "inner lives from their oppressors."[37] Chisholm wrote both *Unbought and Unbossed* and a second book, *The Good Fight*, which documents her presidential run, to ensure that she controlled her own narrative. In my previous work, I have suggested that although Black congressional women in the 1970s operated from a position of political power, there were moments when they could maintain that power only by presenting a collegial relationship with male leaders while engaging in a culture of dissemblance that hid their personal thoughts and feelings. Chisholm's public conflicts with male Black political elites during her 1972 presidential campaign, especially with some of her male colleagues in the Congressional Black Caucus, reflected her struggles in maintaining a public perception of solidarity among Black leaders.

Chisholm was speaking, writing, and creating public policy at the nexus of the civil rights, Black Power, and Black feminist movements. She served in the New York State Assembly during the height of the Black Power movement that was burgeoning in Bedford-Stuyvesant. As a Black feminist she not only would develop policies that met the needs of Black and Brown women, like increasing the minimum wage for domestic workers and reforming welfare laws, but would also participate in conferences and meetings that collectively mobilized Black women. After leaving Congress she cofounded the National Congress of Black Women in 1984.

From her membership in the National Organization for Women and her support of abortion and participation in NARAL to her role as a founding member of the National Women's Political Caucus,

Chisholm sought ways to expand women's rights and advocate for Black women within mainstream women's spaces. Though she formed coalitions and alliances with white women feminists around abortion rights and workers' rights, she also addressed the ways in which white feminist activists failed to conceptualize the full range of concerns faced by Black and Brown women around reproductive justice.[38] Historian Ula Taylor argues that this is a pattern in "white women's movement building," in which "white women followed the tradition of their foremothers by 'developing their feminism' in a movement to rid the country of legal and/or racial injustices and ultimately created organizations endemic to their needs as white, economically elite, professional women."[39] Black and Brown women like Aileen Hernandez, Florynce Kennedy, and Shirley Chisholm would do the heavy lifting, pushing traditional white women's organizations to understand the socioeconomic nuances that affected women of color differently with regard to abortion and other intersectional issues. Chisholm's advocacy around family planning was inextricably linked to her insistence that abortion was not genocide.[40] Her writings and speeches on abortion aligned with those of her Black feminist peers, whose advocacy for reproductive justice went beyond a woman asserting her right to choose and also spoke to the racial and economic inequities that existed for women of color. A choice to have an abortion was just as fundamental as the right to have safe and accessible options for family planning—options that included birth control and policies that addressed Black and Brown maternal deaths. Chisholm's congressional remarks about population control highlighted the racial discrepancies between white and nonwhite women's maternal death rates. Today, as the Black maternal mortality rate far outstrips that of whites, Chisholm's speeches and advocacy continue to highlight the pervasive racism and dangers surrounding Black women in childbirth.

Black feminists of the 1970s refused to limit their fight for liberation to conventional modes and areas of critique. They interrogated domestic and international powers as well as dominant economic and political structures. Opposition from Black men added a layer to their freedom struggle, compelling them to form organizations, theories, and artistic productions that publicly addressed Black male sexism and explored the contradictions revealed in the fight for Black liberation. Like Chisholm, some Black feminist organizers operated between Black nationalism and feminism, refusing to be placed in the margins. Subsequently, they created spaces that centered their identities and realities despite external efforts to deny how sexism and racism existed within various movements. Chisholm would deal with the double jeopardy described by Beal by refusing to abide by a silent patriarchal code that "protects Black men," and also by committing to strip away the facade of a unified sisterhood with white women. Challenging both paradigms, Chisholm and her contemporaries created a Black feminist imaginary that was not static within identity politics but transformative; hers was an advanced framework of radical humanism that is critical for universal liberation. It is in this context of a Black feminist intellectual tradition that we see Chisholm in her totality as an intellectual, an activist, and a politician.

In her poem "9 Haiku: For Freedom's Sisters," Sonia Sanchez writes of a group of Black women freedom fighters: Kathleen Cleaver, Betty Shabazz, Rosa Parks, Fannie Lou Hamer, Charlayne Hunter-Gault, Barbara Jordan, Myrlie Evers-Williams, Dorothy Height, and Shirley Chisholm. The verse dedicated to Chisholm states,

We saw your
woman sound footprinting
congressional hallways[41]

One of the few poems, if not the only one, that identifies Chisholm as one of a collective of Black women freedom fighters, it provides a perspective that allows Chisholm to be fully seen and heard. This collection of speeches, writings, and position papers should allow us to listen profoundly to what Chisholm has to say to both new and older generations. *Shirley Chisholm in Her Own Words* illuminates the richness of her words and the actions that would follow her demand that progress requires an "implementation of ideas."

Notes

1. Jennifer Steinhauer, "2019 Belongs to Shirley Chisholm," *New York Times*, July 6, 2019.

2. Manning Marable, *Living Black History: How Reimagining the African-American Past Can Remake America's Racial Future* (New York: Basic Civitas, 2005).

3. Deborah Gray White, "Mining the Forgotten: Manuscript Sources for Black Women's History," *Journal of American History* 1, no. 74 (June 1987): 237-42.

4. Quoted from Kristopher Burrell, "Black Women as Activist Intellectuals: Ella Baker and Mae Mallory Combat Northern Jim Crow in New York City's Public Schools during the 1950s," in *The Strange Careers of the Jim Crow North: Segregation and Struggle outside of the South*, ed. Brian Purnell and Jeanne Theoharis with Komozi Woodard (New York: New York University Press, 2019), 91.

5. Shirley Chisholm, *Unbought and Unbossed* (Boston: Houghton Mifflin, 1970), 30.

6. On the norm for Black women organizers to operate behind the scenes, see Barbara Ransby, "Behind the Scenes Organizer: The Roots of Ella Baker's Political Passions," in *Sisters in the Struggle: African American Women in the Civil*

Rights-Black Power Movement, ed. Bettye Collier-Thomas and V. P. Franklin (New York: New York University Press, 2001), 42–55. Also see Belinda Robnett, *How Long? How Long? African American Women in the Struggle for Freedom and Justice* (New York: Oxford University Press, 1997).

7. James H. Cone, *Black Theology and Black Power* (New York: Seabury Press, 1969).

8. See Ira Reid, *The Negro Immigrant: His Background, Characteristics and Social Adjustment, 1889-1937* (New York: Columbia University Press, 1938), 146.

9. James Haskins, *Fighting Shirley Chisholm* (New York: Dial Press, 1975).

10. Shirley Chisholm, "On Busing," *Congressional Record* 117, no. 30 (November 4, 1971): 39310.

11. Shannon Norton, "More Discrimination as a Woman," *Wichita Beacon*, October 20, 1970.

12. Shirley Chisholm, "Chisholm: Dream Still That for Many," address at University of Notre Dame, January 19, 1988, *South Bend Tribune*, January 20, 1988.

13. Shirley Chisholm, "Progress through Understanding," *Congressional Record* 115, Part 12, Extensions of Remarks (June 16, 1969): 15973.

14. Shirley Chisholm, "The Black as a Colonized Man," speech delivered at Atlanta University, October 20, 1969, p. 6. Shirley Chisholm Papers, MC 1194, Box 1, Folder 13, Special Collections and University Archives, Rutgers University Libraries, New Brunswick, NJ.

15. Chisholm, "The Black as a Colonized Man," 6.

16. Chisholm, "The Black as a Colonized Man," 12.

17. The groundbreaking work on Black women intellectuals, specifically public intellectuals, includes but is not limited to Gloria Hull, Patricia Bell Scott, and Barbara Smith, *All the Women Are White, All the Blacks Are Men, but Some of Us Are Brave: Black Women's Studies* (New York: Feminist Press, 1982); Beverly Guy-Sheftall, *Words of Fire: An Anthology of African-American Feminist Thought* (New York: New Press, 1995); Paula Giddings, *Where and When I Enter: The Impact of Black Women on Race and Sex in America* (New York: Bantam Books, 1985); Bettye Collier-Thomas, *Jesus, Jobs, and Justice: African American Women and Religion* (New York: Alfred Knopf, 2011); Carole Boyce Davies, *Left of Karl Marx: The Political Life of Black Communist Claudia Jones* (Durham, NC: Duke University Press, 2007); Nell Irvin Painter, "Representing Truth: Sojourner Truth's Knowing and Becoming Known," *Journal of American*

History 81, no. 2 (2008): 461–92; Darlene Clark Hine, *Hine Sight: Black Women and the Re-construction of American History* (Bloomington: Indiana University Press, 1998); Keisha N. Blain, Christopher Cameron, and Ashley D. Farmer, eds., *New Perspectives on the Black Intellectual Tradition* (Evanston, IL: Northwestern University Press, 2018); Elsa Barkley Brown, "Mothers of Mind," *Sage* 6 (Summer 1989) 4–10; Brittney C. Cooper, *Beyond Respectability: The Intellectual Thought of Race Women* (Urbana: University of Illinois Press, 2017); Robyn Spencer, *The Revolution Has Come: Black Power, Gender, and the Black Panther Party in Oakland* (Durham, NC: Duke University Press, 2016).

18. Guy-Sheftall, *Words of Fire.*

19. Patricia Hill Collins, *Black Feminist Thought: Knowledge, Consciousness, and the Politics of Empowerment* (Boston: Unwin, Hyman, 1990), 3.

20. See Harold Cruse, *The Crisis of the Negro Intellectual: From Its Origins to the Present* (New York: William Morrow, 1967).

21. Antonio Gramsci, *Prison Notebooks*, vol. 2, trans. Joseph A. Buttigieg (New York: Columbia University Press, 1996).

22. Gramsci, *Prison Notebooks*, 2:202.

23. Mia Bay, Farrah J. Griffin, Martha Jones, and Barbara Savage, eds., *Toward an Intellectual History of Black Women* (Chapel Hill: University of North Carolina Press, 2015), 1.

24. Collins, *Black Feminist Thought*, 3.

25. Hattie V. Williams, ed., *Bury My Heart in a Free Land: Black Women Intellectuals in Modern U.S. History* (Santa Barbara, CA: Bloomsbury, 2017).

26. Hattie V. Williams, introduction to Williams, *Bury My Heart*, xiii.

27. My use and analysis of transformative intellectual work is framed from Edward Said's "The Limits of the Artistic Imagination and the Secular Intellectual," *Macalester International* 3 (Spring 1996): 3–34.

28. Cheryl Clarke, *"After Mecca": Women Poets and the Black Arts Movement* (New Brunswick, NJ: Rutgers University Press, 2004), 2.

29. There is a vast scholarly literature on the obstacles that Black women encountered within the civil rights movement and the ways they reenvisioned and reconceptualized Black women's politics. See Charles Payne, *I've Got the Light of Freedom: The Organizing Tradition and the Mississippi Freedom Struggle* (Berkeley: University of California Press, 1995), 204, 209; Ransby, "Behind the Scenes Organizer."

30. Toni Cade Bambara, ed., *The Black Woman: An Anthology* (New York: New American Library, 1970); Frances M. Beal, *Black Women's Manifesto; Double Jeopardy: To Be Black and Female* (New York: Third World Women's Alliance, 1969).

31. Shirley Chisholm, "The Black Woman in Contemporary America," speech delivered at University of Missouri Kansas City, June 17, 1974.

32. Tera Hunter, "The Forgotten Legacy of Shirley Chisholm: Race versus Gender in the 2008 Democratic Primaries," in *Obama, Clinton, Palin: Making History in Election 2008*, ed. Liette Gidlow (Urbana: University of Illinois Press, 2008), 66–85.

33. Beal, *Black Women's Manifesto*, 168.

34. Beal, *Black Women's Manifesto*, 169.

35. Chisholm, "The Black Woman in Contemporary America."

36. Hine, *Hine Sight*, 41.

37. Hine, *Hine Sight*.

38. See Dorothy Roberts's work on reproductive justice and Black women, *Killing of the Black Body: Race, Reproduction, and the Meaning of Liberty* (New York: Pantheon, 1997)

39. Ula Taylor, "The Historical Evolution of Black Feminist Theory and Praxis," *Journal of Black Studies* 29, no. 2 (November 1998): 234–53.

40. Jennifer Nelson, *Women of Color and the Reproductive Rights Movement* (New York: New York University Press, 2003).

41. Sonia Sanchez, "9 Haiku: For Freedom's Sisters," in *Morning Haiku* (Boston: Beacon Press, 2010).

1   *Education*

*We must accept the fact that our role, as educators, should be inseparable
from the concept of the community; that our function is, and must be,
directed toward alleviating economic, political, and social injustice. Indeed,
what else can the purpose of education be?*

"THE NECESSITY FOR A NEW THRUST IN EDUCATION
TODAY" (1973)

During Chisholm's attendance at Brooklyn College in the early 1940s, she
became intimately aware of the racism and sexism that existed within the
American educational system. Before the political revolutions that erupted
on campuses in the late 1960s forced administrations to establish Black
studies departments, Chisholm joined the Harriet Tubman Society, where
she was one of the student leaders who advocated for a Negro history
course at Brooklyn College. Long before the famous historian John Hope
Franklin would join Brooklyn College in 1956 as its history chair, and the
establishment of the Africana Studies Department in 1970 after years of
struggle and protest, Chisholm believed that education was a liberatory
process that began with Black history. As an intellectual, she thought
deeply about the field of Black studies and its potential for being a transforming force in Black communities. For a Black woman in the 1940s who
aspired to be a professional, the field of education was one of the few occupations that provided access for her. The young Shirley Anita St. Hill would
have to fight just to become a teacher's aide. Subsequently, education

would become the most important legislative area for Chisholm. In the state assembly, she sponsored the SEEK program to provide financial and logistical support for minority students. As a congresswoman, she was the leading expert in early childhood issues. Most politicians of the era considered education a far less important target for appropriations than war and criminal punishment, but Chisholm understood it to be a national priority. Despite her years in Congress, she would return to higher education after leaving office, affirming that teaching was her true love.

"The Necessity for a New Thrust in Education Today"

An address delivered at the convention of the National Science Teaching Association in Detroit, Michigan, March 31, 1973.

Henry Adams once said of our profession: "A teacher affects eternity, he can never tell where his influence ends." I am inclined to agree. Our function as educators is to teach—to impart knowledge.

But what concept do we attempt to convey when using these words? To most of us "teaching"—the imparting of knowledge—has meant disseminating to our students the body of facts that mankind has accumulated. We have taken this definition and demanded that our education system evolve around it. Education is a world of excitement, dreams and success; it is also a world of frustration, failure, and impossible problems. Education is charged with being irrelevant to the present and future needs of society, and much of it is, but in our frenzied haste to become "relevant" we often detest all that was of the past and love all that smells of newness without analyzing in depth and without, in a sense, being objective about the situation.

Published in *The Science Teacher* 40, no. 5 (May 1973): 20-24. Courtesy of the National Science Teaching Association.

I submit to you that before we, as educators, ask how we can better our capacity to educate we must first ask what is our function as educators. Before we look toward more and better legislation, before we talk about more money and better school buildings, we must ask ourselves the hard questions.

As I view the problem, we have stressed the intellectual aspects of education at the expense of the emotional. We have instructed our students in languages and numbers, but we have failed to educate them in self-respect, leadership, cooperation, and understanding. In a word, we have failed to help them—to allow them—to self-actualize, to come to know and respect themselves as human beings, as individuals with intrinsic value and worth.

Our primary function as educators must be to break from tradition when that tradition does not serve the present or retards the future; to reorient our school systems, not in terms of instruction in basic knowledge about the natural world, as we have done in the past, but in terms of imparting to our students and children a sense of self-respect, a sense of hope, a sense of belonging, a sense of power. Our primary function as educators must be to recognize that to educate is to "lead out."

Directly related to this, I believe, is the situation we are faced with in attempting to combat the problem of the drop-out in our educational system. When we begin to realize that the "inferiority myth," formerly advanced as the primary reason for the dropping out of the Black student, has been exploded; when we begin to realize that it is not merely lack of interest that causes a student to leave school; when we begin to realize that dropping out is not merely the inevitable result of a student's individual personality hang-ups; when we begin to realize all of this, perhaps then we can come to see that the problem is the sense of futility that the student experiences, often unconsciously.

Why should one remain in school until he becomes the recipient of a diploma, when it is apparent to him that he is in no way better prepared to cope with the outside—the real world? When he is in no way more capable of understanding himself? To the dropout, an education in terms of present public schooling curriculum is irrelevant, that is, not meaningful to what he sees and understands of the world around him.

We must demonstrate to all students that there is a very real reason for being in school and that real reason is to be taught, to be educated, to be *led out* of low income, high unemployment, poor health care, inadequate housing; to be *led out* of ghetto life.

But how can we do this? Projects begun after the child has become a student are remedial rather than preventive; they are an attempt to work within the prevailing organization of our schools, an organization which has itself resulted in failure.

Notwithstanding efforts which have been made, children who go to school in minority areas do not feel that they are treated equally, do not have the same chance of success academically, and are disadvantaged in finding good jobs in a society which increasingly insists on educational attainments for positions more and more of which require sophisticated skills. This in turn causes increasing numbers of such young people to conclude that effort to learn in school is a waste of time. In such an environment, even the best teachers face discouragement, a fact which contributes to the vicious cycle.

Learning today is often aimed at raising scores on standardized short-answer tests geared to knowledge of specific facts. Such tests are the easiest to grade, and they allow comparisons (invidious or otherwise) between students, teachers, and schools—in turn intensifying concentration of effort on teaching for the test rather than any other goal. Even teachers who abhor teaching by the criterion of a test rather than of the children are subjected to pressure to cover material which will be the subject of examinations on which the school may be rated. And the future of the children often depends on how they do on such examinations at every stage of their career. The result is that interest in exploring exciting questions in man's discovery about the world in and around him is often stifled. The search for understanding and the ability to deal with situations intelligently is slighted in favor of knowledge of routine standardized information and the ability to guess what the examiner wants you to answer.

In many schools, classes are large. Obstreperous pupils often monopolize teacher attention. Instruction is often by standardized methods (such as in the lower grades the "Look John, Look, John, See the Dog" type of readers). The individual child is thus deprived of the individual attention which he needs in developing freshness of insight and his interest in learning "Why" and "How" as well as "What."

In much of education, the role of the student is strictly passive: to absorb information ladled out and then to prove he has absorbed it in order to get a grade or other sign of approval. The end result of this is often boredom and apathy or vehement revolt, expressed as young people grow older in many kinds of defiance of what they believe is the behavior expected by others.

Because of the salary scale of teachers compared with other professionals, the impact of overcrowded and over-large classes, and pupil resistance due to lack of motivation, combined with pressure from above for results on tests, teachers lack the independence and status to work most effectively. This is compounded by community attitudes that teachers should "make the children learn" and that everybody knows as much as teachers do about education.

What is needed is to realize that our education structure is too large, too insensitive, too out of touch with the problems unique to the various communities within each of our major cities to be able to deal with them effectively. We have lost sight of the fact that the community should have a voice in what goes on in the school. We have lost sight of the fact that the community and the school should be inseparable. American culture is not a culture of homogenous values. When we attempt to indoctrinate our entire population into a middle-class value system, a system that is not thrown open to all of us, when we attempt to reinforce through our school systems social values basic to only one segment of our population, when we attempt to do this, it can only result in a sense of frustration, hopelessness, and rage in those who have not had the benefit of the "system's" values in their preschool experiences. What we must do is to concentrate our thoughts upon the concept of community control.

Community control is not a panacea. I must preface my comments on it with that statement. But it is, as I view it, the most effective and immediate means of achieving our goals. We have all too often heard and made the cry that as teachers, our power is minimized by our principals; as principals, by our superintendents; as superintendents, by our school boards; as school boards, by our legislature. The cries are true, no doubt, and permit us some justification in viewing ourselves as being not totally at fault. But the time for rationalizing is well beyond us. The changes, if they are to be forthcoming, must be initiated by those of us who are on the inside, whose function it is to educate.

That you have come here today is an indication to me that you are, at the very least, interested, and concerned with what must be done. And what must be done is to free our teachers, our principals, our superintendents, and our school boards. Free them, emancipate them, from the outdated restrictions that have inhibited meaningful progress in education; free them from the fear of having economic and social sanctions imposed against them by superiors who may or may not have the interest of the students and the community in mind; free them from the possibility of being passed over by department heads for attempting to strike out in innovative ways.

We must force ourselves, as teachers, to question openly and honestly the goals, tactics, and values of principals and supervisors. We must encourage ourselves to continually fight off the feeling of helplessness that has resulted from our present structural system. We must encourage this because it is the only way I know to up-grade our quality as professionals.

Just as many of our students become drop-outs because our system has no relevant use for them, many highly competent teachers are lost to the educational world because that world does not permit them, in a word, to become "relevant." We must allow for variety, for experimentation, for innovation, for individuality. We must allow for them, and seek to achieve them. We must not be so desirous of keeping within our ranks those who fit well within the educational world, those who are weak-minded and content to preserve the status quo, for by doing so we force out those who are concerned and capable and willing to try innovative ways. We force these teachers out because of their overwhelming sense of frustration.

In effect, we must free ourselves from those whom we have served in the past—our professional superiors—and submit to those whom we should serve in the future—the community. As specialists, we should have been the first to appreciate the fact that we can no longer prepare curricula in a vacuum without consulting with the community.

The result of the curriculum production process looks like any other modern staple. It is a bundle of planned meanings, a package of values, a commodity whose "balanced appeal" makes it marketable to a sufficiently large number to justify the cost of production. Consumer-pupils are taught to make their desires conform to marketable values. Thus they are made to feel guilty if they do not behave according to the predictions of consumer research by getting the grades and certificates that will place them in the job category they have been led to expect.

In fact, healthy students often redouble their resistance to teaching as they find themselves more comprehensively manipulated. This resistance is due not to the authoritarian style of a public school or the seductive style of some free schools, but to the fundamental approach common to all schools—the idea that one person's judgment should determine what and when another person must learn.

Being so close to the young, we should have been the first to realize that in their preoccupation with long hair, "bizarre" music and clothing, that in their preoccupation with the use of drugs and their experimentation with sex, the young were attempting to show us their sense of frustration with the world; and much of that young world is controlled by us; controlled by educators. We trouble ourselves over these preoccupations, yet we have never understood them. Never understood that, as individuals, our youth are in need of, hunger for, search for things which are immediate to them, things over which they feel they have control; vehicles by which they believe they can attain a sense of power. Their preoccupations are merely a negative reaction to the unhappiness, the senselessness, the hopelessness, they perceive in the world. But we must understand that these preoccupations become important, not for themselves, but only as a means of better coping with this world.

I do not wish to say that because the use of drugs can be attributed to an effect rather than a cause that [sic] the problem is any the less frightening. I do wish to say, though, that we should take that observation and begin to mark our direction in terms of it; that as educators, in the valid sense, we must accept the fact that our role, as educators, should be inseparable from the concept of the community; that our function is, and must be, directed toward alleviating economic, political, and social injustice. Indeed, what else can the purpose of education be?

The larger problem is not nearly as much one of finance as it is of power and wresting this power from the hands in which it presently lies and placing it where it belongs. Certainly, education is in need of increased funds, but no amount of funds will provide a more useful, meaningful education unless the effort is made at the local level.

Why do I advocate the use of community control? Perhaps the most immediate reason is that community control can provide us with the means of checking and balancing, at all levels.

Community control can be the vehicle by which school and community, now separate entities, become one; can be the vehicle by which teachers, now transmitters, become developers; can be the vehicle by which teachers, now advocates of the system, become advocates of the student; can be the vehicle by which parents, now spectators, become participants.

It permits members of the community to express an effective voice, not merely an ineffective opinion, concerning the goals of the schools which their children attend. It permits the community to hold principals and teachers accountable and forces the latter to become concerned with what the community feels its primary educational needs to be. Progress is rarely made where the views of those who are governed have no impact, where the men who guide and control our activities are not amenable to our sanctions. This is the situation that parents, students, teachers themselves, all those people that the term "community" embraces, find themselves in today. They have no voice in policy because those who should listen, those who are in charge of making policy, are far too removed from them, in terms of geography, ideology, and security, to worry about listening. And those who must listen, those who act as principals and superintendents, those who are themselves the subjects of power in the overall scheme, are too ineffective to achieve results.

We must localize the structure of the school system and allow the administrator and teacher to be answerable, in a sense, to the immediate and pressing needs of the community they serve rather than to the far-removed desires of those who sit above them.

We must bring the educator closer to the problem and force him to put things in perspective, to consult with parents, to consult with students, to get a full view from all sides as to what needs to be done.

We must force the system to become aware of our needs and then force it to take them into account in setting its goals. In this way, then, education takes on a relevant meaning. The parent is able to meet with the teacher and the principal to discuss the specific problems of his child and of the environment in which the school exists.

We must not fear placing our trust in the community. We must not fear turning authority over to local boards, giving them some power to hire and fire and some power over curriculum and budgeting matters. We must not fear being held accountable. For within the concept of accountability lie the seeds for a part of the restructuring process, namely, that an educator's ability would be measured by, and dismissals, transfers, promotions, and pay raises would be based upon, performance and not merely seniority. Our system now protects the mediocre, not the qualified.

Community control is a way of providing the much-needed link between the school and the area's residents, whom it serves. By involving parents in this type of endeavor, it forces the curriculum to become relevant—relevant in terms of reflecting the cultures of Black and Puerto Rican communities; relevant in terms of no longer being influenced by those who refuse to reach out to the community. Undoubtedly, this will mean that there will be a rise in the percentage of Black and Puerto Rican teachers, but it would be to raise a red flag to say that only such teachers would be permitted to teach within that community. What is required is an administrative and teaching staff that adequately reflects a cross-section of the particular community involved. By communities I mean all those who have a stake in the product so the school. Only in such a manner can we avoid the problem of lack of identification between teacher and students, between school and parent, and insure an emotional closeness between the two, a bond which is almost non-existent in ghetto area schools as they now exist.

There are those who ask if community control will lay the concept of integration to its final resting place. I find I am most often approached on the issue by the very same people who fought against integration in the name of decentralization and the neighborhood concept. To me, it is but another red flag raised by these people who are now to be seen fighting against community control in the name of integration.

The question is not whether integration will die, but whether it was ever meant to live. For the integration of our day has been defined in terms of giving a white child a locker next to a Black child; bussing 100 seven-year-olds from slum to suburb; hiring a Puerto Rican staff member to improve the public relations image of a school. To me, this concept was lifeless even before it took on its present form.

Integration, if it is to live, if it should live, must be seen not only in terms of race but "in terms of culture, a coming together of different peoples in a social esthetic, emotional, and philosophical manner, not in terms of mechanical juxtapositions. It must be seen in terms of pluralism rather than assimilation; it must be based on a respect for differences rather than on a desire for amalgamation. It must be seen as a salad bowl rather than a melting pot." [*Science Teacher* note: Quote taken from NEA's Task Force on Urban Education, *Schools of the Urban Crisis*].

If this is what people have in mind when they ask me about integration and community control, then my answer must be that the two are not only compatible, but they are inseparable.

But regardless of the answer on this question of integration, the most crucial issue is still the quality of the education that we and our children are to receive. Community control seems to hold out a promise in this regard, a promise to bring education that needed step closer to being relevant to creating an environment that is truly democratic and rife with equal opportunity at all levels.

I have referred, quite often, to the word "relevancy." In some instances, no doubt, I have used it improperly. Rather than saying "irrelevant," I should have said "harmful." For it is harmful rather than irrelevant to instruct a child in the meaning of values, in the meaning of "good" while forgetting that the concept of "good" is based upon adult standards which are foreign to him. It is harmful rather than irrelevant to teach a child that in school he will remain docile and passive and obedient, harmful because when he is no longer in school he must forget these ideas and somehow learn to be creative and aggressive. It is harmful rather than irrelevant to raise a generation of what John Holt has referred to as "answer-producers," those who have the ability to "parrot" properly; harmful because their reward for doing so is merely to be led into lives of complacency and dullness. And as for those who are incapable of "producing answers," for them there is shame, fear, resentment, and rejection of others.

These, then, are, as George Dennison describes them in his essay "The First Street School" appearing in *New American Review #3*, "the most familiar waste products of our school system—complacency and rage."

Again, it is harmful rather than irrelevant to subject our children to compulsive processes, aversive processes, to attempt to force the child into unnatural surroundings and situations and then demand of him that he learn. "You must go to school." "You must sit." "You must remain silent." These are situations in which the student finds himself daily—confronted with a void of stimulation, an atmosphere totally lacking in the seeds of curiosity, an atmosphere that demands of the student that he force himself to memorize and thereby "learn."

As Marshall McLuhan has stated in "The Medium Is the Message," the young are merely confronted with "instruction in situations organized by means of classified information, in subjects which are unrelated and visually conceived in terms of blue-print." It is, in its most exposed form, a suppression of the natural direct experience of the young, a process which we utilize every minute while outside the classroom, to assimilate and digest. In these words we find the implicit demand that education must shift from "instruction" to "discovery," from "goal-orientation" to "role-orientation," an employment of total involvement dealing with human problems and situations, not fragmented and specialized goals or jobs. "Education must shift from *structure* to *environment*."

In preparing my address to you, I gave considerable thought to including within it proposals dealing with specific curriculum changes, such as the instruction of sex education courses, courses on religion, and on education itself. I considered discussing the merits of employing in our educational approach newly advanced psychological concepts such as Skinner's concept of "arranging the contingencies of reinforcement." I could have discussed with you the idea of rearranging our teaching day, of shortening classroom time so as to permit home visits and individual work. I could have discussed what the federal government's role in educational policies should be. I could have discussed these topics and many more, but I have chosen not to. My reason for choosing is basic. It is based on the belief that we must first put our full efforts to the task of reversing direction, and only then, only after that has been brought about, can we afford ourselves the luxury of getting down to specifics. Institutions resist change; power concedes nothing. If we forget this we are lost.

If I may leave you with one thought; if I can implant within you one example, one reminder for all I have tried to express here, let it be this: The student brings to the classroom his *entire* person. Let us, then, educate the whole of it. If we are really to affect eternity, let it be to our credit!

Thomas Jefferson observed, "The earth belongs to the living generation."

"The Day Care Dilemma"

An article published in the Wall Street Journal *on April 26, 1976, in response to President Gerald Ford's veto of the Child Day Care bill.*

Economists who evaluate the governmental costs of social welfare programs present varied analyses of both the cost effectiveness and the residual potential of such programs as AFDC, Medicaid and food stamps. There is, in my opinion, widespread acceptance that some public monies must be applied to the problems of the poor and the near-poor in this country. The debate surrounding these "people programs" centers on how much should we spend, and what do we expect to get in return.

Should we measure the success of social welfare programs by how many low-income families enter the middle class? Or, should we acknowledge that we will always have low-income unemployables whose livelihood must depend upon government subsidies? I contend that those of us engaged in this debate have not adequately solved this dilemma, nor have we found meaningful ways to accommodate an economy which, even in the most prosperous of times, defines "full employment" as 4% unemployed.

I have long been an advocate for federal support of many of these life-sustaining programs for reasons other than the monetary

---

In the Shirley Chisholm Papers, MC 1194, Special Collections and University Archives, Rutgers University Libraries.

return to society. But, the current administration has sought to make the poor the most expendable during the current recession, arguing that we must cut health, education and social services budgets because we can no longer "afford" them. Because of the lack of persuasion those human arguments seem to have, given the current national mood of fiscal conservatism, I have found myself justifying social service outlays on a cost-effective basis.

These programs are defensible because they contain a savings potential—if we administer them properly and fund them adequately.

A LACK OF UNDERSTANDING

Yet, for all the preponderance with tax savings, there is a basic lack of understanding of the economics of welfare among some of my own colleagues and, especially, the current administration. Nowhere has that been more evident than in the day care crisis now brewing. And President Ford, by vetoing the Day Care Services Act earlier this month, made a decision that is not only politically unwise, but financially unsound. For without this legislation, we are guaranteed retroactive financial penalties imposed on state budgets, increased welfare costs, and more unemployment.

More than any other social welfare program, day care is tied directly and specifically to the labor market. Through provisions of Title 20 of the Social Security Act, we subsidize the child care women need in order to participate in the labor market. A large percentage of the children enrolled in these centers are from families which have long histories of welfare dependency but which are now entering the middle class because of the availability of child care facilities.

There has been only a modest commitment on the part of the government to provide this necessary program, despite the fact that the need is escalating because of the changing nature of the American family. The social portrait of the nuclear family in which the father is the breadwinner and the mother remains at home happily tending the kids might be the idyllic vision of family life represented on television and in our literature. But that view is far from reality.

In the past decade, for example, the number of single-parent households increased 10 times more than two-parent families. This translates into a national situation in which one in every seven children is raised in a family in which the father—because of death, divorce, separation or out-of-wedlock birth—is absent. Most of these families are headed by women, and a large percentage fall below the poverty line.

It is this group, then, which stands to benefit from day care expenditures, since the dual role of caring for children while providing their financial support falls to these women. With subsidized day care, they can be assured that their children are cared for and can join the labor market and become taxpaying citizens. Without it, they find that their best option is to collect welfare and care for their children themselves.

The availability of day care has resulted in transferring thousands of women from welfare rolls into fulltime jobs and cutting the cost of welfare in the process. Now, because of a series of events, day care programs may be severely curtailed and the women who have been able to utilize child care will be forced back onto the welfare rolls.

The emergency is one of a budgetary nature. In 1972, President Nixon imposed a ceiling on federal spending for day care which has not been amended to accommodate the growing costs of personnel, facility maintenance and nutritional costs. Thus, federally-supported centers have been operating on budgets fixed four years ago.

In 1974, Congress attempted to improve the quality of day care by mandating that day care centers comply with their own state health and safety codes, and that they adhere to federally-established staff ratio requirements. But Congress did not make funds available in order to let states come into compliance with these requirements. And so the attempt to upgrade these child care facilities actually created a mechanism through which a good portion of day care centers could be closed down—since centers out of compliance with federal guidelines stand to lose their funding.

Last fall, faced with that predicament, Congress suspended the enforcement of staff ratio requirements on the assumption that these federal requirements were the ones centers were not complying with. A state-by-state survey conducted by the Senate, however, provided some surprising results. The Senate survey found that most states were close to compliance with staffing requirements, but were in need of funds to meet health, safety, and nutritional standards—regulations which had not been suspended.

Senators Long of Louisiana and Mondale of Minnesota co-authored legislation which would remedy the problem. Their bill, the Day Care Services Act (H.R. 9803), was designed to provide the monies the states reported that they needed in order to bring their centers into compliance with federal requirements.

Since the operation of day care is linked to work availability and incentives, Long and Mondale included a provision which allows states to hire welfare mothers for those staff positions which were open. They correctly assessed that this would result in additional savings to state and local governments by decreasing welfare outlays.

THE EFFECT OF THE VETO

Since the President vetoed this bill, however, we can expect welfare costs to soar. In some states half the day care centers with Title 20 enrollments will be closed. The state of Illinois, where HEW auditors are right now, reports that of the 40,000 children now being served by this program, 35,000 will no longer have facilities available.

In addition, states will be assessed penalties totaling their operating budget for each month they are out of compliance with any one regulation. Thus, if a program is found in violation of health standards in June of 1976, that center will not only be closed, but the state can be fined by the federal government penalties back to October 1975, and will be forced to pay money already spent. For states out of compliance with staff ratio requirements, fines will be imposed back to February 1976, the date the suspension of these requirements was lifted.

The cost of back penalties to the states is enough to cripple their social service budgets for some time to come. Add to this the number of women who will return to welfare because they will have no place for their children to go, and it is obvious that we will be facing a crisis of major proportions at a time when we are supposed to be embarking on plans for economic recovery.

If there is any one program that is a proven cost-effective investment into the lives and welfare of our lower-income families it is day care; more than any other program, day care provides the impetus for women to break the devastating cycle of poverty, which has relegated them and their children to lives of despair. Whatever our national objectives for welfare spending are, we can count on day care to provide a direct monetary return and, at the same time, enhance the quality of life for our greatest natural resource—our children.

Obviously, the need for day care will not go away. Our current economic difficulties have forced more women—many from middle-income families—to look for day care since they must now work to supplement incomes rendered inadequate by the spiraling cost of living. Yet, with his veto, President Ford has eliminated that possibility for these families.

I am certain that many state offices share my concern for the day care program; governors know that, unless this veto is overridden when Congress resumes after the Easter recess, they will face nearly insurmountable fiscal problems. President Ford and his economic advisers have been advocating a posture which is supposed to bring us out of the worst economic crisis in 40 years. Yet, by his action on this bill, he missed an obvious opportunity to relieve the welfare rolls, decrease unemployment, and help two million of our most needy youngsters in the process.

Closing Remarks

Delivered at the University of Massachusetts, Amherst, conference "Black Studies and Women's Studies: An Overdue Partnership," April 23, 1983.

The partnership of Women's Studies and Black Studies has the potential for addressing questions of racism in the Women's Rights

---

Transcript in the Shirley Chisholm Papers, MC 1194, Special Collections and University Archives, Rutgers University Libraries.

Movement as well as the problem of sexism in the black experience. The various theoretical perspectives on feminism whether bourgeois, radical or socialist do not reflect the experience of black or other minority women. The isolation and compartmentalization in many Women's Studies programs reflects an attempt to narrowly define "women's issues." The class bias in Women's Studies also skews the economic concerns of women to issues like "pension reform" and "comparable worth" while ignoring the plight of domestic workers and migrant women. Black Studies can offer a more "holistic" approach to women's issues. On the other hand Black Studies departments have all but ignored the sexism faced by black women. Our male colleagues, in this field, are the principal culprits of this policy. Women's Studies can bring a breath of fresh air into courses like "Economics in the Black Community." By focusing on the "feminization of poverty" and the increasing percentage of black female-headed households, the special concerns of black women can be more fully integrated into the curricula. These issues have been largely ignored by the respective programs. Today's conference offers a basis for a much greater exploration of the problems of racism and sexism in American society. Many people have been excited and surprised by the mere theme of this conference. This effort is really long overdue given the historic origins of these programs.

History really binds Women's Studies and Black Studies in the common struggles of the student protests of the '60's and '70's. Both disciplines are an outgrowth of student demands for a different kind of option in their educational development. These modern linkages only mirror earlier political responses to racism and sexism. Just as the "suffragette movement" was, in many ways, spurred by the abolitionists of the 19th century, numerous civil rights workers from the 1950's and the 1960's have emerged as feminist academics in the 1970's. In fact, the evolution of Black Studies provided a model for Women's Studies, in some cases. For example, in mid-1970 in one of the first essays to discuss the neglect and distortion of women university courses and curricula, Sheila Tobias, in "Female Studies—An Immodest Proposal," called for a new program of "Female Studies" at Cornell University, justifying her stand with an analogy to Black Studies.

As these programs emerged, however, it became obvious that their acceptance as respectable academic additions would depend on the extent to which their structures, purposes and course offerings approximated traditional programs. As evidenced by our discussions over the last two days, this tension between the "non-traditional programs" survival in a "traditional atmosphere" remains a problem for both Women's Studies and Black Studies. The crux of this problem lies with the multidisciplinary nature of these programs. University campuses have generally rejected "interdisciplinary scholarship"; thus Women's Studies and Black Studies have been plagued by a widespread suspicion that they lower academic standards and in general pollute the intellectual atmosphere. In addition, because of their origin, these programs offer a much more activist orientation than their "sister" departments. Considering the sheltered "Ivy Tower" attitude of academia, in general, political activism is not an inducement for additional F.T.E. positions.

Without academic respectability, Black and Women's Studies programs are destined to remain marginal units. We must examine creative ways to break this cycle of marginality. In this regard, both programs have something to learn from each other.

The double purpose of Women's Studies—to expose and redress the oppression of women—reflects the widespread attempts to restructure the classroom experience of students and faculty. Periodic small group discussions, use of first names for instructors as well as students, assignments that required journals, "reflection papers," cooperative projects, and collective modes of teaching with student participation all sought to transfer to Women's Studies the contemporary feminist criticism of authority and the validation of every woman's experience. These techniques, borrowed from the Women's Movement, also were designed to combat the institutional hierarchy and professional exclusiveness that had been used to shut out women. Collectivity in teaching and in program governance has been deemed the radical and vital contribution of the Women's Movement to educational innovation. Despite the emphasis on cooperative and group experience, however, Women's Studies courses made heavy demands on students and teachers.

Where Black Studies programs have attempted similar efforts, they have been widely attacked as offering "mick" courses. Black students are partially responsible for this image. While strong advocates for more black professors and more courses in the "Black experience," few students choose to major in Black Studies because "they don't want those courses on their transcript." Women's Studies appears to be more successful in retaining students as majors. While continuing their innovative teaching methods, perhaps Black Studies practitioners need to become more rigorous in their demands on student performance. Our students need to be constantly reminded that their skin color is not an excuse for incompetence. If scholarship is not demanded of students, particularly at the undergraduate level, then we have little hope of developing future Black Studies' scholars to maintain this discipline in the future.

On the other hand, Black Studies can offer Women's Studies a model for a multi-disciplinary program. As one Black Studies chairman suggested: the "real obligation of Afro-American studies" is "to transform and redefine the academic mainstream." To adequately foster this transformation, some Black Studies programs require more coursework in the traditional social science disciplines. For example, if students wanted a strong economics element in their work then they would have to learn economic theory in other departments; while there may not be such a thing as "Black Economics," a variety of different economic techniques of analysis can be applied to a variety of concerns. In this case, the concern would be Afro-American.

This approach has promoted a kind of cross-fertilization from other departments. For example, Harvard's Afro-American Studies Department has sponsored a general education course on the development of race as a concept. The course was team-taught with professors from Zoology, History of Science, Anthropology and the Medical School. The course dealt with race as a concept in science—historically, biologically and politically.

Women's Studies programs have been reluctant to attempt an interdisciplinary approach because of a fear of "co-optation" by the traditional disciplines. One approach suggested by Christine Garside Allen would combine introductory and advanced-level "interdisciplinary" courses with intermediate courses work in the traditional "Letters and Sciences" disciplines. This structure offers undergraduates a foundation for future graduate work in a traditional discipline while preserving a strong Women's Studies program.

Women's Studies and Black Studies also share the commonality of negative internal battles: the integration into Women's Studies of women of color and lesbians remain critical issues; Black Studies varies widely in its inclusiveness of the Afro-American, Caribbean and African experience. Debates on a departmental structure versus a collective approach will continue to be an important administrative issue. The unique example of the department of Ethnic Studies and Women's Studies at California State University at Chico proves that a "true partnership" between the two programs is possible. As academicians who are breaking new ground, we must strive to improve the quality of Women's Studies and Black Studies programs. We should "borrow" from the successes of these programs but as black women we must also integrate these disciplines whenever possible. As Barbara Smith, a pioneer in Black Women's Studies, suggests, a Women's Studies Program committed to research, writing and teaching that makes the experience of black women immediately accessible to all women "would necessarily require and indicate that fundamental political and social change is taking place."

The political origins of these programs demand that we remain committed to an "alternative method" of analyzing the experiences of women and minorities in American society. Since we have chosen to compete on the academic stage, we must ensure that "the props are in place and that we have to memorize the dialogue correctly." Certainly greater demands are placed on Black Studies and Women's Studies programs to "compete" effectively in academia. We should not be cowed by this challenge; after all, women and blacks have always had to exhibit superior qualities to be accepted in this society. We must remember that "no one will save us but us." Surely Women's Studies and Black Studies are worth preserving, even at the cost of great sacrifice. I urge you to use this weekend's exchange as a catalyst for the struggles ahead. Thank you.

"Black Struggle in History for Excellence in Education"

The subject of this lecture, delivered in Washington, D.C., on February 19, 1984, reflects the national theme for Negro Heritage Week that year, selected by the Institute for Afro-American Studies.

Thank you for the opportunity to discuss with you one of my favorite topics in education, "The Black Struggle for Excellence in Education." The first thought which comes to mind in this vein is the historic importance of the traditionally black post-secondary institution. The achievements of black college graduates continue to reinforce the necessity for maintaining our traditionally black institutions of higher learning. I would like to direct your attention to several key issues that are important to black colleges.

As I am sure many of you are aware, it has become popular in some circles today to talk about the growing irrelevancy of a college degree. In higher education journals and in the popular news media, articles abound which question the wisdom of continuing to encourage young people to seek college degrees in the face of a changing and tightening job market. But while this information may reflect accurately the experience of some, it does not reflect the experience of blacks. For blacks, higher education continues to be a significant factor in professional achievement. A study recently brought to my attention indicates that in recent years the trend has

---

Transcript in the Shirley Chisholm Papers, MC 1194, Special Collections and University Archives, Rutgers University Libraries.

been to increase rather than decrease the importance of the college degree. In 1959, for example, black men ages 25–29 who had graduated from college were earning 71% of the earnings of comparable white men. In 1969, the percentage was 83%. By 1973, this same study showed that black earnings had achieved parity with whites for those who had attended college. At the same time, high school graduates were earning only 69% in 1959, 77% in 1969 and 79% in 1973 of their white counterparts.

These statistics demonstrate an indisputable fact: despite changes in the job market, despite economic crises, for blacks the best route to increased earning potential and other measures of professional success continues to be the attainment of the college degree.

Because the attainment of higher education is so vital for blacks, the forces who undermine that opportunity are a serious threat to the survival of a viable black community in this nation. Before examining the plight of blacks in higher education, we must understand the current malaise faced by black children as they matriculate through the nation's school systems. Increasingly, our public schools are under attack as deteriorating in both quality and environment. The struggle to keep drugs off the playgrounds of elementary school receives more time and effort on the part of teachers than teaching multiplication tables and the rudiments of reading. Tuition tax credits are increasingly looked upon as the saving grace not only for the white middle class but for blacks as well. Thus, the children of the poor remain in substandard schools with new threats of further cuts in the Title I education program for the disadvantaged and little support for public schools.

A concerted effort is needed to prepare these children with a sufficient education so that they can have the option of choosing vocational education or some other training as well as a college career. We should not apologize for the fact that college is not for every student. But every child should have that option available to him or her. Parental involvement continues to be the best guarantee for a good education. The nation's public schools will continue to educate the large majority of American children. Those of us concerned with the education of black children must fight for a decent education through the public schools. This commitment means that we must insist on continued federal education aid for the disadvantaged; parental involvement must increase and community-police efforts must be developed to combat crime and drugs in our schools. Without a real turnaround in our public schools, we are only kidding ourselves that our children will be prepared for a college career. Programs such as "biomedical sciences," a program to encourage junior high school students to pursue science and medical careers, must be removed from Reagan's education block grant and targeted to institutions with a commitment to increasing minority representation in these fields. Efforts of this kind at the elementary and secondary education level will enhance our youth's chances for a successful college career or the world of work, if they choose not to attend college. The same commitment that we give to preserving our public schools must also be given to the nation's black colleges.

Unquestionably, the greatest support for blacks in higher education has been our control over our own institutions, our black colleges. Today, 70% of all black graduates receive their undergraduate degrees from black colleges. The historically black college continues to offer the best educational opportunity for poor, black students. Despite many of these students' poor academic preparation, black colleges are able to provide the necessary one-to-one counseling and remedial assistance to make these students successful. The academic success stories from these schools make charges of financial mismanagement all the more troubling. Many of the problems evidenced by our black colleges occur as a result of staff and resource limitations. Because the site and character of the student body have drastically changed at some of these schools, many colleges are almost wholly dependent upon federal support to keep their doors open. Pell Grants are a major source of institutional support for the low-income students who attend these institutions. In this regard, President Reagan's budget proposals in the student aid area provide the greatest threat to the survival of our black colleges. While the president's executive order on black colleges, 12232, calls for the enhancement and support of these colleges, there is an internal inconsistency in the administration's actions when they claim support for black colleges at the same time that financial aid is being cut back.

Under current law, students can receive some amount of a Pell Grant even if their family's income is as high as $25,000. The president's budget calls for students to provide 40% of their financial need, from non-governmental sources, before they are eligible for a Pell Grant. Fortunately, Congress has consistently rejected the Administration's proposals on financial aid.

I might add that the student body, at many of our black institutions, are unable to find summer jobs which pay enough to set aside a portion of these earnings for tuition contributions, so these schools are loath to pass tuition increases based upon this expectation. Moreover, middle class students who [formerly] enrolled in black colleges in large numbers and who *could* be expected to make a financial contribution toward their own college education now attend predominantly white institutions with increasing frequency.

In reality, this situation means that 90–95% of the financial support at many black colleges is derived from the federal government either in the form of Title III, "Strengthening Developing Institutions" funds from the Higher Education Act, or as the administrative share of student financial assistance monies. The extremely tight financial dilemma at many of these schools has forced college administrators to sometimes use these funds, which are earmarked for a specific purpose, to meet payroll or other institution obligations. Furthermore, the lack of modern accounting techniques and machinery sometimes results in the misappropriation of federal categorical funds. College administrators *must* take the responsibility for instituting better financial management. Restricted funds cannot continue to be used for unauthorized purposes.

Black college presidents are aware that they cannot increase tuition beyond the stipend award available under the Pell Grant program or they run the risk of pricing their institutions out of the student market they draw upon. This dismal catch-22 financial situation locks these special purpose schools into an unrealistic tuition scale which is hardly adequate to pay competitive faculty salaries or purchase modern administrative services.

With pressures to fully integrate higher education, black colleges also face competition for both black students and faculty. Blacks are attending white higher education institutions in greater numbers than ever before. Their parents' tax dollars have supported public higher education for a number of years and consequently these students feel that they have just as much right to attend a state university as anyone else. The private, Ivy League schools can afford to financially support young, talented blacks in a way that is not feasible for the average black college. Large research universities are very attractive to the black scholar who once would have been confined to a black college because of segregation. The "hand to mouth" existence of the colleges also restricts the quality of their libraries, laboratories and other research and auxiliary facilities and low salaries and as a result contributes to the "brain drain" problem.

One area where resources have been sorely lacking is black land grant institutions through congressional action in 1890. Tuskegee Institute was designated as a land grant institution in 1899. Until 1981, these institutions lacked the equipment and facilities that would enable them to have a competitive research capability in the areas of food and agriculture. The 97th Congress passed a "Facilities Support Bill" as part of the 1981 Farm Act which authorized $50 million to enhance the research facilities of these colleges. Ten million dollars was appropriated in FY 1983 and an additional $10 million has been requested by the Department of Agriculture for Fiscal Year 1985. Black land grant institutions, however, continue to be shortchanged by the Agriculture Department. In 1979, the total resources received by all black colleges, from the department, was only $28 million in comparison to $430 million received by all land grant institutions.

Other factors also contribute to the loss of black faculty. Quite frankly, many black faculty members, who are actively recruited by white universities, are often stifled by the traditionally tight administrative controls exercised by many black schools. Therefore, we must accept that efforts to integrate blacks into the faculties and student population of white universities will mean that many of these people will be lost to black colleges. Also, however, these "affirmative action" efforts will mean that increasing numbers of white professors will join faculties at black colleges and integrate the black student body. This trend has the potential to drastically change the character of black institutions as we know them.

The *Adams* decision represented the first attempt to apply the principles in *Brown v. Board of Education* to the desegregation of higher education institutions. The *Adams* litigation sought the termination of federal funding to stateside systems which continued to perpetuate dual systems of post-secondary education. Eleven years after the *Adams* decree, the Department of Education initiated enforcement with respect to the compliance status of eight states in addition to North Carolina, who was originally charged in the suit in 1970. Alabama, Delaware, South Carolina and West Virginia were notified in January of 1981 of the failure of their state public education systems to comply with Title VI. Kentucky and Missouri received similar notices that same month as did Ohio. The Reagan Administration has adopted different civil rights policies which resulted in "withdrawal" of these notices and diminished enforcement efforts. This action should come as no surprise given the recent debacle with the U.S. Civil Rights Commission. However, as a result of the plaintiff's monitoring of the Department of Education's enforcement effort, Judge John H. Pratt indicated that he would establish ". . . some deadlines" for desegregating public colleges in twelve Southern and Border States. The Department of Education, last May, also issued new enforcement guidelines and reporting requirements. In the general area of the black public college, black state legislators have a unique role to play in ensuring that these schools receive fiscal support from the State Treasury. Many of these desegregation agreements require that the states commit new money to these colleges. For example,

Texas is committed to $20 million to strengthen and enhance Prairie View A&M Texas Southern University. South Carolina State is supposed to receive over $11.5 million to implement new academic programs as part of its state's desegregation effort. These commitments will not be fulfilled without constant monitoring on the part of black legislators in those states.

Admittedly, some black colleges have been "lost" through integration. This phenomenon has occurred, however, only in the "Border States" of West Virginia, Missouri, and Kentucky. Poor white students have entered West Virginia State, Bluefield State, Lincoln University and Kentucky State's Master's program because no other higher education institution exists. This trend appears to be confined only to "Border States."

In recent weeks, I am sure that we have all heard about the plight of Fisk University. Certainly the threatened closing of one of our most prestigious black colleges brings home the precarious financial positions these schools are in. The Congress has offered some relief in the form of a challenge grant program. This program is designed to promote increased state and private sector investment in developing institutions. I am excited by the potential this program represents for the stimulation of the states and private enterprise to take a more active role in achieving the goal of financial stability among black colleges. This provision is one that I pushed during the reauthorization of the Higher Education Act in 1979 and I am pleased to see that Congressman Paul Simon has continued his support for challenge grants by reporting our legislation which would allow 20% of a challenge grant to be used for endowments. The Senate has refused to act on this legislation this far. If this bill could be enacted, then black colleges could begin to build an independent resource base.

Outside of the black college setting, we cannot afford to ignore the problems of black students at traditionally white institutions. Needless to say, these problems are not exclusively attributable to financial aid shortages. For example, the Southern Regional Education Board studies indicate that although there has been substantial progress for blacks in higher education in predominantly white colleges, the vast majority of black students will still earn their baccalaureate degrees from historically black institutions.

These findings appear to confirm an argument often voiced by black students and educators that while white universities have opened their doors to black students, and to a lesser extent, black faculty, many of these students "fall through the cracks" before graduation. We often find these statistics to support the continuing need for black colleges but they are also an indictment of the true commitment of white post-secondary institutions to the minority student. We must demand that these colleges and universities provide the necessary financial and academic support to black students. Certainly, the presence of black faculty, with tenured positions, would serve as an anchor for students who find the university campus to be an alienating environment. As taxpayers, we have an obligation to ensure that these institutions do a better job of serving our community. We support the University of Virginia, CUNY and SUNY campuses in New York and the University of California system with hard-earned tax dollars. Black and other minority youngsters deserve a fair chance at these prestigious campuses. It is a demand that is often ignored in our legitimate quest to preserve black colleges but it is one that we can no longer afford to let fall by the wayside.

In conclusion, let me say that many of you are now probably thinking, "There goes Chisholm again," asking us to act on all fronts. Many people thought my retirement would quiet me down. In fact, since I am no longer a public official, I take great delight in saying just what is on my mind. And I believe that for blacks not only to move forward in the educational arena but to prevent us from losing ground we must act in all areas of education. Parents need to join their children's local parent associations; we need to make regular financial contributions to our black colleges not only when there is a crisis situation; and finally we need to insist on quality educational experiences for both black faculty and students at traditionally white colleges and universities. This challenge may seem to be an awesome task but we have many historical role models that show us that it can be done. Booker T. Washington and Mary McLeod Bethune started black colleges in barns and woodsheds without knowing where the next dime would come from to realize their dreams of an education for newly-freed slaves. Tuskegee Institute and Bethune-Cookman College stand as a testament to the fact that hard work and perseverance hold great rewards. Despite Fisk University's current troubles, it would not exist today but for the sacrifice of nine Fisk students in the late 1870's who formed the Fisk Jubilee singers to raise money for their school. It is a little-known fact that eight of these students gave up their own academic careers in order to save Fisk. Only one graduated from Fisk despite their immeasurable contributions to the school. The fight for a black academic high school in Washington, D.C., which led to the establishment of the famous Dunbar High School, exemplifies the determination of black educators for quality education.

I am sure that there are many other examples of triumphs by black educators against the odds. We are far better off than they were and we should not ignore this legacy. Education has always been the saving grace of the black community. Without this reservoir for the development of our people, our communities will face severe setbacks in the near future. The hour is growing late; let us redouble our efforts, on all fronts, to enhance the quality of education for black America.

2   *Colonialism*

*In rising, I remind America that I am a representative of the black people,
an American captive.*

"ON CAPTIVE NATIONS WEEK" (1970)

During the Great Depression, the worst economic downturn of the industrial world, Chisholm migrated from Brooklyn to her mother's homeland
of Barbados. The experiences of spending her early childhood years on the
British-controlled island and then living under an American apartheid in
Brooklyn's poorest neighborhoods shaped her intimate understanding of
colonialism and imperialism. This worldview stamped her fight as an organizer who sought to break the stranglehold of white supremacy in New
York City politics. Entering Congress, Chisholm developed an instinct for
recognizing all forms of political subjugation. Debating on Capitol Hill
amid the Cold War, she boldly condemned U.S. government officials for
operating as colonizers of nonwhite U.S. citizens, cailng them "hypocrites
in the eyes of the world" for using "freedom" as a pretense to control land,
markets, and populations across the globe. Judging by her activism and
position papers, a President Chisholm would have championed the rights
of all communities, in the U.S. and globally, to define their own future free
from colonial violence and exploitation.

"People and Peace, Not Profits and War"

The Congresswoman's inaugural floor speech on Capitol Hill, Washington, D.C., March 26, 1969.

Mr. Speaker, on the same day President Nixon announced he had decided the United States will not be safe unless we start to build a defense system against missiles, the Head Start program in the District of Columbia was cut back for the lack of money.

As a teacher, and as a woman, I do not think I will ever understand what kind of values can be involved in spending $9 billion— and more, I am sure—on elaborate, unnecessary, and impractical weapons when several thousand disadvantaged children in the nation's capital get nothing.

When the new administration took office, I was one of the many Americans who hoped it would mean that our country would benefit from the fresh perspectives, the new ideas, the different priorities of a leader who had no part in the mistakes of the past. Mr. Nixon had said things like this: "If our cities are to be livable for the next generation, we can delay no longer in launching new approaches to the problems that beset them and to the tensions that tear them apart." And he said, "When you cut expenditures for education, what you are doing is shortchanging the American future."

But frankly, I have never cared too much what people say. What I am interested in is what they do. We have waited to see what the new administration is going to do. The pattern is now becoming clear. Apparently launching those new programs can be delayed for a while, after all. It seems we have to get some missiles launched first. Recently the new Secretary of Commerce spelled it out. The

---

Congressional Record 115, pt. 6 (March 26, 1969): 7765.

Secretary, Mr. Stans, told a reporter that the new administration is "pretty well agreed it must take time out from major social objectives" until it can stop inflation.

The new Secretary of Health, Education, and Welfare, Robert Finch, came to the Hill to tell the House Education and Labor Committee that he thinks we should spend more on education, particularly in city schools. But, he said, unfortunately we cannot "afford" to, until we have reached some kind of honorable solution to the Vietnam war. I was glad to read that the distinguished Member from Oregon (Mrs. Green) asked Mr. Finch this: "With the crisis we have in education, and the crisis in our cities, can we wait to settle the war? Shouldn't it be the other way around? Unless we can meet the crisis in education, we really can't afford the war."

Secretary of Defense Melvin Laird came to Capitol Hill, too. His mission was to sell the anti-ballistic-missile insanity to the Senate. He was asked what the new administration is doing about the war. To hear him, one would have thought it was 1968, that the former Secretary of State was defending the former policies, that nothing had ever happened, a President had never decided not to run because he knew the Nation would reject him in despair over this tragic war we have blundered into. Mr. Laird talked of being prepared to spend at least 2 more years in Vietnam. Two more years, 2 more years of hunger for Americans, of death for our best young men, of children here at home suffering the life-long handicap of not having a good education when they are young. Two more years of high taxes, collected to feed the cancerous growth of a Defense Department budget that now consumes two-thirds of our Federal income.

Two more years of too little being done to fight our greatest enemies, poverty, prejudice, and neglect here in our own country.

Two more years of fantastic waste in the Defense Department and of penny pinching on social programs. Our country cannot survive 2 more years, or 4, of these kinds of policies. It must stop—this year—now.

Now I am not a pacifist. I am, deeply, unalterably, opposed to this war in Vietnam. Apart from all other considerations, and they are many, the main fact is that we cannot squander there the lives, the money, the energy that we need desperately here, in our cities, in our schools.

I wonder whether we cannot reverse our whole approach to spending. For years, we have given the military, the defense industry, a blank check. New weapons systems are dreamed up, billions are spent, and many times they are found to be impractical, inefficient, unsatisfactory, even worthless. What do we do then? We spend more money on them. But with social programs, what do we do? Take the Job Corps. Its failure has been mercilessly exposed and criticized. If it had been a military research and development project, they would have been covered up or explained away, and Congress would have been ready to pour more billions after those that had been wasted on it.

The case of Pride, Inc., is interesting. This vigorous, successful black organization here in Washington, conceived and built by young inner-city men, has been ruthlessly attacked by its enemies in the Government, in this Congress. At least six auditors from the General Accounting Office were put to work investigating Pride. They worked 7 months and spent more than $100,000. They uncovered a fraud. It was something less than $2,100. Meanwhile, millions of dollars—billions of dollars, in fact—were being spent by the Department of Defense, and how many auditors and investigators were checking into their negotiated contracts? Five.

We Americans have come to feel that it is our mission to make the world free. We believe that we are the good guys everywhere-, in Vietnam, in Latin America, wherever we go. We believe that we are the good guys at home, too. When the Kerner Commission told white America what black America had always known, that prejudice and hatred built the Nation's slums, maintains them, and profits by them, white America would not believe it. But it is true. Unless we start to fight, and defeat, the enemies of poverty and racism in our own country and make our talk of equality and opportunity ring true, we are exposed as hypocrites in the eyes of the world when we talk about making other people free.

I am deeply disappointed at the clear evidence that the No. 1 priority of the new administration is to buy more and more and more weapons of war, to return to the era of the cold war, to ignore the war we must fight here—the war that is not optional. There is only one way, I believe, to turn these policies around. The Congress can respond to the mandate that the American people have clearly expressed. They have said, "End this war. Stop the waste. Stop the killing. Do something for our own people first." We must find the money to "launch the new approaches," as Mr. Nixon said. We must force the administration to rethink its distorted, unreal scale of priorities. Our children, our jobless men, our deprived, rejected, and starving fellow citizens must come first.

For this reason, I intend to vote "No" on every money bill that comes to the floor of this House that provides any funds for the Department of Defense. Any bill whatsoever, until the time comes when our values and priorities have been turned right-side up again, until the monstrous waste and the shocking profits in the defense budget have been eliminated and our country starts to use its strength, its tremendous resources, for people and peace, not for profits and war. It was Calvin Coolidge I believe who made the comment that "the Business of America is Business." We are now spending $80 billion a year on defense—that is two-thirds of every tax dollar. At this time, gentlemen, the business of America is war, and it is time for a change.

"The Black as a Colonized Man"

A lecture given at Atlanta University, Atlanta, Georgia, October 20, 1969.

There is little doubt that in some ways the Black American is a colonized man. One need only point to the ghetto as proof of at least one aspect of his colonization.

However, colonization is more than living together in the same areas. Since the situation of the Black American, past and present, differs so radically from that of other colonized people in many ways I would like to examine it in some depth.

There are two basic groups of colonized people, immigrants who migrate to a country and natives of a country which some other more powerful country conquers. Black Americans, it is obvious, fit into neither of these categories.

The immigrant usually leaves his homeland by choice. There may be many factors such as religious, economic, social or political persecution that influence him but it is still generally true that he is looking for a better way of life.

Transcript in the Shirley Chisholm Papers, MC 1194, Special Collections and University Archives, Rutgers University Libraries.

If he has somehow acquired the necessary social and cultural tools, or if his own culture is not too divergent from that of the host-country, he may be able to move directly into at least the economic mainstream. If he hasn't the requisite tools—knowledge of the host-language, some needed or desirable labor skill and at least a rudimentary education, he must find some way to acquire them and to survive at the same time.

What he does then, of course, is seek out people like himself—often a sister, brother or a friend—for help, advice and security. Even more often he does this before leaving his home country. Eventually, this process creates a colony, from which individuals filter out slowly into the host-society. Often these colonies are called more simply neighborhoods—the Italian neighborhood, the Jewish neighborhood and so on.

The situation for the Black American differed in that 1) he was transported largely against his will; 2) his own culture was intentionally obliterated and destroyed; 3) the skills that he had were of relative little use to the host-country; 4) his own language was destroyed for the most part by deliberately separating him from his fellow tribesmen and the language that was used by the slave masters to communicate with him emanated from the whip and the club; 5) his family and social ties were deliberately broken; 6) there was no way in which he could build a group economic basis; and finally 7) there was no way in which he could build group martial or political power. There are, of course, other differences but these seven constituted the major ones.

In the case of the colonial native—those persons who owned and occupied the land before the interloper—the colonist—forced his way in—there was also a situation that differed significantly from that of the first Black Americans.

First, guns and clubs were only moderately successful in destroying his culture even though they served to keep him docile. The native had in that respect the same advantage that the immigrant had over the first slaves. He could maintain his language, family structure, village or tribal ties, religion and other basic elements of his culture. Therefore, because he could retain the transmittants of his culture, he was free to perpetuate at least a facsimile of his former lifestyle.

For the newly arrived slave there was the future of deliberate and constant breaking of cultural ties that I mentioned.

Even more important was the fact that the major ingredient of his life-style was the force and violence perpetrated upon him. From dawn to dawn—twenty-four hours a day—it was the driving force of his life and was used by the slave masters to accomplish the governing of every aspect of his life, whether it was planting, harvesting or breeding.

There were few exceptions; there existed still vestiges of various African crafts such as weaving, wood-working and iron-working; drums were used for communication and music; work songs and spirituals showed African influence; and because it was virtually impossible to separate people from the same tribes completely, there were vestiges of the African languages left.

The other major exceptions were the "house Negroes" and the relatively few freedmen. Both of these groups had already begun the process that E. Franklin Frazier euphemistically calls "acculturation."

The fact that the vast majority of Black slaves lived in a cultural void is one of the prime reasons that the situations of Black Americans, even today, should not be seen as strictly analogous to colonialism.

The colonized native can choose between retaining his own culture or accepting the colonialist's, or as in the case of the immigrant, the host-culture.

For the Black slave there existed a void not only culturally but politically and economically also. It was the political and economic void that was to prove the most damaging to him.

The end of the Civil War freed some four million slaves and it was at this point that Black Americans "en masse" were faced with the most crucial decision—accept return to an Africa that most had never seen; accept the life-styles and cultural norms of the dominant society; or, somehow, build a new life-style and cultural base from scratch.

I use the word decision because in retrospect it would seem to have been a decision. In truth the die was already cast. The freedmen, North and South, had already set their feet upon a path—the uneducated, almost decultured Black masses had no real choice but to follow. There was nothing to do but to accept the dominant Western culture.

Before I go any further there are two factors that it is essential to establish. The first has to do with the different situations of the colonial native and the immigrant to, particularly, a capitalistic country.

Frantz Fanon, in *The Wretched of the Earth*, gives an excellent insight into the motivating factors of both the colonial and the capitalistic worlds. He pointed out that for the "native" in the colonial world the dividing line, the frontier, is clearly delineated by the barracks and the police station; the intermediary between the powerful and the powerless are the soldiers and the police.

He counterposes against this system of open force and brutality the capitalistic systems of using "education" (and I put that in quotes), the passed-on structure of moral reflexes, the gold watch or medal at the end of long and faithful service and other "esthetic expressions that are designed to lighten the task of policing" that the exploiter must have performed.

When we talk about the Black American as a "colonized man," it is important to remember that he has always lived in a capitalistic democracy that has not hesitated to use violence as well.

The second factor that is essential to establish at this point is the political and social context of the South at the end of the Civil War. It was then that I feel that the black American began to become "colonized."

The nation, and particularly the South, was in tumultuous disorder, politically, socially and economically. The country had fought a war based primarily on economics that the North had disguised as a war for social justice. Even the President had said that the most important factor was the non-dissolution of the Union. The country, North and South, found itself with two problems it was ill-prepared to solve. The abolishment of slavery had been accomplished but the Nation was still split asunder. The second problem was, of course, what to do with four million freed Negroes.

Dr. Rayford Logan described the situation thusly: "Quite apart from considerations of race and class, the elements of a community that have long exercised exclusive control of government do not generally relinquish that control without a struggle. The contest in the South, however, was initially embittered by the difference in race and culture."

The years immediately following the Civil War were perilous and trying ones for the Southern Black. Most white Southerners either participated in, or condoned, the political frauds that brought "home rule" back to Tennessee, for example, as early as 1869 and to three more states the next year. Many white Southerners also either condoned or participated in the intimidation by violence and terror as exemplified by the Ku Klux Klan and similar groups.

Some of the most significant advances in many Southern State Constitutions were accomplished in that period but in most cases as soon as "home rule" returned they were either wiped out or replaced by the infamous "Black Codes."

In fact, throughout the entire period everything that looked as if it *might* benefit Black folks was systematically destroyed, either by law or by violence.

Unfortunately, it was at this point that education, or more to the point—the lack of education—had its greatest impact upon the new Black American.

Education has always had as its primary task imparting not only the history of a culture but, in fact, the transmission of the culture itself.

Now, for Frantz Fanon's "colonial native" or for the immigrant, education was a process of cultural superimposition at best or cultural transplantation by choice and design at worst. Education, for the freed slave, was cultural implantation; he had no choice.

What I am saying is that in order to continue to exist—to do simple daily things like feeding one's family, if one had a family—the freed man had to begin to submit to the cultural norms of those who seemed "superior" to him. In short, to make it in Charley's world he had to imitate Charley.

At least three white groups in the South were aware of the impact that education for the masses of Blacks would have on their own conceptions of, and goals for, a future society. They were the Northern white Liberals and the Southern white Conservatives and Moderates.

For the Northern Liberal, education for the Negro was the best way toward an entirely new social order and they, as Horace Mann Bond stated it, "wished to use the schools for the Negroes as the instrument for leveling all vestiges of the past."

For the Southern Conservative education for Blacks meant potential Black political and economic power—two factors that would be fatal to their goal—a New South, constructed from the patterns of and shaped in the mold of the Old.

The white Southern Moderate saw education of Black people in what was perhaps the clearest context: a method and means of continuing control of the lives of Black people.

Needless to say, both groups of Southern whites saw the danger of allowing the Northern white Liberal to educate Black people.

The Northern Liberals, composed mainly of Abolitionists, church groups and missionary societies, were not just idle dreamers. Barely six months into the Civil War the American Missionary Society established a day school for what the Union Commander of the area called "contraband of war" at Fortress Monroe, Virginia.

That school still exists; today it is the Hampton Institute. Hampton set the tone for the rest of the emergent Negro schools, especially those established by the Liberals. The schools were intended to impart thrift, piety and industry primarily and they did.

It must be remembered that the schools were operated and controlled for a number of years by the same people who were setting up and running missionary schools throughout the world. It must also be remembered that thrift, piety and industry were the cardinal virtues of the religio-ethical background of the majority of those founders.

I don't mean to disparage the work of those good people but a few things must be pointed out. First, what they were doing was imposing a culture upon Black people. Secondly, they didn't fully comprehend the political and social context in which they found themselves; they were "educational carpet-baggers."

They had, though, a very impressive saving grace. They believed and helped demonstrate on a significant scale that Black people could be educated and this factor had telling force, particularly upon Black people themselves.

There was another major force involved as far as Southern education was concerned—the Bureau of Freedmen. It is important to note the presence of the Bureau for at least two reasons: one, it was involved in establishing and sustaining a number of schools and two, the charges of graft and corruption that hung over it provided further fuel to feed the Southern whites' anger.

Southern opposition to education for Black people took many forms, not the least of which were school-burnings, teacher-beatings and the siphoning off of funds intended for Negro schools.

Another formidable and effective weapon was the smear campaign instituted by Southern whites. They claimed that the Negro child wasn't worth educating, that he couldn't or wouldn't learn. They claimed that the moral standards of the "Yankee school-marms" left a great deal to be desired.

Some of this may seem irrelevant—it isn't. The job of making the Black American a colonized man, an accultured neo-native, had only begun. Education was to finish the task and these were the forces that shaped education for the Negro in the South.

A strange, unholy alliance took place in the period that followed Reconstruction. It was left to the Southern Moderates, black and white, to "cast down their buckets" and make the best of what was an intolerable situation for both.

As I indicated earlier, the white Moderates realized that the brand of education dispensed by Northern white Liberals spelled absolute doom for the hope of salvaging anything at all of the pre-war Southern life-style. Most of them also recognized the fact that some form of education was inevitable.

These two factors combined to give them the impetus to do two things. First, they involved themselves in maintaining schools for Blacks, often at private expense. Secondly, they moved to control public education of Black students.

The Black leaders realized the absolute need for any kind of education for the masses of Black people. They were also extremely aware of the political and social context in which they existed.

No one can say for sure whether those early Negro schools and educators would have survived at all if they had become embroiled in the political and social holocaust that was raging in the South. Therefore no one can say that they were completely wrong in their choice of curriculum and direction. We do know, though, some of the results of the emphasis on "industrial education." W.E.B. DuBois has pointed out that such an emphasis would mean that Negroes would no longer demand the right to vote, the same public education as whites, or integration. He said that such an education was intended to make Black students docile and servile. There were other factors, it is true, but in essence I believe that DuBois was right.

The majority of graduates from Negro schools went into teaching in other Negro schools, carrying with them that colonialized attitude—spreading it.

I cannot say that they were wrong just as I cannot say that the schools were wrong. In many ways the schools and teachers of that day—in that time and place—were as militant and courageous as were the students and civil rights workers of the 1950's and 1960's.

But it must be said that the type of education available on the one hand and the lack of education for many on the other produced a break between the classes of Black people that made it easy to maintain control or colonization, if you will, of all Black people.

I have taken almost an hour saying to you what Malcolm summed up in this brief paragraph: "The slavemaster took Tom and dressed him well, fed him well and even gave him a little education—a *little* education; gave him a long coat and a top hat and made all the other slaves look up to him. Then he used Tom to control them. The same strategy that was used in those days is used today."

The reason that I have taken so much time is to show you that there were extenuating circumstances in those days. I must remind you that there are very few today. You no longer have good reason to perpetuate or succumb to innocuous mind-deadening education designed to control you.

Many students today want to know about power, especially economic and political power. That is true whether they are studying medicine, law or physical education.

Black educators, North and South, are going to have to involve themselves in both of those areas. Particularly in the South is this important since almost eighty per cent of the Black students who received B.A.s last year were graduated by Southern schools that were predominately Black.

Just as important to the Southern schools and therefore presumably to all Black Americans is the financial crisis that these schools are facing. In order to overcome it those who run the schools, those who attend the schools and those who support them are going to have to become knowledgeable in economics and politics very quickly.

The education that you will receive in trying to save their lives as institutions will have to be transferred to students as soon as you possibly can do it.

As I said, students want to know about power—they want that power to make some important changes. Changes not only in the colonial status of Black Americans—but in the fabric of the country itself.

It would behoove us to give them access to that knowledge for two reasons. One, it is their birthright and two, they intend to make those changes with or without sophisticated knowledge.

The passage I quoted from Malcolm is wrong in one sense. The leadership styles will no longer work effectively today. And educational leaders of today must involve themselves in the life of the community that swirls around them.

"On Captive Nations Week"

Congressional floor speech, Washington, D.C., July 17, 1970. Captive Nations Week was originally established by Congress in the early years of the Cold War to bring attention to Soviet-controlled Eastern European nations.

Mr. Speaker, I rise today in recognition of Captive Nations Week, which has been proclaimed as July 12 to 18. Americans have been urged to express their concern for the future of individual rights in Central and Eastern Europe and wherever else those rights are being violated and threatened.

Congressional Record 116, pt. 18, extensions of remarks (July 17, 1970): 24932-33.

I acknowledge this occasion and, in rising, I remind America that I am a representative of the black people, an American captive. There can no longer be any thinking and aware person who does not understand the reality of my position. Bedford-Stuyvesant and Harlem in New York, Chicago's South Side, Roxbury in Boston, Watts in Los Angeles, all these are "ghettos." A resident of one of these or a similar area seems to have no rights that anyone is bound to respect. Every action of an individual must have the approval of an outside authority.

The killings of innocent students at Jackson, the shootings of black men in Augusta, these, and more recorded infamous deeds, make it impossible for black people to determine and realize any of their own goals. In most areas, the old saying about the black neighborhood being on the other side of the tracks remains true.

While black people are the largest "ghetto," they are by no means the only racial or economic group to be subject to America's whims or to be set apart from the mainstream. Mexican-Americans, or as they prefer, Chicanos, white migrant workers, Puerto Ricans, and, still, the American Indians are in the same predicament. Indeed, women are also a captive nation.

These six groups can do nothing that the Americans have not officially approved. Indians are forced to live on reservations; migrant farm workers—white and Chicano—are forced to work for next to nothing on a precarious seasonal basis in miserable conditions; Puerto Ricans are confined to the lowest menial jobs in the cities where they abound.

Mr. Speaker, Chinatown, Harlem, and El Barrio are not historical, different, exciting, or flavorful places to visit. They are the preserves for the United States captive nations.

Presidential Campaign Position Paper No. 1: Foreign Aid

The first of ten position papers that were distributed to the public and press by the Chisholm presidential campaign beginning in January 1972 for that year's Democratic primary contest.

The legislative debacle which occurred in 1971 over the Foreign Aid Bill has shown clearly that the American Foreign Aid Program, in operation for 25 years, has reached the point where its future is in real doubt. Congress has appropriated less funds for the program than ever before. The reasons for the widespread discontent with the program are varied. Some argue that it has been a rat hole into which the U.S. has poured countless millions of dollars for nothing. Others argue that we have given aid to "Communist" or "Leftist" governments who have used it against American interests.

The most serious criticism of Foreign Aid, however, is coming from those who have always staunchly supported aid. We are concerned that Foreign Aid seems to be failing to achieve its own prescribed objectives. We feel that our Foreign Aid is in fact retarding long-term growth abroad, including political development of the poor nations. For this reason, many of us have come to realize the necessity for a radically different approach. We are therefore not talking of abolishing Foreign Aid but of restructuring and revitalizing it.

We know that the gap between the rich and poor nations of the world is widening. We know that this gap increasingly threatens international stability. We have seen in the past decade internal uprisings and continuing domestic political and social turmoil in country after country in the developing world. Let us make no mis-

Shirley Chisholm Project Archives (SCPA), Brooklyn College.

take about it—this is an historic period in international affairs. Throughout the developing world there is a revolution going on involving radical, structural change in the political, social, and economic systems. It is in our interest, I suggest, and in the interest of humanity that this revolution be peaceful. The tragedy of our Foreign Aid Program—and what has caused its near wreckage—is the fact that our Foreign Aid policy has for too long combined an offering of lip service to broad structural change with the systematic lending of actual support for the status quo. Under the guise of an unending, paranoiac anti-Communist crusade, we have shipped guns and napalm to self-serving and cynical dictators all over the world to use against those among their own countrymen who have tried to make real in their nations that which we have so piously declared we faithfully support everywhere—freedom, democracy, and self-determination. Our Foreign Aid has too often provided a source of patronage and political strength for the existing power structure in poor nations. All over the world, it is American weapons and the assistance of U.S. military groups which repressive dictatorships have used, and are still using to stifle real reform.

Under the Foreign Aid program, the United States has become the chief arms supplier of mankind. Where we once proclaimed proudly that America was the "Arsenal of Democracy," we have become in the eyes of many the "Arsenal of Reactionary Violence" on the international scene. Having devoted so relatively little to the effort to deal with the actual causes of misery and social conflict overseas, we have repeatedly intervened, as in Vietnam and as in the Dominican Republic in 1965, to prop-up repressive or incompetent regimes confronted with the explosive discontent of their own peoples. Instead of providing sufficient sums of aid to poor countries to help them build roads, provide electric power, and improve education, we have rushed tanks, airplanes, guns, bombs, and military advisors to such reactionary governments as those in Spain, Brazil, Portugal, Greece, and Cambodia. Since 1959, for example, Portugal has received nearly $400 million in American aid under NATO—and used a large part of it in Black Africa to repress liberation movements seeking political self-determination. This has been a clear violation of NATO Treaty terms. In Greece, our aid has only served to create the impression among countless Greeks that we are singlehandedly upholding a government which has imposed and maintained martial law on its people for over 4 years, with no prospects for a return to constitutional democracy.

Why is it that we are always shipping murderous weapons to dictatorships to repress their poor and dispossessed? Why shouldn't we be sending economic aid to benefit the poor and to help eradicate those conditions which cause their discontent in the first place?

The United States is the richest country in the world, yet our Foreign Aid has decreased to the point where, under the Nixon Administration, it has reached the lowest level ever. Among the 16 members of the Development Assistance Committee, formed in 1961 under U.S. leadership, America ranked 13th among the wealthy nations in terms of its public and private Foreign Aid disbursements when measured as a percent of the Gross National Product. Today in Latin America, the social revolution is under way with elements of the church, universities, and trade unions pushing for reform in their countries. Yet, the Nixon Administration has gutted the Alliance for Progress and the Peace Corps—two imaginative programs which so favorably impressed people everywhere not so long ago as products of the youthful idealism which America once symbolized. In the last few years, in Latin America,

Americans have been kidnapped and assassinated, a once close ally has freely elected a marxist government, and other countries have nationalized American companies operating there.

The Foreign Aid Program has become too tied-up with the supply of guns, rather than butter, to continue to serve its original, lofty purposes. It has become too often a political tool with which ambassadors could curry favor with the governments to which they are accredited. It has led America, a self-professed revolutionary nation, to become identified as a part of that bulwark of resistance to the profound changes now sweeping the third world. We have given much aid—but too often of the wrong type and to the wrong governments—and that is why the Foreign Aid Program is self-defeating and therefore no longer acceptable.

A new approach to Foreign Aid must be based on the premise that it is not only right for those of us who have, to help those who have not, but that we ignore the frustrations of poverty at home and abroad at our own risk. We must create among the poor everywhere new confidence in our desire to help, rather than hinder, this contemporary demand for social justice. We must work to reduce hunger, disease, ignorance, and poverty with the ultimate goal of higher living standards, more open and liberal societies and a stronger world community.

In so doing, we will prove that this great nation is in step with one of the great movements of history, and that it truly believes in the need to turn our swords into plowshares.

Economic and social development abroad is not something that can be precisely measured or that will be peaceful or even always consistent with our own perceived interests. Substantial progress is being made in many countries. Aid is not obsolete or a boondoggle or a giveaway, and economic aid is no longer a political orphan. Those of us who support reduced military aid and greater economic aid abroad will continue to speak out for a more sophisticated and objective view of aid. If we wish the world to be secure and prosperous, as I am sure we all do, we must show a common concern for the common problems of all people. By so doing, we will demonstrate that international leadership is a matter of performance, and imagination[,] rather than of arm twisting and distribution of largesse. We must provide a clear and confident commitment to the future, rather than the past, and I propose such initial steps as the following, many of which have been proposed by experts, to reshape our Foreign Aid Program:

1. Greatly increased economic aid (to amount to 1% of total U.S. GNP) to assist the poor countries in their struggle against ignorance and poverty;

2. Greatly decreased military aid abroad, including elimination of aid to repressive regimes such as those in Spain, Greece, Portugal, and Cambodia;

3. Gradual abolition of the Agency for International Development and elimination of the American ambassador responsibility for the administration of U.S. assistance programs;

4. Increased multilateralization of aid through strengthened international and regional agencies including the World Bank, the International Development Association, the Inter-American Development Bank, and Regional Development Banks;

5. The opening of the developed countries' markets to exports from developing countries by the creation of an open, non-discriminatory preference system featuring reduced tariffs and reduced excise taxes on imports from poor countries,

with an immediate reduction of duties on Latin American goods exported to the United States;

6. Focusing of technical assistance on family planning, agriculture, education, and vocational training;
7. Maximum funding for development loans;
8. The absence of paternalism or expectations of immediate economic or political reward;
9. Two years' authorization for aid funds rather than annual authorization in order to save Congress time and to provide greater time to organize and implement approved programs.

Presidential Campaign Position Paper No. 2: The Middle East Crisis

The second of ten position papers that were distributed to the public and press by the Chisholm presidential campaign beginning in January 1972 for that year's Democratic primary contest.

The renewed tragic conflict in the Middle East continues unresolved into the fourth year, presenting to the peoples of the area and to the world a source of misery and profound danger. The enormous military budgets of the countries of the region destroy possibilities for progressive economic and social development. A constant exchange of threats, political assassination, and the face to face confrontation of the big powers are all aspects of this terrible problem, with tensions and fears percolating insidiously while at this very moment diplomatic discussions appear to be going nowhere.

Shirley Chisholm Project Archives (SCPA), Brooklyn College.

There often seems to exist a gulf or mutual incomprehension between Arabs and Israelis as to the nature of each other's fears and the nature of a settlement by which the two peoples could peacefully coexist in the Middle East. Thoughtful Americans are appalled at the resulting carnage wrought by three wars there in the past 25 years, and they are deeply saddened that, during that period, they seem to have lost the goodwill and trust of the Arab people and gained simultaneously only the suspicions and doubts of the Israelis.

What is so tragic about this development is that Americans have genuine historical and spiritual ties with the peoples of the Middle East, Arabs and Jews. As school children, we learned about the birth of great religions and the growth of great civilizations. We marvelled at the accomplishments and contributions which the cultures of the Mesopotamia and the Nile Valley made to the development of Western civilization. Jerusalem, with its incredibly rich and diverse history, retains a special place in our hearts and minds as a great international city.

Today, Arabs and Jews live in the United States, enrichening our society and contributing to its cherished diversity. An increasing number of Americans, young and old, want to travel to these lands to see their architectural wonders, to meet their peoples, and to learn about their customs.

All of us, Arabs, Israelis, Americans—everyone—lose by the political confrontation in the Middle East. Choices have been forced for too long, passions have been inflamed, and foreign powers with alien and hostile ideologies have sought to gain strategic advantage in the region. A new approach to solving this dilemma is crucial if we are to get off the treadmill of fruitless talks and new outbreaks of violence.

I wish to state first that I personally appreciate the unique problems of Israel and of Jews the world over. I should know about discrimination and persecution. The idea of a national homeland for the Jewish people was a noble and perfectly logical idea in view of the monstrous horrors they had faced for so long. The creation of the State of Israel in Palestine was meant as a form of ultimate moral redress by the West for the atrocities committed against Jews throughout their long history. We Americans have always sincerely encouraged their efforts to build a modern and democratic nation, and we have naturally desired that they live in growing prosperity and peace with their Arab neighbors.

Yet, I suspect that too many people failed to recognize another very real human factor in this historic international political development. They failed to see and understand the personal implications of that development on [sic] those human beings who had lived in Palestine prior to 1948, those people still referred to as the "Palestinian Refugees."

In the midst of rejoicing at the creation of a national homeland for the Jews, the world overlooked the hardship and misery created for the Palestinians. The Palestinians have been forced to live in wretched refugee camps, their homes gone, many of them stateless citizens, living on UN relief supplies. A generation has grown up in the Palestinian ghetto, and, like the young who have survived their early years in our ghettos, these Palestinians have made clear that they will no longer tolerate the injustice of their condition. Those refugee camps have become emotionally festering sores for many young Palestinians who rightfully believe that the deplorable conditions in which they were raised must be drastically altered. Their acts of desperation in recent years have shocked us, perhaps unnecessarily, for we should have learned from our problems here at home the inevitable result of social injustice and poverty. Yet the Palestine dispute has appeared regularly on the annual agenda of the United Nations General Assembly for over 20 years. Soviet Communism has not been slow to seek political gain from this state of affairs.

Dr. Cham Weizman [*sic*] once said that the Arab-Jewish conflict with regard to Palestine is a clash between two rights, not between right and wrong. While we must protect Israel's very existence against outside threat by giving her whatever assistance she truly needs, we must also finally launch a new effort to resolve the root cause of this Middle East conflict, the Palestine dispute.

The Nixon Administration is uniquely unqualified for this change in focus. A law and order administration which has proved completely ineffective in dealing with the causes of lawlessness and revolt at home is temperamentally incapable of attacking the problems of the poor and dispossessed in the Middle East. Just as this Administration has found that an imposed peace will not long survive in our ghettos, neither will it prove successful in the ghettos of the Middle East.

Because of this shortsightedness, we have allowed the Soviet Union to posture as the Real Friend of the poor in the Middle East. While courageous governments in Libya, Egypt, and the Sudan, for example, struggle to maintain their freedom and independence from Soviet influence, we have been sidetracked into forgetting about the Palestine problem and simply engaging in endless maneuvering with the Soviet Union.

Instead of talking around each other or not even talking to each other, let us stop to realize that Arabs and Jews groan at their arms burden, the continuing brutal loss of life, and the hatred. I favor the following steps in an effort to move to what should be recognized as the heart of the Middle East conflict:

1. A United Nations guarantee, supported by the United States and the Soviet Union, to guarantee the stability and territorial integrity of all states in the Middle East;
2. A limitation on all arms shipments to the area;
3. Resumption of diplomatic relations with all Middle East governments;
4. Increased economic aid to the less developed nations of the region;
5. Full representation for the Palestinians in all negotiations concerning the return or compensation for Palestinian Arab property; and
   a. Immediate consideration of the problem of the lack of status of the several hundred thousand people who left Israeli held territory in 1948 and 1967.

If we stop to remember the human element in international affairs, rather than relying on deceit and threats and cheating, so much of a part of great power politics, we will be attacking the Middle East problem at its root—Palestine. It is a tragedy for the suffering peoples of that area, as it now is for the poor of our own society, that the present American government has become so enamoured of its game plans, its glamorous world travels, and its great schemes by which it intends to spin the world around like a top, without any hitches or mistakes, that it has completely ignored the desperate problems of human beings. Unresolved they keep our world in turmoil. Will this Administration ever learn this stark fact of life? Is it merely a coincidence that the Administration has done virtually nothing to help the Vietnamese refugees, the Pakistani refugees, and the Palestinian refugees while it is also steadily eliminating aid to our poor in America?

Presidential Campaign Position Paper No. 3: Equality of Commitment—Africa

The third of ten position papers that were distributed to the public and press by the Chisholm presidential campaign beginning in January 1972 for that year's Democratic primary contest.

This Administration's policy towards Africa, like that which it has followed toward its own Black citizens, has been one of "benign neglect," if not simply plain neglect. The Nixon Administration has ignored the tragic problems facing the poor nations of Black Africa. It has wiped out of its consciousness, if indeed such a notion ever existed there, the idea that the richest country in the world—Christian, young, and revolutionary in origin—should be able, and is morally obligated, to help the Africans in their fight against ignorance and poverty.

This policy is therefore identical to that which has been followed towards Americans. Just as the Nixon Administration has refused to allocate the resources necessary to help the poor in this country, so President Nixon has cut foreign aid to the lowest level in the history of the program, admitting that his 1969-70 program was the lowest aid recommendation proposal since the program began.

The spirit in which generous and useful economic aid programs for Africa were established and in which the Peace Corps was created in the early sixties has, in fact, been replaced by a great moral vacuum, cynically filled only by another expensive and empty vice presidential junket to various African nations having authoritarian governments. In the meantime, we have watched as some Africans

Shirley Chisholm Project Archives (SCPA), Brooklyn College.

begin to look elsewhere in recent years for the sympathy and help which we once gave them. An open and rather understandable public contempt for the American Government has developed among Africans and other poor peoples of the world as a result of this Government's attitude towards them.

Africa has, of course, been swept in and out of the vortex of cold war politics on numerous occasions. With Soviet interest in Africa apparently low for the moment, the Nixon Administration has also decided to ignore the area, so long as it seems to be free from the threat of "communist subversion." At home, the same attitude prevails—ignore the ghettos unless they blow up, and then send troops.

So, in the absence of a clear external threat to Africa, this Administration has consistently pursued the same kind of callous, insensitive, and reactionary policy toward Black Africa that it has toward Black Americans. It recently ignored, for example, UN economic sanctions against Rhodesia in order to permit the importation of Rhodesian chrome. It has refused to condemn in clear and categorical terms the white minority governments of Rhodesia, South Africa, and Portugal. It has tolerated the insulting refusal of the South African Regime to permit Arthur Ashe, one of the finest tennis players in the world, to play there. It has coldly ignored the struggling liberation movements in Angola, Mozambique, Namibia, and Zimbabwe. It has no meaningful and systematic contact with the Organization of African Unity.

Yet, despite this policy, or non-policy, this Administration is still capable of flying into a rage and sulking when African nations oppose us in the United Nations, as many did regarding the seating of China. In Africa as at home, we should clearly understand that the Nixon Administration is a minority government, representing the wealthy and vested interest. As such, it is on the defensive, confronted by a coalition of not only the non-white minorities but any of their poor white people as well. This particular Administration is distrusted because of the narrowness of its vision and rigidity of its attitudes towards the poor majority of the world's peoples. There should be no surprise then, that the position of the United States in the United Nations and in the world at large has seriously eroded during the Nixon Administration.

The racial attitudes of this Administration are well-known by Blacks here and in Africa. The negative image of the character of this Administration is shared by Black Americans and Black Africans. President Nixon has not only failed to bring this nation together, but he has, through his attitudes towards Africa, contributed to racial and economic polarizations so great that they pose a threat to the entire international community. In so doing, this government has blithely permitted African-American relations to disintegrate to the lowest level in recent history, ignoring the blood relationship which binds so many Americans to Africa and oblivious of the consequences which are sure to come.

I wish to stress that I do not propose a huge giveaway program to Africa in the face of our enormous needs here at home, nor am I calling for world-wide revolution against the powers that be. I offer rather a new attitude of sympathetic solidarity with the poor in Africa and a policy which would include at least these key elements:

1. A fresh look at our relations with those European states maintaining racist policies in African countries, a review of our relations with each African nation, and the development of an understanding of the causes for which the various liberation groups in Africa are now fighting;

2. The appointment of highly qualified Black Americans to top positions in my cabinet, the courts, and the diplomatic service to let Africa and the world know that America is a multiracial nation and proud of it;

3. Preferential trade agreements with Black African countries and support for reduced air fares between Africa and America;

4. Increased economic aid to Africa, to be administered by recognized and efficient international organizations, in close cooperation with the World Bank and International Monetary Fund;

5. The systematic condemnation in word and deed of the racist policies of white minority governments in Rhodesia, South Africa, Mozambique, and Angola. With respect to South Africa and its barbarous system of apartheid, I would propose a ban of new American investment; a total ban on South African participation in international athletic events; abolition of the sugar quota. With specific respect to Portugal, I would propose a review of the need for our base in the Azores, followed by the expulsion of Portugal from NATO. With specific respect to Southern Rhodesia, I support all United Nations measures thus taken and I refuse to lend my support to such ludicrous so-called settlements as that to which Great Britain has just agreed;

6. A presidential visit to those African countries struggling to develop progressive and liberal governments;

7. Finally, I intend to make known to Africans in every possible way, that the Government of the United States understands and sympathizes with them in their struggle against the terrible problems of tribalism, multiplicity of languages, lack

of investment capital, lack of jobs, and lack of even minimal health and sanitary necessities. We will help Africa as we are best able, and Africans will realize that compassion and respect for their humanity are once again the underlying attitudes behind American policy in Africa.

3   *Criminal Justice*

The prison system in America today remains a tragic failure and waste of money, and the prisons themselves remain reserved for those with dark skins, little money, and different lifestyles.

"PRESIDENTIAL CAMPAIGN POSITION PAPER NO. 5:
JUSTICE IN AMERICA" (1972)

Generations before mass incarceration gained mainstream exposure, Black activists were resisting the monstrous growth of the police state. A witness to the explosion in the prison population and the war on drugs as they unfolded in real time in Bedford-Stuyvesant and Brownsville, Chisholm understood how the government created a penal system that dominated its most economically desperate and politically vulnerable citizens. She would be one of the two elected officials trusted by Attica inmates to visit and negotiate with the Corrections Department. In her Attica testimony, she described the slaughter of inmates as a humanitarian crisis long in the making. Her fifth presidential position paper clearly predicted how Nixon's "tough on crime" policies would only deepen the wounds of social violence without putting an end to crime, and would continue to oppress marginalized communities who were the likely victims of criminal activities.

"The Attica Prison Uprising: A National Tragedy and Disgrace"

Congressional floor speech, Washington, D.C., September 15, 1971.

Mr. Speaker, I thank the gentleman very much for yielding me his time. I am going to be very brief.

I want to say at the outset, in a very realistic way, that I knew it was going to happen. Perhaps people might be rather surprised at my stating the case in this way, but it is because for over 15 years, at least, in the City and in the State of New York, I have witnessed the appointment of all kinds of investigatory commissions, and investigatory bodies, Governor's committees, and special community committees, to go into the prisons and the jails to observe the conditions under which these men, who are paying certain penalties already prescribed by the law, are undergoing, and these committees had indicated quite clearly that the lid would explode and at some time in the very near future many lives would be taken.

I particularly feel very deeply about this because I have had the opportunity to be in two of these situations within the past year, one where we spent 3 days—if not almost a week—along with our distinguished colleague from the Bronx, Congressman Herman Badillo, when we had an outburst in the Long Island prison.

I want to tell you that I do not think that many of us who are responsible for implementing our laws can readily recognize why we are doing these things to human beings whose individual liberties and just, basic, personal freedoms are denied so that because of this they eventually become dehumanized and depraved, and do

Congressional Record 117, pt. 24 (September 15, 1971): 31985–89

that which they have to do in order to dramatically bring to the attention of the world what is happening.

When I went into that prison—and never will I forget it—for 3 days—and again I say never will I forget what I saw—I could not believe it.

It was a very interesting thing to know that even though many of these prisoners were there for very serious crimes—basically the overriding question and the overriding consideration and issue was, "We know we have to pay our penalty, but have you forgotten that we are human beings who are entitled to just a few basic things—" such as my friend, the gentleman from New York (Mr. Koch) has mentioned—a bath, a daily shower, soap, toothbrushes; and to be able to have gone into those cells, just two-by fours, and to see those prisoners in despair—and to walk through urine and feces only because these men are not important in the eyes of many persons in this country. That is because, as someone has so eloquently phrased it—they are not voters.

I say to you in conclusion, to the gentleman in the well from Illinois (Mr. Mikva), and all of those who are interested in dealing in legislation and having more investigations—I do not want to sound pessimistic—it is necessary for us to get at the bottom of what happened in Attica prison. But I hope to God that as a result this Congress must now take action, and that is to take the leadership in setting some basic guidelines and basic rules for the deprived and depraved men, in a real sense that we may be able to implement something realistic, something that will give them the hope that at least with the death of over 25 persons we have finally come to understand what has happened. Let us hope that those deaths will not have been in vain; let us hope that perhaps we can move on the case.

Presidential Campaign Position Paper No. 5:
Justice in America

The fifth of ten position papers that were distributed to the public and press by the Chisholm presidential campaign beginning in January 1972 for that year's Democratic primary contest.

It is in the field of civil rights and criminal justice, or what the President calls "Law and Order," that the Nixon Administration must be most severely condemned. This Administration has virtually declared war on blacks, non-whites, and the young in this vitally sensitive area. The fundamental rights guaranteed all Americans by the Constitution have too often been flagrantly and willfully ignored in the Nixon Administration's discriminatory and repressive approach to criminal justice and civil liberties. This Administration has talked a lot about law and order, but its blatantly political and partisan administration of justice is, in effect, undermining American democracy while real crime of all types continues to rise.

There is no question that crime is a valid and burning issue today. Crime crosses all social and economic boundaries whether in the manifestation of violence or in the fear of its eventuality. America today is a nation barricaded into safety. Americans are fleeing to the suburbs, restaurants' business activity is down during evening hours, and bus companies have fewer riders at night. Burglar alarm sales are up 40 to 60% over last year in Los Angeles. There are now more private police than public police, with the number of private police and security guards rising to approximately 800,000. The Library of Congress, lying in the shadow of the dome of the Capitol, has had to change its working hours so

Shirley Chisholm Project Archives (SCPA), Brooklyn College.

that the majority of its 4,000 employees can begin the journey homeward before the sun goes down. Of every 10,000 women, seven are raped but 4,300 fear they might be. While the problem of crime preys particularly on the ghetto dweller, it has now invaded America's suburbs and rural areas as well.

The President who came to power in 1968 on a "Law and Order" platform has completely failed to halt the rise in crime, while simultaneously adopting various police-state tactics and methods whose constitutionality is in real doubt. The lack of positive leadership in fighting crime becomes clear when one looks at the sins of omission of this Administration in moving against the sources of serious crime.

The President has given no meaningful support to the effort to control the open sale of guns whose easy availability is unquestionably responsible for so many of the violent crimes committed today. He has procrastinated and then acted with too little, too late to halt the increase in drug abuse until it has risen to epidemic proportions. He has failed to generate prompt and sweeping reform of our 200-year old prison system, which everyone now recognizes to be a monstrous failure with no pretense of rehabilitative treatment. He has failed to achieve meaningful reform of our courts which too often violate standards of fairness, due process, and common justice. He has ignored the recommendations of experts from his own crime commissions to reduce the number of acts considered crimes, thereby freeing the police for serious police work. He has refused to support efforts throughout the country to eliminate police corruption and brutality.

Of perhaps even greater seriousness are the sins of commission of the Nixon Administration and law enforcement agencies throughout this nation during the past four years, actions and policies which have not only failed to halt the increase in crime but which are leading to a severe curtailment of freedom for all Americans. The Nixon Administration has encouraged an institutionalized counter-violence which has given the green light to every local law enforcement or vigilante group in the country to act as it wishes in the execution of its perceived tasks.

Moreover, the Administration has politicized this nation's Justice Department. The powers of the government have been too often marshalled, not against the actual criminals in the nation, but against those who oppose this Administration politically. The harassment of newsmen who dare to criticize Administration policies; expanded wiretapping, room-bugging and surveillance of the poor and black and even those attending "Earth Day" ceremonies; governmental overkill in the press and courtroom—all represent a conscious and deliberate drive to encourage adjustment to the reality of life in "Nixon's America" rather than stimulating a creative means of changing some of the intolerable unfairness and inequities which still trouble the nation.

In its broad retreat on civil rights enforcement, in its attempt to place on the supreme court of the land men with records of such negative racial attitudes or juridical incompetence that members of the President's own party have felt compelled to vote against them, the Nixon Administration has provoked widespread shock and dismay among millions of Americans that their government has become an "enemy" to its own people.

The demonstrable failure of the Nixon Administration to effectively reduce crime lies in the fact that the President has chosen to neglect the miserable conditions in which crime is born and festers. Instead of attacking causes rather than symptoms, the Administration has encouraged response to violence by counter-violence and a policy of instant justice.

During the last three years we have seen a proliferation of bloody night-time raids with the killing of unarmed students at Kent State and Jackson State; the brutal and insane slaughter of prisoners and guards alike at Attica; and mass, unlawful arrests in the Nation's capital last Mayday.

The Nixon Administration's preference for repression and persecution of political dissenters has taken greater precedence than court, police, and prison reform. The record suggests that the Administration's appalling lack of concern for the rights of the individual is exceeded only by its deeply ingrained authoritarian and reactionary instincts, fearful and dangerous perhaps because it rests on such a narrow basis of electoral support.

Let us look at the details of this record:

NO GUN CONTROL

The nation's chiefs of police have appealed for urgent efforts to control the sale of guns in this country. Private guns have caused more American deaths since the turn of the century than wars have caused since the beginning of the nation. America today has the highest gun accident rate in the world. Three beloved American leaders have been murdered in recent years by men who should never have been able to obtain the guns that fired the fatal bullets. Such an obvious link to crime cries out for attention, and I am baffled by the President's seeming indifference to this life and death issue.

It has been said that 95% of the women incarcerated in the District of Columbia correctional institutions are drug addicts. Estimates of drug related crimes in New York run above 50%. For the past three years, the Nixon Administration virtually ignored the scope of the drug problem—as long as its major effect appeared to be only on the poor and minorities. The Drug Abuse and Education Act of 1969, sponsored by 85 members of Congress, passed the House by a vote of 294 to 0, in spite of the Administration's statement that the bill was "unnecessary."

The President later admitted that he thought the answer to the drug abuse problem could be remedied by stiffening the penalties, but that he had a change of heart when it became clear that "the problem is not confined to a particular segment of society, but one which has begun to reach the upper middle classes." In other words, as long as the problem of drug abuse did not affect the children of the upper middle classes, stiff penalties and punishment would be his only answer to the problem.

Similarly, the President waited until the epidemic of heroin addiction among American servicemen in Vietnam was revealed to the public before he wheeled out his version of a crash program to counter it. This action came almost a year after a Senate Subcommittee issued warnings that an epidemic was growing rapidly in the armed services, and the President later contradictorily announced a hiring freeze for staff in Drug Rehabilitation Centers in Veterans Administration Hospitals.

Moreover, the Nixon Administration has consistently hampered Congressional initiatives in the fight against drugs during the last three years. It has opposed legislation to establish a National

Institute on Drug Abuse and drug dependence to coordinate existing programs and agencies. It has opposed Title I (National Institute of Drug Abuse) of the comprehensive Drug Abuse Prevention and Control Act, even though it was sponsored by the entire Labor and Public Welfare Committee of the Senate. It opposed greater controls on amphetamines, over half of whose production reaches illegal channels. It opposed the Senate amendments to the Economic Opportunity Act for community drug and alcoholism programs.

Even though 60 to 70% of the nation's communities have expressed interest for funding for drug programs, the Administration offered no plans to assist with new community projects to lease drug treatment facilities; no plans to assist new community projects to build drug treatment facilities; no plans to fund more than four initiation and development grants for treatment and rehabilitation facilities for the entire country; and no plans to fund more than a few new education, research and training projects in drugs. The Administration's incredible lack of leadership in this critical field has made far more difficult the efforts of those of us who are determined to eliminate this major source of crime and human misery, once and for all.

NO PRISON REFORM

In the past three years, riots have broken out in New York's Tombs Prison, San Quentin, Attica, the Indiana Reformatory and elsewhere as inmates protested the cruel and degrading conditions of America's dungeons. Many experts have long attacked the punitive basis of our prison system, which has succeeded only in bringing out the worst in men and assuring their life-long careers as criminals. The President's own Crime Commission, describing the system, found "overwhelming evidence of institutional shortcomings in almost every part of the United States." New York's Joint Legislative Committee on Crime reported that ¼ of all inmates in the state prisons believe "with reason" that they are victims of a "mindless, undirected and corrupt" system of criminal justice.

The 1972 budget for the Federal Bureau of Prisons calls for $189.7 million—an increase of only $66 million over the 1971 budget. Most of the increase, unfortunately, simply goes for new buildings and facilities. The Legal Enforcement Assistance Administration Administrator, Richard W. Velde, estimates that a modern prison building program could cost $15 billion. The LEAA fiscal 1972 budget for corrections showed $97.5 million, but this money was allocated to the states in block grants over which the LEAA has little or no control. There is no federal guarantee that this money will be used as hoped.

The prison system in America today remains a tragic failure and waste of money, and the prisons themselves remain reserved for those with dark skins, little money, and different lifestyles.

NO COURT REFORM

No amount of money spent to reform prisons nor any program of inmate rehabilitation, no matter how carefully conceived, would be effective without an essential restructuring of our chaotic court system. The Nixon Administration had vowed to reform the system. Chief Justice Burger has called for a major overhaul of the courts as have many, yet the Nixon Administration has again taken virtually no action to make the tools available. Its tinkering has been largely ineffectual and has not changed the fact that for those who are poor, powerless, and non-white, sentencing is too often grossly disparate, illogical, and unprincipled. Excessive bail continues to be the norm for these people.

With Administration encouragement, the courts have developed mass production procedures in routine criminal cases, making a mockery of the trial process. Plea bargaining now receives full judicial approval. Administrative inefficiency and judicial or prosecutorial incompetence continue to create pressures in which defendants and society can only come out losers. Some courts give [up] the counsel requirement entirely, others pressure defendants into signing a waiver of that right. The Chief Judge of the District of Columbia Superior Court has been moved to describe the courts as "factories where defendants are quickly processed like so many sausages." Instant justice has become the hallmark of Nixon justice, with overcrowded courts dispensing assembly line justice.

The danger in the present criminal justice system is that it is cynical and unfair to blacks and other minorities, including migrant workers. The law appears to be an instrument of oppression; to the poor, a barrier to alleviation of an unjust status quo; to the young, a coercer of conformity to middle class, puritan virtues. Most of us recognize that there are gross inequities in the American criminal justice system, a system which guarantees the second-class status of minorities and poor people, combats differing life styles, and silences those who might challenge the status quo.

One seldom hears these days about the prosecution of business leaders for such widespread and socially harmful crimes as deceptive advertising, pollution, selling dangerous merchandise and violating antitrust laws. Real estate agents are rarely prosecuted for blockbusting or practicing illegal racial discrimination in renting and selling. Election laws limiting political campaign contributions are violated regularly every two and four years, and there are no enforcement policies. Where are the prosecutions of white collar criminals committing crimes of falsification, fraud, libel, bribery, health code violations, perjury, income tax evasion and price fixing? Where are the convictions of slumlords, polluters, and those who make unsafe autos? To these people of "respectable" background go the written warnings and mild penalties.

The New York Joint Legislative Committee revealed that several thousand arrests of organized crime figures in the last decade had resulted in prison sentences in only 5% of the cases. A class nature of law enforcement process continues to exist under the Nixon Administration, functioning to maintain a racist relationship between the white majority and the black, brown, red, and yellow minorities. Not only do the powerful manage by and large to escape the sanctions of the criminal justice system, but they also manipulate the system for their own political ends. Thus, James R. Hoffa is given a Presidential pardon while others, non-white and less influential, are passed over.

Laws forbidding armed robbery and burglary have a very different impact for a millionaire and for an unemployed young black male in a ghetto where the unemployment rate is 25%. The evil of racism and the indignities of second-class citizenship still characterize America's system of criminal justice[;] the power of the purse appears to remain decisive to an Administration manifesting thinly concealed contempt for the racial minorities, the poor, and the young who remain disproportionately victimized by law enforcement.

Rampaging police brutality and summary justice in the black community, and evidence of widespread police corruption, as in New York, have for too long characterized police work. Excessive police violence, discriminatory treatment of Chicano juveniles, biased enforcement of motor vehicle regulations, racial discourtesies, the excessive use of "stop and frisk" laws are all various forms of police harassment and intimidation common to the poor and non-white communities. Vigilante squads and right-wing political repression have sprouted from coast to coast.

The Administration has shown its lack of concern for this intolerable abuse of police power by simply giving more arms to police forces and by promoting Orwellian police tactics such as "No Knock," which strikes at the fundamental right of every American to be secure in his home. No meaningful federal assistance has been offered for minority hiring or significant increases in salaries, which would help draw better police personnel. Not unexpectedly, the Law Enforcement Assistance Administration, the Justice Department's liaison with local police forces, has been charged with a "grossly inadequate" civil rights performance by the U.S. Civil Rights Commission, in connection with its legal responsibilities in this area.

BLOCKING CIVIL RIGHTS PROGRESS

In adopting the "Southern Strategy," the Nixon Administration served notice that it would systematically eliminate the government's crucial role in ensuring the civil rights of all Americans. It has not only said nothing when black school children's buses were burned or black votes thrown away. It has instead spoken out to strike popular governmental political notes against school busing and adopted a policy of refusal to enforce civil rights statutes, particularly in the fields of employment, housing, education, agricultural services, labor programs, public accommodations, and public facilities.

The record is clear. This Administration has moved to wipe out the effectiveness of the legal services program, a part of the Office of Economic Opportunity. The Attorney General failed to use the powers accorded him by the 1970 voting rights act and allowed a discriminatory new voting law to go into effect in Mississippi. In 20 counties, the registration rolls were wiped clean, and registrants were told to re-register. This meant that over six years of registration efforts were wiped off the books. The Federal District Court in Biloxi, Mississippi, reviewed the law and stated that it failed to meet the burden of proof in court, and criticized the Attorney General for taking a "Pilate-like" and "obtuse" illegal course in the enforcement of Federal Voting Laws. In May 1971, the House Judiciary Subcommittee on Civil Rights accused the Nixon Administration of inadequate enforcement of Federal Voting Laws and inviting "irresponsible" people to disregard them. The Attorney General was charged to set an example for the country for obedience of the law, rather than complain about existing law. Civil rights lawyers have quit this Administration en masse, and a suit was filed in district court by civil rights attorneys, charging the Attorney General and Assistant Attorney General with failure to enforce the laws.

In short, the cause of Civil Rights and Human Rights has been systematically jeopardized by the Nixon Administration. The "Southern Strategy" has opened the door to the past, as shown in the recent statewide elections of Mississippi where intimidation of black voters and the ignoring of black votes once again undercut American democracy.

CRUSHING OF POLITICAL DISSENT

Under the Nixon Administration, America has entered a new phase of political repression against the activist forces struggling for change. While crime ravages our cities, a policy of overt political reaction and the expansion of police power have been given top priority by this Administration. Spying is out of control, with the Army at one point spying on Senators, the proliferation of FBI wiretaps and bugs, revelations of networks of paid informers, and the political persecution of the Chicago 7, the Berrigans, Angela Davis, and Daniel Ellsberg.

America has entered the road to 1984, with the President refusing to fire an FBI Director who systematically and fearlessly abuses his power and by politicizing a justice department bent on restricting individual liberties and monitoring the lives of countless Americans. The Nixon Administration has devoted its efforts to crushing political opposition with the result that force, intimidation, and repression are undermining our democracy, rather than insuring an orderly society in which human dignity can flourish. Many of the hack politicians in the Justice Department appear to be men who see order as the rigid freezing into place of the America they have made and who think law has no higher function than to preserve that order.

I am terribly concerned about crime in America. I believe that the abatement of crime lies not in police hands, but in reducing the stresses and strains which produce in some, disrespect for the law, and in others, a sense of grievance expressing itself in violence and crime. Criminal justice is dependent upon and largely derives from social justice. The only solution for the problem of class and race bias in the courtroom or by the police and correctional systems is the eradication of bias from American life—we must do away with oppressive functions and with social prejudices and inequities to significantly reduce crime.

The Nixon criminal justice approach is adding to the increasingly dangerous polarization of conflict in America. Instead of strengthening the belief in the legitimacy of authority, it has generated cynicism and bitterness. Our entire society will inevitably suffer from this blindness in our national leadership. While working for social justice throughout the nation, I propose the following steps as a beginning for reform of our criminal justice system and the reduction of crime:

1. Federal prohibition of handguns, strict licensing and registration of all other weapons;

2. Appointment of more blacks, non-whites, and women as judges and wardens, to the FBI, police forces and all law enforcement agencies, and as parole board members, probation officers, minority prison guards, etc.;

3. FBI reform by immediate replacement of FBI Director Hoover, and by giving the FBI greater responsibilities in civil rights enforcement and combating white-collar crime, including organized crime;

4. Prison reform, including open visitation, creation of programs to allow prisoners to obtain college degrees, and a bill of rights for prisoners to include:
   a. Freedom of threat from physical abuse;
   b. Freedom of worship;
   c. Unrestricted access to legal assistance;

5. The creation of special courts or judges for alcoholism, petty larceny, and civilian review boards for police corruption;
6. Greater financial support for local and state police with emphasis on attracting higher grades of personnel into police work;
7. Beefing-up local and federal anti-crime efforts with the sharing of information in order to allow a coordinated attack on organized crime in all areas, especially in drug traffic;
8. Full support for the U.S. Civil Rights Commission and a non-political Justice Department;
9. Applying of criminal laws uniformly;
10. Doing away with indeterminate sentencing and minimizing discretionary powers of police, judges, and other judicial functionaries;
11. Separation of treatment and punishment, making therapy and counseling available to all prisoners on a truly voluntary basis;
12. Greater enforcement of antitrust laws.

4 *Race, Racism, and Civil Rights*

Racism is so inherent in the bloodstream of this country that you cannot see beyond a particular limit.

"ON BUSING DESEGREGATION" (1971)

Coming into political leadership at the height of the civil rights movement, but not engaging in the acts of civil disobedience that were most prevalent in the South, Chisholm would be part of the northern movement that focused on advocating for Black access to jobs, social services, adequate housing, and political representation. She never approached race from a singular view; her analysis always included gender and sexism. Yet at the center of her public policy analysis was the inherent racism that exists within the U.S. Whether in debates around education and busing, immigration policies toward Haitian refugees, police brutality, or housing, racism rears its head. Chisholm spoke and wrote about the hypocrisy of creating a narrative of American freedom and democracy that did not reckon with the white supremacy and racism found among its citizenry. She wrote, "In the end anti-black, anti-female, and all forms of discrimination are equivalent to the same thing: anti-humanism." Her many intellectual engagements with civil rights reaffirm her dedication to radical humanism.

"Racism and Polarization"

Congressional floor speech, Washington, D.C., February 17, 1971.

Mr. Speaker, no nation in human history has the promise that even approaches that of the United States of America. It was, as you will recall, "conceived in liberty and dedicated to the proposition that all men were created equal." And "from the mountain to the prairies, to the oceans white with foam," it is endowed with resources that are the envy of the world. Its people, drawn from the nations of the earth, have used their education, their driving energies, and their creative minds to develop dimensions of wealth that stagger the imagination. And yet, we are a nation in agony, beset by problems and currents and forces that are shaking its foundations and threatening to destroy it. It is [a] paradox that demands the attention of our best minds and the highest priority on our national agenda.

What has gone wrong, in this, of all nations? A nation with more churches than all of the Christian nations combined. A nation that spends billions of dollars on education and boasts the finest universities in the world.

What is wrong is that we are suffering the agony of race and racism, despite the fact that more than a century has passed since the Civil War and despite the hundreds of court cases, many of which have gone the judicial distance to the Supreme Court, and despite the great civil rights laws of the 1960's.

And the problem fundamental in discriminatory and racist practices is the willingness of the majority of Americans, both

Congressional Record 117, pt. 3, extensions of remarks (February 17, 1971): 2957–58.

silent and vocal, to resist necessary change or to be callously indifferent to it.

The National Conference of Christians and Jews, one of the Nation's best known human relations agencies, has recognized a situation that is critical to all Americans.

In an effort to do something about the solid resistance and indifference the National Conference of Christians and Jews is sponsoring a national committee for commitment to brotherhood in 1971. The purpose is to urge all concerned citizens to support organizations, which, together with the NCCJ, work to effect rapid, yet peaceful social change and bring about brotherhood through the eradication of racism and polarization.

The committee advocates support for and involvement in the National Association for the Advancement of Colored People, the National Urban League, and the Southern Christian Leadership Conference—organizations which work for the rights of all people regardless of color, religion, or national origin. These interracial organizations have records of positive accomplishment achieved by nonviolent approaches in seeking an end to social injustice.

This marks the first time that a national human relations agency has undertaken to obtain support for other such groups.

The national committee for commitment to brotherhood is composed of a cross section of influential men and women dedicated to broadening the mutual concern for the rights of all, so vital to national unity.

During 1971, the committee will foster public support, involvement and cooperation for the NAACP, NUL, and SCLC throughout the United States through educational programs and cooperative projects.

Local NCCJ chapters will participate in the brotherhood commitment.

I salute the National Conference of Christians and Jews for its project and I think it is time our country's leaders began to exercise some strong moral leadership in this area. We cannot tacitly condone nor encourage any more deadly polarization.

"On Busing Desegregation"

Congressional floor speech, Washington, D.C., November 4, 1971.

Ladies and gentlemen of this Chamber, the time has come that we must face a real reckoning of many things that many of us have been trying to avoid through parliamentary maneuvers and parliamentary tricks. Liberals show one face here in Washington, D.C., and something else in their representative home districts.

Let me say this: My heart bleeds this evening for all of those who are addressing themselves to the fact that we must not and cannot have young children being carted from one district to another in order to be able to give them the kind of education that is necessary to cope with a highly automated and technological society.

Where have you been for these many years? The black and Spanish-speaking children in the Southern and Western parts of the United States have been bused right past the white schools in your communities in order to go to the dilapidated buildings reserved for them to acquire some kind of education. Where have your voices been for those children through all those years?

Congressional Record 117, pt. 30 (November 4, 1971): 39310.

Now it is the same old pattern, and because it now affects a certain segment that have been the beneficiaries of the status quo in America, it takes on a highly different picture now. The same thing is happening with respect to the drug problem in this country. Where have you been all these years when drug addiction has seized certain groups in this Nation? Now everybody is crying out about what drugs are doing to the children, the youth of this country. Everybody is crying about what cross-busing is doing to the children.

You know, let me bring it right down front to you. The fact of the matter is racism is so inherent in the bloodstream of this country that you cannot see beyond a particular limit. You are only concerned when whites are affected. If you were indeed concerned about the busing of young children for the sake of getting educational equality, your voices would have been raised years ago in terms of the fact that black and Chicano, Spanish-speaking children were getting an inferior education by being bused right past the white schools in their neighborhoods in which they lived to the dilapidated schools in the outlying districts.

Come out from behind your mask and tell it like it really is. Are we going to believe in the United States of America that we are going to try to bring about a society where every man and woman and child will be judged not on the basis of his race, but on the basis of his capabilities and his potentialities for realizing the dream we all speak so glibly about during political times?

I say to the Members: Where have you been? Where were you when the black children were being bused right past the white schools in the community? Nobody has addressed himself this evening yet to that particular issue, but it is very understandable why the Members are not addressing themselves to this issue.

There is a chance this evening to come out from behind your mask. Forget they are white children. Forget they are black children. Forget they are Spanish-speaking children. Just remember one thing: They are America's children. They are the children who are going to carry this country on when we pass off this scene, and the hope of this Nation really lies with these children. So for God's sake, let us be done with this amendment and deal with it objectively. Listen to the children of this Nation.

We would not be confronted with the problem we are confronted with tonight—at what time is it?—it is 10 after 9, unless it is because we have practiced sham and hypocrisy for so long, and it has finally caught up with us.

Mr. Chairman, I hope the Members vote down this amendment.

Presidential Campaign Position Paper No. 8: Housing

The eighth of ten position papers that were distributed to the public and press by the Chisholm presidential campaign beginning in January 1972 for that year's Democratic primary contest.

Twenty-three years ago, in the Housing Act of 1949, Congress committed this nation to "realization as soon as feasible of the goal of a decent home and suitable living environment for every American family." Yet in 1972, some ten million American families—one out of every six in the nation—are still living in housing that is, as one housing authority put it, "steadily deteriorating, grossly unhealthy, or utterly wretched." It is doubtful that most of these families will soon, if ever, move into decent housing. A nation

Shirley Chisholm Project Archives (SCPA), Brooklyn College.

beset by racial conflict and a President far more interested in foreign travel than critical domestic needs still refuse to come to grips with what is surely one of the most fundamental problems of the world's wealthiest nation—the lack of a "decent home and suitable living environment for every American family."

OPEN HOUSING—A MYTH

Failure to integrate housing remains a yardstick by which to measure our lack of progress toward achieving an integrated society in America. The fact is that two distinct housing markets exist today in America—one black and one white. Not only have real estate agencies traditionally refused to show houses outside ghetto or transitional areas to blacks, but even if properties in white residential areas become available to blacks, lending institutions have been reluctant to grant blacks mortgages for properties in the areas. For all practical purposes, blacks are limited in their residence selection to houses within segregated or transitional neighborhoods. As sufficiently prosperous whites invariably look for property only within the white housing market, residential segregation is perpetuated, and ghettos are the result.

Moreover, the supply of housing available to blacks being severely restricted, the demand increases due to rapid urban migration. Comparable housing units therefore bring a higher price in the black than in the white sector of the market. This price differential is known as a "color tax." A Chicago Urban League study of rental housing (which constitutes four-fifths of the black housing market) conducted during the mid-1960's found that blacks pay 10% more than whites for comparable rental units.

Let us look for a moment at how America's ghettos came about. The creation of the black ghetto in Bedford-Stuyvesant, which is in my own Congressional District, illustrates the problem. Before the 1930's the neighborhood consisted of the large homes of the relatively wealthy. When the Depression hit in 1929, many owners found that they could no longer maintain their homes; the cost of running them was too high; they were unable to pay for servants; and taxes were increasing. At this point, the technique known as "blockbusting" was initiated by some real estate salesmen. Blockbusting consists of getting a single black family to move into a house in a formerly all-white neighborhood. The real estate operator then contacts all the other white owners in the neighborhood and offers to buy their homes because "the neighborhood is changing." Fear that the changed neighborhood will force a drop in the values of their homes causes the whites to sell to the real estate operator at a low price. The real estate firm then finds other black families to whom it sells the houses at high profits. The black families pay the higher prices because they have less choice and cannot "shop around" to find something equally good for less money. This technique, used in the 1930's, launched the Bedford-Stuyvesant ghetto of today, as well as countless other ghettos throughout America. There is no need to describe in graphic language the horrors of life for the American slum-dweller. Jacob A. Riis wrote as far back as 1890 about the miseries of poorly heated, rat-infested, crowded and crumbling housing and the traumatic psychological effects on the children who have no place to play and are exposed to manifold dangers and accidents. I know, from the ghettos in Bedford-Stuyvesant and elsewhere, how deep is the anguish and helplessness of the poor.

Whether they want to or not, the overwhelming majority of blacks in the city live within the confines of the ghetto. They shop in the ghetto where the absence of competition encourages high prices, and their children go to school there. Absentee landlords prey on slum-dwellers. They make few repairs and encourage overcrowding and the sharing of bathrooms and kitchens. Often they give little heat or hot water. Since taxes are low, their profits are high. In short, a substantial number of landlords and merchants in America today profit from the miseries of the poor.

The tragedy for the American slum-dweller is that there seems to be no way out. The average cost of a new single-family home in the city today is about $25,000; with a typical mortgage and average maintenance, utility, and other costs, this demands a monthly housing expenditure of about $250—or a $12,000 a year income. Buy an old house? The average price for existing old houses is itself in the $20,000 to $25,000 area. Apartments? More than 80% of the new rental units on the market are priced at more than $150 a month—and the larger apartments, which poor families most often need, are, of course, more expensive than the average.

The lack of opportunity for blacks in housing is obviously related to their servile position in other sectors. Housing segregation and a declining urban tax base, resulting from the suburbanization of industry and middle-class urbanites, means that schools in black neighborhoods tend to be older, understaffed, and overcrowded. An inferior education is usually the result.

Housing segregation, in addition to its effect on the quality of education, has an immediate bearing on economic opportunity. Job opportunities are moving to the suburbs. The less skilled jobs for which inferior education has prepared the slum-dweller are declining with the advance of technology, and outright discrimination in hiring or promotion by employers and in membership in unions further diminishes opportunities for employment and advancement. Inadequate public transportation in most large cities makes it difficult to cross town every day even should the poor man manage to find a job.

Segregation in housing also obviously reinforces segregation in personal relations and in access to community facilities. Thus, the system of institutions is mutually reinforcing. For whites, dominance in one sector reinforces dominance in another; for blacks, subordination begets subordination.

In short, our residential segregation virtually precludes the possibility that a poor black man can be a productive citizen in contemporary America. The black man naturally senses this. No one should be surprised when the ghettos explode as they have in Watts, Detroit, Newark, and elsewhere. No one should be surprised that ghettos are often hothouses of crime. The fact is that slums are not simply broken-down hovels; they are a state of mind. That state of mind is inevitably hostile and potentially dangerous to the larger community. The huge cost, to this nation, in wasted lives and manpower, in crime and social turmoil as well as in expensive welfare programs, is a monumental tragedy.

WHITES ALSO HAVE HOUSING PROBLEMS

The housing crisis in America is most serious for the inhabitant of the ghetto, but it strikes at the nation's poor whites and the middle class as well. Although in 1960, substandard housing was far more prevalent among non-whites than in the overall population, $\frac{1}{8}$ of whites were still living then in housing characterized as substandard (serious defects in ventilation, light, heating and sanitary facilities, presence of noxious or foul odors from nearby industry, etc.).

Census data in 1960 revealed that 9 million of 53 million occupied housing units were labeled substandard, ⅓ were classified as dilapidated. 1970 figures show that 25 million Americans are still defined as "poor," so there is little reason to believe that the 1960 figures have changed appreciably.

Exorbitant interest rates and sky-rocketing property taxes have brought home to the middle-class evidence that for its benefit also this nation must give a much higher priority to the entire subject of housing if we are to eliminate the tensions, irrationalities and frustration which currently permeate so much of our national life.

Everyone knows that urban blight is spreading in America's cities, and there are signs that it is invading the suburbs as well. Whites, as well as blacks, are still flocking to the cities from rural areas, looking in vain for jobs in decaying central cities already made up largely of the poor, the childless, and minority groups, and surrounded by burgeoning stretches of monotonous suburbs populated by middle and upper-middle income white families.

So the problem gets worse with every passing year. Business moves out of the cities, with revenues lost to city government. Increasing urban land and building costs minimize the volume of unsubsidized private construction for low and moderate income families. Exclusionary zoning practices in the suburbs further slam the door shut on the lower-income family, black or white. The cities of America are dying, and this trend represents an enormous, intolerable cultural loss for all Americans.

Americans are now asking why it is that the society that sends men to the moon and returns them safely cannot use its ingenuity to provide housing for all of its people on earth. The problem is that in eliminating the nation's housing deficits, the perfection of technology, as challenging as that may be, is ultimately the least of the problems.

A sound housing policy must provide both lower costs and government subsidies. Simply spewing out subsidies without seeking to reduce the costs of housing and thus of the subsidies themselves is wasteful and wrong.

When most people think of reducing housing costs, they have in mind technological advances that would permit houses and apartments, or at least their major components, to roll off assembly lines as bountifully as new cars in Detroit. But while technological advances are important, more than just improved technology is needed if housing costs are to be lowered in America. Just as vital are drastic reforms in the nation's zoning, building, and property tax laws, all of which affect housing costs.

Cost-cutting won through construction technology can easily be lost by increases in the other components. For a $15,000 house with a forty-year mortgage, a single percentage-point rise in the mortgage interest rate, from 6 to 7 percent, has the same effect on the monthly housing expenses as a 13% increase in total construction development costs. As one government-ordered study suggests, a cost-lowering program "must work on all the bits and pieces that make up the initial costs of a housing unit and its subsequent operating and maintenance costs."

The pursuit of "bits and pieces" takes us right to the heart of the nation's economic and social problems. The Nixon Administration chose to fight inflation by a tight-money policy, raising interest rates in the hope of slowing down the economy, thereby forcing a rise in the cost of mortgage financing. Housing has been given an unfair share of the burden of economic stabilization. It is ridiculous that so fundamental an industry as housing should bear the brunt of anti-inflation measures. Preserving a steady supply of credit at moderate interest rates is all important in keeping housing finance costs down.

One major element in the housing crisis is the fact that the cost of land to build on has risen steeply in the recent years of heavy demand. In the major metropolitan areas, the average price of raw land is double what it was twenty years ago. Still another element is, as mentioned, soaring property taxes, especially in the big cities. Rising education costs mean property taxes will continue to go up even further.

Another problem is that of the fear of people fleeing from city to suburb with large numbers of additional children to educate which has led many suburbs to "zone out" apartment construction and low- and moderate-income homes. Where, then, are some of the major areas in which partial answers may lie to solving the housing crisis?

END TO EXCLUSIONARY ZONING

The U.S. Government must address itself to the problem of bringing housing for the inner-city poor into areas now excluding them. The mass of zoning laws, along with a jungle of more than 8,000 local construction codes, has helped to stifle the kind of high-technology home-building industry that would contribute, however modestly, to cost reductions. The advance of housing technology depends in great part on the existence of a mass market for fairly standardized structural and utility elements. But such a market has generally been impossible where large areas of land are closed to many types of housing, and antiquated or unnecessarily rigid local construction laws remain inconsistent even in a single county.

Strong pressure is needed by Washington on state and local governments to end exclusionary zoning. One tactic might be to withhold federal water and sewer grants, highway development aid and the like from communities that effectively zone against lower-income and minority families. The exclusion is clearly often racially motivated so that 23% of the central-city population, and only 5% of the suburbs, is black. Such steps as withdrawing government business from companies that move to areas that do not provide housing opportunities for poor and middle-income families is a must item in a new federal housing policy.

REDUCED PROPERTY TAXES

Federal spending priorities must be realigned to permit more funds to flow from Washington to the cities so that they can reduce the steep tribute, the equivalent of a 30% sales tax in some places, that they now must exact from housing. One possibility which I strongly support is federal assumption of all welfare costs, a backbreaker for the cities. There must also be another method of financing public school education that does not rely on the local property tax. The revenue reforms must succeed in bringing more money to the cities and not just increase it in some categories of aid while decreasing it in others.

GOVERNMENT SUBSIDIES FOR HOUSING

Even if the unlikely occurs and the social, economic and technological problems are solved, and the cost of housing is reduced, the price of decent shelter will probably still be beyond the reach of most poor families and even many moderate-income ones. Only government subsidies can lower prices further. Since the Great Depression, the federal government has subsidized the construction, rehabilitation, or acquisition of some 2.1 million homes and apartments for low- and moderate-income families—about one-fifth of the current estimated need of ten million, based on Census Bureau statistics.

About half of the 2.1 million completed units have been produced in the past three or four years, an indication of the utterly meager levels of the federal housing subsidy effort for most of its three and a half decades. The history of government housing-subsidy programs has clearly been "woefully inadequate," as the President's Committee on Urban Housing stated in 1968. The progress that has been made in recent years largely stems from the housing legislation of the Johnson Administration, particularly the 1968 Housing and Urban Development Act.

Although at present, subsidized housing production is proceeding at half a million units a year, there continue to be troubling signs that the government still has not found an effective approach to meeting the housing needs of the nation's lower- and moderate-income families. A disturbing number of projects are bankrupt or in serious default. Reasons for this situation appear to include rising operating costs; poor market choices; the legacy of "quick-buck" speculators more intent on a swift and fat profit or tax shelter than on building durable housing and managing it well; Congressionally mandated construction-cost limits that may also have hindered sound construction; and the inevitable influence of general slum conditions that make some of the new developments as undesirable for upwardly mobile families as the tenements they replaced. Public housing is too often "cold, impersonal and cheerless."

I have always supported this program which recognizes the fact that problems of slum housing are intimately related to problems of local government, city planning, poverty, unemployment, ill health, and inferior education. It suggests that merely rebuilding houses is no longer enough. Urban renewal has too often meant urban removal of Blacks and other non-whites when the poor moved out and the middle-class moved in. Instead, a whole city or at least a large part of its rundown sections, must be rehabilitated, not only to provide better housing, but also to improve the total welfare of the people of the community.

NIXON SPENDS MORE FOR SPACE AND DEFENSE, LESS FOR HOUSING

The above-mentioned approaches to deal with America's continuing housing crisis cost money. In its new budget, the Nixon Administration has once again called for increased military spending and decreased spending for housing. The nation's big-city mayors recently declared that "we are dismayed by the proposed cut of $765 million in several major programs of the Department of Housing and Urban Development. These cuts affect cities in areas dealing with their efforts to rehabilitate their slums and older neighborhoods. This is a federal downgrading of a high urban priority." They noted that "the actual appropriations available in fiscal 1972 for urban renewal, water and sewer systems, open space, public housing and rental assistance for apartments is $2.4 billion, while the Administration's proposed level for fiscal 1973 is only $1.65 billion, a $765 million reduction in effort."

Much of this reduction was not apparent in the budget, which showed the bulk of the programs continuing at about the same level as that for this year. But Milwaukee Mayor Henry Maier said that in a number of categories the Nixon Administration was not spending all funds appropriated for this year but carrying the amounts forward for spending next year. He observed that "the main item involved is urban renewal, for which Congress appropriated $1.46 billion this year. But the Administration is reserving $500 million of this to pay for relocating families under a new law that requires the Federal Government to pay the full cost of moving families whose homes were taken by renewal projects begun before January 2, 1971."

Although urban renewal has been paying relocation costs since 1956, the Mayors said that they did not believe the costs would run that high and they objected to the amount being carried forward into next year, constituting half of the budgeted amount of $1 billion.

Under his general revenue sharing plan, the President has budgeted $5.3 billion for next year, which would be shared among the states, counties, and cities of all sizes.

"If we separate out the dollars budgeted for revenue sharing," the Milwaukee Mayor said, "we find that the budget leaves urban areas with very few dollars more in direct aid to cities than they are receiving in this fiscal year." He concluded that overall, the budget this year reflected more than ever a lack of commitment to renewing the cities. "We're gearing-up for a space shuttle by adding $250 million to the earth orbital program, while we're cutting back substantially on funds for low-income housing," he said. "The total allocation for research and development in space and the military in fiscal 1972 is $12.4 billion. The total research and development effort for civilian programs is $5.4 billion. Of this, only $60 million is for the Department of Housing and Urban Development."

The Leadership Conference on Civil Rights, a coalition of 126 civil rights organizations, declared that President Nixon had "diagnosed a cancer and prescribed aspirin as the remedy." The Conference urged that the Administration require communities to provide for low-income housing needs or lose all federal aid, not just housing or urban renewal money. The Conference also urged that the Justice Department challenge any local zoning that barred the poor and minorities.

The Nixon Administration's consistent reluctance to act in civil rights matters generally and in housing in particular is illustrated by a case in Black Jack, Missouri. In November 1970, HUD asked the Justice Department to prosecute a zoning case where zoning had been set to avoid the planned building of a racially integrated apartment complex. The Justice Department said no. In January 1971, the ACLU brought the case to court without the help of the Justice Department. After the President's statement of policy in June, the Justice Department finally announced that it was suing the city of Black Jack, charging racial discrimination in zoning— seven months after HUD had asked it to step into the case.

The conservative and callous policies of the Justice Department under John Mitchell help account for the fact that open housing laws have not radically altered the existence or operation of the dual housing market. Whites in the American South are now discovering what whites in other regions of the country have known for some time, that legal sanctions are not really necessary in order to maintain institutional racism so long as the racial norms are operative and the government remains aloof. The spate of civil rights laws of the 1960's has modified racial norms only slightly rather than wiping out the subordination prescriptions. At best, recent legislation has created a situation in which a little less discrimination is considered normal. The U.S. Civil Rights Commission, for example, recently reported that "racial data which HUD has, indicates that there are serious problems of racial and ethnic segregation in current housing programs subsidized by HUD."

It is this persistent indifference toward and incomprehension of the urban problems of America, with all that despair and rage at their root, which has characterized the Nixon Administration's attitude toward so many American citizens. An Administration of right-wing politicians, Wall Street lawyers, and advertising men appears temperamentally incapable of sensing how crucial to the general well-being of our nation is an end to the housing crisis.

Richard Nixon was elected President in 1968 on a shrill and shrewdly designed platform of "law and order." He plans to win in 1972 by convincing Southerners and other Americans that he opposes busing. It is small wonder that, as with desegregation of schools and busing, the Federal and state courts have spearheaded whatever fair housing progress that has been made. Nowhere in his speeches or actions can one find any appreciation of the crucial importance of adequate housing in rebuilding our cities, or even of minimal, strong and positive leadership by the President himself in this regard.

NEW HOUSING AND NEW PROGRAM FOR HOUSING

The American Public Health Association has taken the lead in promulgating housing standards. APHA regards the primary criterion for housing adequacy to be its influence on health. It includes as contributing to health, "safety from physical hazards, and those qualities of comfort and convenience and aesthetic satisfaction essential for emotional and social well-being." The sense of frustration caused by living in a substandard house, APHA observes, "may often be a more serious health menace than an unsanitary condition associated with housing."

It is obvious that open housing has not yet been achieved. It is equally obvious that the integration of society and elimination of the slums, as well as elimination of the crime, delinquency, ill health, and inferior education that are all associated with the slums, essentially depend on open housing. The achievement of open housing is also dependent on the black's level of employment and living standards. As the economy improves, he will be able to exercise his economic power to buy a house or rent an apartment wherever he wishes.

In short, progress toward the goal of 1949 has been intolerably slow. Providing a "decent home in a suitable living environment" for lower-income families, black and white, is going to require both rising income levels for families in this group and changes in social attitudes and in legislation to do away with the practices that have confined them to the slums of the central cities.

The following are specific steps which I support to achieve this long-deferred goal:

1. Total slum clearance, an investment in human life and the key to all urban problems, to be accomplished by 1976, the 200th anniversary of the United States. This would involve:
   A. Greatly increased aid for rehabilitation of existing housing (Federal programs have not yet sufficiently emphasized renovation of decaying but basically sound buildings);

B. Greatly increased expansion of Federal funds for Urban Renewal and Model Cities and other community development programs so that communities have a major voice in determining policies to be accomplished;

2. Spread low-cost housing out over metropolitan areas through formation of metropolitan housing agencies and;

   A. Legislation to end exclusionary zoning in suburbs;

   B. Withhold all Federal aid of all types from communities lacking open, low-cost housing;

   C. Require that a community show it can provide adequate housing for moderate and low income families before a new state or Federal facility could be located there (Senator Cranston's 1971 bill, S. 1282);

   D. Encourage and aid local governments in the development of communities both in inner cities and in suburbs, which would house diverse age, race, ethnic, and income groups;

3. Consolidation and simplification of Federal housing subsidy programs, replacing existing programs with a "single-subsidy mechanism" for all rental, cooperative and private housing aided by Federal money. Under this approach, any family found unable to afford decent housing in the private market would qualify for a Federally subsidized unit. The tenant would pay a portion of his income, perhaps 25%, for his quarters while the difference between the total cost and the rent would be made up by Washington;

4. Federal government interest-free construction loans and long-term loans for housing for low-income citizens;

5. Legislation to protect the small homeowner by a limitation of a one percent levy of property taxes for homes under $30,000;

6. Give the Federal Division of Highways responsibility for adequate relocation of residents prior to receiving funds for construction of highways and other public projects;

7. End discriminatory policies against women by FHA (a single man earning $10,000 a year may buy a home under the FHA, but a single woman earning the same amount may not);

8. Legislation providing that no individual may lose his, her, or their home due to natural disaster or inability to pay taxes;

9. Legislation to subsidize cities' efforts to make landlords fulfill their legal responsibilities to tenants;

10. Improved police, fire and health protection for low-income communities through Federal assistance;

11. Immediate, intensive Federally-sponsored programs to develop skilled managers for housing projects.

"The White Press: Sexist and Racist"

An article originally published in The Black Scholar, *September 1973.*

The all-male, all-white Gridiron Club has invited myself and 12 other carefully selected token women to its annual dinner. I refused this invitation because the absence of women and minorities in the Gridiron Club is symbolic of the racism and sexism which pervades the news industry.

Normally I don't consider integrating all-male bars and similar activities as a priority item in the fight for equal rights. I have made an exception in this instance because I believe that this invitation is nothing but a lame, token gesture. Under the rules of the Club,

---

The Black Scholar 5, no. 1 (September 1973): 20–22.

women journalists are still excluded. Although there is no formal written prohibition against minority members, there are, in fact, no black, Mexican-American, Puerto-Rican, Indian or other minority group members.

The members of the Gridiron Club and the press as a whole must realize that women and minorities are through with tokenism. We are not going to be "bought off" by a few select dinner invitations. Our price is much higher. The price is full equal opportunity, not only in terms of hiring practices but in terms of pay, promotion and assignments. To date the record of the news industry has not been equal to the lofty admonitions in support of equal opportunity that appear on the editorial page.

Just how bad is the situation? Lest I be accused of spouting unsubstantiated rhetoric, I had a journalism student intern in my office do a survey of the hiring practices of the press. Not all of our inquiries have been answered but the information we have received thus far clearly documents the charges of racism and sexism. I intend to print all of the information we have collected in the *Congressional Record* when the survey is completed but until that time, here are some examples of what we found.

To start, we checked the bureaus of 18 major papers, most of them from cities with substantial minority populations. Five bureaus had women reporters and none had black reporters. Of the 73 reporters employed by these bureaus, only seven were women. This is especially significant because Washington is the news capital of the world and an assignment to a Washington bureau is considered a "plum" in the journalism field.

When the focus switched to individual papers, the picture was even more appalling. The *Los Angeles Times*, for example, emanates from a city with a population of 2,800,000. Included in this total are half a million blacks and 138,000 other minority group members, 22.8% of the population. There are 100,000 more women in Los Angeles than men. But the *Times*, with 175 reporters, employs a grand total of 20 women, four blacks and one Mexican-American.

St. Louis, with 622,000 residents, is 41 percent black and has 50,000 more women than men. The *St. Louis Post-Dispatch*, which actually has one of the better records among big city newspapers, employs 25 blacks and 52 women on a staff of 260.

In San Francisco, which has a population of 715,000, there are close to 100,000 blacks and 108,000 members of other minority groups, mostly of Oriental or Spanish descent. The combined minority population is equal to 28.5%. The *San Francisco Chronicle*, with a staff of 223 editorial employees, employs but one person of Japanese descent, one of Chinese descent and one Mexican-American, in addition to eight blacks. Almost a quarter of the staff is female but a third of these women do only women's news.

The venerable *New York Times*, in a city with 1,850,000 or 23.4% non-white citizens, employs 20 minority group members on its editorial staff of 557. In a city with almost half a million more women than men, it employs but 62 women.

Here in Washington, the population is 71% black, the highest percentage in the country. Yet at the *Washington Post*, of a total editorial force of 310, only 19 are black and 34 are women. The Washington *Daily News* has only one black reporter but does have three black reporter trainees and will have three black summer intern reporters.

As the head of the Ridder News Service Washington bureau put it quite honestly, hiring minorities "is not in the nature of this business. They look at everything through white, middle-class eyes." When those eyes are also male, the problem becomes quite blatant.

One woman reporter recently urged her paper, which had done analyses of black, white-ethnic and Wallaceite voters, to analyze the women's vote. The paper refused—after all, everybody knows that women vote for the handsomest candidate. That's why Kennedy beat Nixon in 1960, right? (Wrong, more women were polled as voting for Nixon than for Kennedy.)

Each year, businesses with more than 100 employees are required to submit to the Equal Employment Opportunity Commission figures on the racial and sexual composition of their workforce. Let's look at what figures for the newspaper industry showed.

Newspapers with more than 100 employees had a combined total nationwide of 217,000 employees. Thirteen thousand six hundred (13,600), or 6.2%, were members of minority groups, a sorry enough figure. But when we look at the classification of "professionals," the category that would include reporters, the percentage drops to 2.6%.

But a better indicator of newspaper employment practices is gained by comparing the percentage of minorities employed by the newspaper industry in a city with the percentage of minorities employed by all industries put together in that city. We looked at seven different cities. All of them 20 or more percent black in population.

In all seven cities—Washington, Miami, New York City, Los Angeles, Chicago, Houston and San Francisco—the percentages both for minorities hired on the whole in all classes and in particular for the professional class were higher for all industries averaged together than for the newspaper industry. In other words, the newspaper industry is behind industry as a whole when it comes to employing minorities, especially among the professionals, who are the reporters—the eyes of a nation.

Although the EEOC does not break down these figures into percentages for women, even the raw figures show what sort of discrimination exists. Close to a quarter (49,000) of the 217,000 industry employees are women. But when we look at the class of professionals, where reporters are included, the percentage drops to one-fifth, 5,700 out of 25,000.

Newspapers are not the only villains among the media. EEOC statistics for periodicals, for example, show that while minorities are better treated by magazines than by newspapers, the minority employment rate is still only 9.7 percent for the whole magazine industry and 4.5 percent for the professional class. Women make up over two fifths of magazine professionals but that figure is nowhere near their 52 percent of the population.

In the electronic media, we find the situation not much better. Although the FCC yearly requires reports from each television and radio station on their employment of racial groups and women, it apparently does not place a very high priority on compiling totals for the television and radio industry. Reports filed last May are still waiting around for someone to finish a computer program that will allow them to be processed. By the time the reports are finally compiled in usable, statistical form, the 1972 reports will be coming in.

Although the National Association of Educational Broadcasters cared enough to go through FCC files and compile by hand information about its member stations, the statistics it compiled are hardly encouraging. The percentage of minority persons employed by public television stations, for example, dropped from 12 percent to eight percent in one year (from 1970 to 1971). The reason for this is the decline in private contributions to support public television. As usual, minorities are last hired and first fired. In this case, I will admit, minorities were fired first for a unique reason—because in public television blacks and other minorities are concentrated in the job levels of professionals and technicians rather than the usual levels of service workers or laborers. It is the nature of the television industry that when staff cutbacks are made, they come first in the production department in the professional and technician levels.

So we see that newspapers are not the only media outlets at fault. They are, however, the most hypocritical, for they speak loudest in favor of equal employment on their editorial pages. For example, when I tried to find out the equal employment record of the New York Post, my aide was told, "It is our firm policy that we do not reveal these figures to anyone except a governmental agency doing an authorized study." What we have here, it seems, is a king-sized case of "Do as I say, not as I do."

And in the face of this hypocrisy, the Gridiron Club adds insult to injury by inviting token women to dinner.

My price is much higher. The price of women is much higher. The price of minorities is much higher. We are not bought off so easily.

Gentlemen of the Gridiron Club, guess who's not coming to dinner!

"U.S. Policy and Black Refugees"

An address delivered at the "African and Caribbean Refugees" symposium at the 25th Annual Meeting of the African Studies Association, Washington, D.C., November 6, 1982.

The debate over who is a "legitimate refugee" involves more than just a quarrel over definitions. Haitians and African refugees,

Published in *Issue: A Journal of Opinion* 12, nos. 1–2 (Spring–Summer 1982): 22–24.

largely Ethiopians, have come to our shores in much the same manner as previous groups. The reaction to the arrival of these groups, however, must be seen in the context of legal and political changes in American society.

The "first asylum" phenomenon of persons fleeing to the United States as their first place of refuge from persecution has become the primary focus of any policy decisions affecting our refugee and immigration laws. Further, the "first asylum" issue has blurred the distinctions between refugees and immigrants. The controversy surrounding the "first asylum" issue emanates from two areas: our foreign policy in the Western Hemisphere is based on the perception that "first asylees" flee to the U.S. for economic reasons rather than a "well-founded fear of persecution on the basis of race, religion, political opinion or membership in a social group," the definition for a refugee and/or asylee as embodied in the Refugee Act of 1980. Secondly, the new "asylees" are overwhelmingly persons of color in comparison to earlier immigrant groups, which were largely European.

First, the majority of the people fleeing to this country as "first asylees" come from Western Hemispheric countries like El Salvador, Haiti, and most recently Guatemala. These countries are not simply allies to the United States; their governments receive a substantial amount of military and/or economic assistance from us. In addition, the Reagan Administration has made it quite clear that it will support the existing governments in such countries against any revolutionary or liberating forces. Needless to say, this support often contributes to refugee flight from the Caribbean and Central American nations.

Secondly, the poor economic conditions in countries like Haiti provide an easy excuse for labeling Haitians as "economic refugees." This characterization, of course, ignores the political conditions in the home country and encourages the presumption that nationals from Haiti are fleeing to the United States solely for economic reasons.

The color question overlays the politics of our refugee policies. Clare Booth Luce, who serves on the President's Foreign Intelligence Advisory Board, was recently chastised for her remarks in the September issue of *Geo* magazine where she suggested that America's new immigrants were a threat to American culture. Her remarks are worth repeating here:

> In the Nineteenth Century, the United States absorbed something like forty million immigrants. But the vast majority were of a fundamental culture, and they were all white. They were not black or brown or yellow.

Luce's statement, while perhaps embarrassing to the administration, is indicative of the thoughts behind some of the administration's policy formulations. Refugees, who are people of color, are assumed to be inapplicable [*sic*] of integrating into American society. Ms. Luce forgot that black Americans preceded 19th century European immigrants and that our society is not *white* but rather multi-cultural. That is why jazz remains America's only original art form despite efforts to make square-dancing the official American national dance.

The marked increase in numbers of "first asylum" cases has certainly heightened the debate in this area. In 1980, 125,000 Cubans came to South Florida in the Mariel exodus. Notably, *these* Cubans were of a darker hue than their predecessors in the 1960s. During this same year, it is estimated that 12,000 Haitians arrived on U.S. shores. Over 100,000 Salvadorans entered the United States in 1981. This level of mass asylum is a new concept for U.S. immigration and refugee law. The genesis of the current crisis results from the fact that when Congress adopted the Refugee Act of 1980, the Act was silent on the issue of the United States as a country of first asylum. Needless to say, the Mariel exodus and the continuing flow of Haitian and Salvadoran refugees focused attention on this first asylum issue very quickly.

The next question, of course, is how have we responded as a country of first asylum. As signatories to the U.N. protocol relating to refugees in 1968, the U.S. has certain international obligations toward refugees who are defined as persons who have a "well-founded fear of being persecuted for reasons of race, religion, nationality, membership in the [sic] particular social group, or political opinion." Our own refugee laws, as a result of the Refugee Act of 1980, largely incorporate this definition. Of special significance is the protocol's prohibition of the deportation of a refugee "to the frontiers of territories where his life or freedom would be threatened. . . ." It also requires that its provisions be applied "without discrimination as to race, religion or country of origin." Our problems with "first asylum" issues largely stem from our inability to accept this definition with "political" qualifications.

As a country, the U.S. has been far more interested in responding to refugee concerns when we gained some political benefit than in addressing humanitarian need. In fact, only in the case of Cubans, and to a lesser extent Nicaraguans, has the U.S. responded positively to its obligations as a country of first asylum. In both cases, we perceived that it was in our political interest to accept Cubans as refugees and to grant extended voluntary departure status to Nicaraguans. For example, Haitian political prisoners, who were released from prison through the intervention of U.N. Ambassador Andrew Young, were dissuaded by our own state department officials from applying for political asylum in the United States. In this instance, we obviously saw no political gains from accepting Haitians as political prisoners. Geo-political considerations reveal far more about why we have pre-judged Haitian asylum claims as frivolous and rejected Salvadorans as refugees than any other explanation. These considerations raise the question generally of whether we have equal application of our refugee laws or differential treatment. Let me cite a few examples.

New York City papers recently carried the story of four Polish nationals who arrived in Elizabeth, New Jersey. They were granted asylum after only six days in the Brooklyn Detention Center and released. Yet Haitian nationals waited over a year before their release from the Detention Center. Two small boats of Cuban refugees have landed in Miami within the last two weeks. The Cubans have immediately been released to their family members while Haitians, with family members in the area, were denied release from the Krome Detention Camp until very recently.

These comparisons only confirm a continuing racial and ideological bias in our refugee and asylum law. Despite a change in our immigration laws to accommodate the U.N. definition of a refugee, we still respond more favorably to those persons fleeing from a communist regime. For example, from January 1974 to May 1975, none of the Filipinos or South Koreans who requested asylum were granted it. The State Department also recommended that asylum requests be denied to sixteen Greeks who sought political refuge before the fall of the Junta, and to the eight South Vietnamese who asked asylum from the Thieu regime. Yet during this same period, scarcely any requests from Eastern European countries were denied. Between 1975 and 1976, the last year for which data is available, 96 percent of the applicants fleeing rightist governments were denied refuge in the United States, while 95 percent of those applicants from communist countries, in the same time period, were granted sanctuary here. In the particular case of Haitian boat people arriving in Florida and requesting asylum eighteen have been granted asylum, less than one percent of the total.

In spite of a humanitarian change in the United States refugee law in 1980, which eliminated any legal basis for discriminating in favor of those fleeing communist countries, fully 95 percent of those whom the United States has admitted as refugees since the change still come from communist countries in Southeast Asia, Eastern Europe, or the Soviet Union. Furthermore, the quick action on the asylum claims of the four Poles, while Haitians forcibly exiled from Haiti in November 1980 have yet to receive a ruling on their requests for asylum, illustrates the priority given to asylum claimants from communist countries.

Yet, the racial issue cannot be ignored here. The plight of Ethiopian nationals in this country is a clear example of the racism inherent in our policies. The State Department's decision to revoke the extended voluntary departure status granted to Ethiopians in August of 1981 was greeted with cries of racism. At the same time that we were granting this status to Poles, the State Department was removing this status for Ethiopians. Here, we have a people who fled a communist-ruled government just like Poland or other Eastern European countries. Yet, they received decidedly different treatment. Skin color is the only differential which explains this policy decision. Fortunately, through the efforts of Congressmen

Jack Kemp (R-NY) and Julian Dixon (D-CA), this decision was reversed.

Generally, our policy toward African refugees has been one of conflicting interests and benign neglect. Despite the presence of 25 percent of the world's refugee population in Africa, our annual admission quotas remain at the low level of 3,000. When challenged on the small numbers, the State Department's defense is three-fold:

1. Africa takes care of its own and there is no need for permanent resettlement in the U.S.;
2. Africans are largely rural people and would not adjust well to American society; and
3. The U.S. compensates for these small numbers by giving economic assistance to refugees in Africa.

Such defenses are only a polite way of saying that African refugees are not a priority. While Africa's response to refugees is nothing short of remarkable, given her resources, many Africans could benefit from resettlement in the United States. The rural argument ignores the fact that Hmong Tribesmen were actively encouraged to apply for refugee admission to the U.S.; in this instance, a rural lifestyle in Indochina was no barrier for U.S. policy-makers. Finally, economic assistance from the U.S. is tenuous at best. Recently, the African Refugee Section, at State, estimated that the U.S. might withhold as much as $25 million in food aid that it pledged at the Geneva Conference on African Refugees in April of 1981. "Unforeseen donations by other countries, carry-overs . . . from previous years and reduced estimates" of refugee numbers prompted this change. It seems that even in terms of food aid, Africans receive second-class treatment.

Finally, we cannot ignore the feelings of the U.N. high commissioner for refugees and African leaders that the U.S. program encourages a "brain drain" from Africa. Individual liberty and choice, however, should not be sacrificed for the sake of governments' prestige. As long as the U.S. maintains a refugee program, Africans and other black refugees must be treated equitably.

Remarkably, these statistics and facts are not the worst aspects of our policies toward black refugees. Legal protection for refugees has been deliberately undermined by the Reagan Administration. The success of the Haitian lawsuits has generated a lot of discussion about eliminating federal court jurisdiction over asylum claims to prevent any future cases like *Haitian Refugee Center v. Civiletti*. These changes in court jurisdiction, of course, are being proposed in the guise of "streamlining the process." The real motive here, however, is to cut Haitians' access to the courts. This action is in direct response to the success of the Center's lawsuit and other lawsuits brought on behalf of Haitian asylum claimants.

The new immigration reform package, the Simpson-Mazzoli Bill, severely restricts judicial review of asylum claims. The bill punishes the victims of discriminatory policies for successfully using our legal system to thwart those policies. This action is not "streamlining the process" for efficiency but rather a blatant drive to cut aliens' access to our courts.

The policy of interdiction is a clear violation of the U.S.'s responsibility for the protection of refugees. Without specific legislative authority, the Coast Guard has interdicted three boats carrying Haitian nationals and returned these people back to

Haiti. There is no definitive information about the fate of these returnees. Interdiction has certainly eliminated most of the Haitian boat traffic but one must ask at what cost in terms of resources and people.

Perhaps the most heinous policy of the Reagan Administration has been the imprisonment of Haitians for the past year. With the exception of the detention of Japanese-Americans during World War II, no other group has been treated so inhumanely. Over 2,000 Haitian asylum-seekers were dispersed in twelve different facilities around the country, including Puerto Rico. At least three deaths occurred during the year-long detention. In addition, federal prisons were used to detain Haitians who had been accused of no crime either in the United States or in Haiti. The racist treatment of Haitians is clear; no other group has been placed in our federal prisons without first being labeled as a criminal.

One must also be mindful of the forced repatriation of refugees processed for admission to the U.S. in Djibouti and the recent debacle with Ethiopians on extended voluntary departure in the U.S. As with Civil Rights issues generally, Human Rights advocates must expect deliberate attempts by this administration to obfuscate its international commitments to refugees when it is politically expedient.

As scholars interested in the peoples of the African Diaspora, we have a responsibility to monitor and influence foreign policies which impact the Caribbean and Africa. Certainly, the plight of black refugees in this country is an issue to which we must all respond. Refugee policy is an adjunct of our broader foreign policy goals. Since U.S. foreign policy is greatly determined by ethnic pressure, it is imperative that black Americans become intimately involved in shaping American foreign policy, including refugee policy. State Department reaction to Polish Martial Law, the Turkish invasion of Cyprus, and the Israeli attacks in Lebanon greatly shaped America's policies in these situations. We must not be tempted by those who use immigrants and refugees as scapegoats for the economic plight of black Americans. We must be willing to advocate for the protection of black refugees now; otherwise, we will be at a distinct disadvantage when the crisis in South Africa reaches its climax, as it surely will in the near future.

FIGURE 1. On the day of the New York City mayoral election, November 2, 1965, New York state assemblywoman Shirley Chisholm studies political statistics. Source: Library of Congress. Photo by Roger Higgins.

FIGURE 2. Freshman Congresswoman Chisholm speaks at an election night rally on November 4, 1969, celebrating New York mayor John Lindsay's reelection. Source: Library of Congress. Photo by Bernard Gotfryd.

FIGURE 3. Rep. Chisholm in 1970, surrounded by participants of the Youth Dialog Program, a part of the Model Cities Initiative aimed at the revitalization of urban communities, including Bedford-Stuyvesant. Photo by Capt. Jay Ruffins.

FIGURE 4. The thirteen founding members of the Congressional Black Caucus, February 1971. *Back row, from left:* Representatives Parren J. Mitchell (D-MD), Charles B. Rangel (D-NY), William L. Clay Sr. (D-MO), Ronald V. Dellums (D-CA), George W. Collins (D-IL), Louis Stokes (D-OH), Ralph H. Metcalfe (D-IL), and John Conyers Jr. (D-MI); Del. Walter E. Fauntroy (D-DC). *Front row, from left:* Representatives Robert N. C. Nix Sr. (D-PA), Charles C. Diggs Jr. (D-MI), Shirley A. Chisholm (D-NY), and Augustus F. Hawkins (D-CA). Source: Library of Congress.

FIGURE 5. One of Shirley Chisholm's 1972 presidential campaign posters combines her 1968 campaign slogan, "Unbought and Unbossed," with a statement of her intersectional vision of unifying the underrepresented populations of the United States into a transformative people's coalition. Source: Library of Congress.

FIGURE 6. On the third day of the Democratic National Convention, July 12, 1972, supporters of Shirley Chisholm demonstrate alongside supporters of segregationist George Wallace (who also competed for the Democratic nomination), showing the wide divisions in the Democratic Party. Source: Library of Congress. Photo by Thomas O'Halloran.

FIGURE 7. After fulfilling her pledge to lead her presidential campaign and its progressive ideas all the way to the Democratic National Convention at Miami Beach, Rep. Shirley Chisholm gives a speech, on July 13, 1972, to galvanize the disparate factions of the Democratic Party against incumbent Richard Nixon. That night, she became the first African American and first woman to have her name entered into nomination at a major party convention. Source: Library of Congress. Photo by Thomas O'Halloran.

FIGURE 8. Rep. Chisholm in 1973. After her presidential campaign, her national profile grew. She continued to champion women, racial minorities, the working class, and other marginalized groups. Long after retiring from Congress in 1983, she continued to influence the social and political landscape as a political educator, activist, and elder stateswoman. Source: New York Public Library.

FIGURE 9. Rep. Shirley Chisholm and other congresswomen observe as President Ford, on August 22, 1974, signs legislation proclaiming August 26 Women's Equality Day. *From left:* Representatives Yvonne Brathwaite Burke (D-CA), Barbara Jordan (D-TX), Elizabeth Holtzman (D-NY), Marjorie S. Holt (R-MD), Leonor K. Sullivan (D-MO), Cardiss Collins (D-IL), Corinne C. Boggs (D-LA), Margaret M. Heckler (R-MA), Bella S. Abzug (D-NY), and Shirley Chisholm (D-NY). Source: National Archives/Ford Presidential Library.

5 U.S. Politics and Coalitions of the Marginal

*Those of you who have been neglected, left out, ignored, forgotten, or
shunned aside for whatever reason: Give me your help at this hour!
Join me in an effort to reshape our society and regain control of our
destiny.*

PRESIDENTIAL CAMPAIGN ANNOUNCEMENT (1972)

In 1972, when Chisholm ran for the U.S. presidency, her strategy revolved
around being the people's candidate who represented the most marginalized constituencies. Although these groups would differ in terms of race,
gender, sexuality, class, and age, they believed a Chisholm candidacy represented possibilities that went beyond identity politics. For Shirley
Chisholm, oppressed people's best option for obtaining political power
was through coalition building that crossed multiple racial, social, and
generational lines. Creating a coalition of marginalized people was not a
naïve notion; it reflected her belief in a strategy that, if executed,
would allow for substantive change. While Chisholm strongly criticized
the corruption and maintenance of the status quo in U.S. politics, she was
fundamentally committed to working within conventional political avenues and structures. Sitting in between multiple identities and coming
from humble means, she also situated Black women as the foremothers
and political conscience of America.

"A Government That Cannot Hear the People"

An excerpt from Unbought and Unbossed, *originally published in 1970.*

"For the first time in the history of the human race, a great nation is able and willing to make a commitment to eradicate poverty among its people. It will be a great program and it will succeed."

That was President Lyndon B. Johnson's boast as he signed the Economic Opportunity Act of 1964. The war on poverty began with tremendous fanfare and was waged with enormous outlays of money and effort. Thousands of dedicated persons spent all their talents on it. Why did it fail to close the gap between poverty and affluence in the United States? Was it the Vietnam war that stole away the tax money that should have gone into social programs?

Like the crusaders for civil rights, some poverty warriors still do not want to admit that their great venture was a flop. They prefer to blame Johnson's war, Congress, the city hall and courthouse, political crowds, and now the Nixon administration. There is justice in each of those indictments, but the main reason the war on poverty was lost was a failing that was built into it. The antipoverty programs were designed by white middle-class intellectuals who had no experience of being poor, despised, and discriminated against. They looked at the condition of the poor and made their diagnosis: lack of opportunity. All the other problems of the have-nots in our society—hunger, ignorance, crime, disease—were seen to be caused by the fact that when poor people tried to reach out for socially acceptable goals, they found their aspirations blocked.

Excerpted from Shirley Chisholm, *Unbought and Unbossed*, 40th anniversary ed. (1970; repr., Washington, D.C.: Take Root Media, 2010).

So far, so good; this is true. But why is the way upward blocked? The poverty warriors described the cycle of deprivation: hunger, lack of education, lack of social mobility, leading to unemployability or low income potential, leading to frustration and poor motivation, leading in turn to hunger, poor education, and so on for the next generation. Break the cycle at one point and you end its vicious repetition. That was true, too, of course. Where do you start, with schools, health, housing, jobs, or what? Better employment was clearly the key, the planners decided. We will train the poor who are rejected and unhirable, and find them better jobs as they are able to handle them. The only fact left out of the analysis was the fundamental problem: racism.

Most of the poor were poor because they were labeled niggers or greasers or hillbillies or canucks or spics. They belonged to despised, powerless groups. There was no way the antipoverty strategists could see the importance of this factor. They knew about it theoretically, but they had not been there themselves. They didn't know where it was at. If they had gotten together with their "clients" in the poor communities from the start, things might have been different. Such involvement did come later, dictated by the growing understanding of program field workers.

The federal programs were intended to give the poor something tangible, quickly, and without alarming the middle class. Congress, in particular, did not want to cause any disruption of the political structure. The goal was to eliminate poverty without making any other major changes. Slowly the suspicion grew that the poor knew more about what they needed and how to get it than anyone else, if they were given a chance to get in on planning the programs. But this meant organization, and dealing with issues affecting jobs, schools, and housing meant that the organization of the poor soon got to be political. No top policy-makers wanted community action programs to become ways of achieving political power for the poor. Certainly few of the congressmen who voted for the establishment of the Office of Economic Opportunity would have done so if they had foreseen the Pandora's box that could be opened by organizing the poor. It was to have been a self-help program without the self.

Local politicians were quick to see the danger to them, and to demand that "maximum feasible participation" of the poor can be played down in the design of the antipoverty programs. If people started to get together to help themselves, with the resources of the federal government to help them, who would need the ward politicians, the district leaders, the clubhouse lawyers, the courthouse gang? So the local politicians' response was to take charge wherever they could, and usually they could; they made sure the representatives of the poor were hand-picked, middle-class, and "responsible" leaders who had more in common with the existing power structures than with the truly deprived. It did not take long for the mass of the poor to catch on that they were being defrauded once again. After that happens, it is unlikely that real participation in a program can be readily secured, or that it will be orderly and cooperative in nature.

But the antipoverty program is leaving behind it a legacy that was quite unexpected. It politicized blacks and other poor minority groups to a surprising degree, considering that original programs had so little emphasis on organization, and that where effective organizations appeared that they were no longer encouraged by those in power. Black Americans, in particular, partly because of the failures of OEO, began to understand that they had struggled too hard to fight prejudice and make it possible for individuals to win freedom and power, and not hard enough to build organizations on ethnic lines to achieve group power and freedom. Many kinds of economic self-help organizations have started to appear. It has also become increasingly clear to minorities that they cannot ignore the political arena. If they are going to enter the economic mainstream, they will have to become significantly involved in politics.

There is a clear lack of joy in political circles over this trend, which is evidence to me of its importance. Similarly, the fact that the present administration is dismembering OEO and turning its more successful programs over to older, more change-resistant bureaus and agencies tells me that OEO was, in spite of everything, achieving enough success in limited areas to make it worrisome to some people.

The history of the war on poverty shows, among other things, that people are learning to rebel against government that imposes on them policies that they had no hand in forming. The trend is visible in other areas of public life, particularly in education. But nowhere has the conflict between official policy and what the public wants been more bitter and prolonged than it has over the Southeast Asian war and its relation to domestic priorities. I had made my maiden speech against the war after I was forced to realize that the new President was not, despite what he said, acting to bring the war to a quick end. He was also moving to continue the development of fantastic weapons for future wars, at staggering costs, and to do so was quite willing to cut the heart out of social program after program—education, job training, housing, urban redevelopment.

Head Start, one of OEO's most successful programs and one especially significant to me as a specialist in early childhood education, was reduced. The Job Corps, just hitting its stride, was slashed in half. Real job training programs that prepared unskilled persons for worthwhile work were put on the shelf in favor of phony ones, which amounted to subsidizing businessmen so they could hire poor people at low cost to themselves. Those hired were kept in routine jobs for the period of "training" and then laid off when the subsidies ran out. The list was all but endless.

What was happening? How could a President be so unconcerned about the needs of the nation he headed, so unresponsive to the will of its citizens? What barrier kept the voices of the people from reaching him? Before the end of his first year in office, there came the Haynsworth nomination to the Supreme Court. When it was defeated, the Carswell nomination followed. I was aghast at this appeal to a sectional minority. When Carswell's 1948 white supremacist speech came to light, reporters called the black members of Congress for their reactions. I was so angry I instructed my staff not to put them through to me but to tell them: "Mrs. Chisholm has no comment. She says she can't be bothered to make a statement every time Nixon appoints a racist to the Supreme Court."

Then the administration tried to tear the heart out of the Voting Rights Act, the federal law that had made it possible for more black citizens to register and vote in the deep South than ever before. Its cunning scheme was to ostensibly extend the law to the entire country, at the cost of removing the features that had made it work. It was pushed through the House by a coalition of Republicans and southern Democrats. If it had become law it would have left action to protect voting rights in any locality up to the attorney general— the same attorney general who was at that moment paying the administration's campaign debts to the South by wrecking the progress of school desegregation through indefinite delay of legal action against southern school districts.

Southern schools, which had been given fifteen years of grace in complying with the law and the Constitution, began to get further delays. The White House, in mid-1969, issued a "new policy" on desegregation guidelines. It was so vague that no one could make out what it said except perhaps one district judge in Louisiana. Judge Ben C. Dawkins ordered HEW to renegotiate the school desegregation plans of thirty-seven Louisiana districts, of which the judge had earlier approved. Now he was calling the same plans "outrageous" and declaring that the new policy statement "gives us considerably more elbow room."

For more than a year the Nixon administration appeared to be wavering on school desegregation, but actually kept moving, behind a curtain of misdirection, straight toward a policy that would win the President every unreconstructed heart in Dixie. Finally he went all the way with his March 1970 statement on policy, appointing himself the guardian of the "neighborhood school," a code phrase that no segregationist could fail to catch and admire. He proclaimed that the federal government would not require busing beyond "normal geographic zones" and made it clear that Washington would have nothing whatsoever to say about de facto segregation.

The difference between *de jure* and *de facto* segregation is the difference between open, forthright bigotry and the shamefaced kind that works through unwritten agreements between real estate dealers, school officials, and local politicians. What the President said was that, as long as a locality can manage to keep its black, brown, and poor citizens jammed into filthy slums by conspiracy, rather than by statute, it is fine with him and no one in Washington will lose any sleep.

As an outrageous attack on school buses at Lamar, South Carolina, showed immediately thereafter, the Nixon southern strategy was playing with fire, because it encouraged the lowest, most racist elements in the South to believe that their day was not past after all. The result was a tragic setback for all the white and black southerners whose main desire is to progress together in peace and growing understanding. They had been making a beginning at that essential and difficult job. Gains had been made, but President Nixon helped to see that they were undone. It amazed me to hear a President refer, as he did in that statement, to "the notion" that all-black schools are inherently inferior. That "notion" has been the law of the land since the Supreme Court declared it to be in its 1954 decision on Brown v. Board of Education, and the President, by his oath of office, swore to uphold the Constitution.

His school desegregation policies and his Supreme Court appointments made it clear that Nixon does not want to be President of black, brown, and other dark-skinned Americans. His Vietnam policy turned out to be to keep the war going as long as possible, except with Vietnamese troops taking over in the combat areas. This meant that the estrangement of American youth from their own government would continue and grow more serious. And his decision to fight inflation by every means but the one effective one—ending the war—meant that there would be no real efforts made to attack housing, employment, nutrition, and education problems under his administration, because there would be no money in the budget to do it with.

Of all his errors, I believe that President Nixon's cynical, callous attitude toward his poor, black, brown, white, or red fellow citizens will turn out to be the most serious. It will be his undoing. His southern strategy will be his Vietnam. As President Johnson assured his own downfall by edging, step by step, into that disastrous and unpopular war, Nixon is trying to lead this country, step by step, in a direction that eventually, I pray, it will refuse to take.

But will it? My deep misgivings at the answer are not based on mere political opposition to President Nixon, nor even opposition to his Vietnam war policy or his school desegregation and voters' rights policies. The first two years of his administration made him a symbol to me, and I think to nearly every black American. He represents nearly every one of the deep-seated and tragic flaws of this society, as they appear to us. He does not care for his black fellow citizens; he does not even see them until he is forced to, and then deals with them grudgingly. He is able to disregard the misery of poor Americans of every color in order to squander our resources on a foreign military adventure in which this nation has no vital interest. We look to the 1972 election with anxiety. Will part of this nation rejoice at seeing the rest oppressed, and reward a leader who has cunningly manipulated its fears and prejudices? Or will a majority of voters insist on a leader—who he could be I cannot yet guess—who will appeal to their birthright of idealism and their love of justice, instead of to their heritage of racism and special privilege?

Presidential Campaign Announcement

Delivered at Concord Baptist Church, Brooklyn, New York, January 25, 1972.

I stand before you today as a candidate for the Democratic nomination for the presidency of the United States of America.

I am not the candidate of black America, although I am black and proud.

Transcribed from video and audio, New York City Department of Records and Information Services (WNYC-TV Moving Images Collection), Series 1: Film, 1943–1981, Reel 2776. Segments of the full speech are skipped in the video version.

I am not the candidate of the women's movement of this country, although I am a woman and I'm equally proud of that.

I am not the candidate of any political bosses or fat cats or special interests.

I stand here now without endorsements from many big-name politicians or celebrities or any other kind of prop. I do not intend to offer to you the tired and glib clichés, which for too long have been an accepted part of our political life. I am the candidate of the people of America. And my presence before you, now, symbolizes a new era in American political history. I have always earnestly believed in the great potential of America. Our constitutional democracy will soon celebrate its 200th anniversary, effective testimony to the longevity of our cherished Constitution, and its unique Bill of Rights, which continues to give to the world its inspirational message of freedom and liberty.

We Americans are a dynamic people because of our rugged individuality and our cherished diversity, because of our belief in human dignity, because of our generosity and good will to our fellow man—and most importantly, because of our tradition of moving forward, forward to actively confront those problems which plague us in a world growing more complex each year.

Like all human beings, we have made mistakes. Our involvement in Vietnam was and remains at this very moment a terrible tragedy. To have intervened in the civil war in that country, and then later to have intervened in still two more countries, Laos and Cambodia, was an ill-conceived blunder whose consequences all of us have had to suffer. To leave our men there, or to increase massive bombing in the process of withdrawing them, is to compound the havoc and misery which we are inflicting on the peoples of Indochina; [our] own young men who have been killed and mutilated and rendered drug addicts; and ourselves—ourselves, whose hard-earned money has, during a serious economic recession, made up the billions of dollars spent in Vietnam when we so urgently needed these resources at home.

During last year, 1971, more civilians were killed and wounded in Indochina, and many more made refugees, than at any time in our history. And Vietnam continues to cost us one million dollars a day—this despite President Nixon's promise, four years ago, to end this nightmare.

Our unique economic system has made America the wealthiest nation in history. Yet we have undergone another economic recession in which millions of Americans have lost their jobs and are unable to find work—the highest number in ten years. And at the same time, prices have soared on even the essentials of life: food, clothing, and medical care.

And beyond Vietnam and its horrors, which have dominated our newspapers and televisions for eight long years; and beyond the economic recession, which has caused severe hardship at home to so many Americans, is the visible, ongoing destruction of our natural environment, and our loss of a sense of personal security in our own daily lives.

Perhaps even more fundamental is our loss of the feeling of community; shock at the continuing injustices and inequities in the land that we love; our suspicions of pervasive constitutional [sic] incompetence and corruption; our feeling that there's an absence of respectable authority in our nation; and our loss of confidence in ourselves, with apathy or despair arising from the conviction that we are powerless to make ourselves heard or felt in remedying our ills.

Fellow Americans, we have looked in vain to the Nixon Administration for the courage, the spirit, the character, and the words to lift us, to bring out the best in us, to rekindle in each of us our faith in the American Dream. Yet all that we have received in return is just another smooth exercise in political manipulation, deceit and deception, callousness and indifference to our individual problems, and the disgusting playing of divisive politics—pitting the young against the old, labor against management, North against South, black against white.

The abiding concern of this Administration has been one of political expediency rather than the needs of man's nature. The President has broken his promises to us, and has therefore lost his claim to our trust and confidence in him.

I cannot believe—I cannot believe that this Administration would have ever been elected four years ago if we had known then what we know today—that we are entering—we are entering a new era in which we must, as Americans, demand stature and size in our national leadership—leadership which is fresh, leadership which is open, and leadership which is receptive to the problems of all Americans.

I have faith in the American people. I believe that we are smart enough to correct our mistakes. I believe we are intelligent enough to recognize the talent, energy, and dedication which all Americans, including women and minorities, have to offer.

I know from my travels to the cities and small towns of America that we have a vast potential which can and must be put to constructive use in getting this great nation together.

I know that millions of Americans from all walks of life agree with me that leadership does not mean putting the ear to the ground to follow public opinion, but to have the vision of what is necessary and the courage to make it possible—not by force, violence, or intimidation, but by persuasion, example, and law.

We must turn away from the control of the prosaic, the privileged, and the old-line, tired politicians to open our society to the energies and abilities of countless new kinds of groups of Americans: women, blacks, browns, Indians, Orientals, and youth, so that they can develop their own full potential and thereby participate equally and enthusiastically in building a strong and just society, rich—rich in its diversity and noble in its quality of life.

I stand before you today to repudiate the ridiculous notion that the American people will not vote for a qualified candidate simply because he is not white, or because she's not a male. I do not believe that in 1972 the great majority of Americans will continue to harbor such narrow and petty prejudices. I am convinced that the American people are in a mood to discard the politics and the political personalities of the past. I believe that they will show, in 1972 and thereafter, that they intend to make independent judgments on the merits of a particular candidate based on that candidate's intelligence, character, physical ability, competence, integrity, and honesty.

It is, I feel, the duty of responsible leaders of this country to encourage and maximize—not to dismiss or minimize—such judgment. Americans all over are demanding a new sensibility, a new philosophy of government from Washington.

Instead of sending spies to snoop on participants at Earth Day, I would welcome the efforts of concerned citizens of all ages to stop the abuse of our environment.

Instead of watching a football game on television, while young people beg for the attention of their President concerning our actions abroad, I would encourage them to speak out, organize for peaceful change, and vote in November.

Instead of blocking efforts to control the huge amounts of money given political candidates by the rich and the powerful, I would provide certain limits on such amounts, and encourage all the people of this nation to contribute small sums to the candidates of their choice.

Instead of calculating the political costs of this or that policy, and of weighing favors of this or that group, depending on whether that group voted for me in 1968, I would remind all Americans at this hour of the words of Abraham Lincoln: "A house divided cannot stand."

We Americans are all fellow countrymen, one day confronting the judgment of history in our country. We are all God's children and the will of each of us is as precious as the will of the most powerful general or corporate millionaire.

Our will can create a new America in 1972: one where there's freedom from violence and war at home and abroad; where there's freedom from poverty and discrimination; where there exists at least a feeling that we are making progress in ensuring for everyone medical care, employment, and decent housing; where we more decisively clean up our streets, our water, and our air; where we work together, black and white, to rebuild our neighborhoods, and to make our cities quiet, attractive, and efficient; and, fundamentally, where we live in the confidence that every man and every woman in America has at long last the opportunity to become all that he was created of being, such as is his ability.

In conclusion, all of you who share this vision, from New York to California, from Wisconsin to Florida, are brothers and sisters on the road to national unity and a new America. Those of you who were locked outside of the convention hall in 1968, those of you who can now vote for the first time, those of you who agree with me that the institutions of this country belong to all of the people who inhabit it, those of you who have been neglected, left out, ignored, forgotten, or shunned aside for whatever reason: Give me your help at this hour! Join me in an effort to reshape our society and regain control of our destiny as we go down the Chisholm Trail for 1972.

"The Politics of Coalition"

An article originally published in The Black Scholar, *September 1972.*

It is obvious to me that black Americans can no longer look upon our struggle for full participation within American society as one which is isolated from that of other second-class groups. Discrimination against blacks because of the color of our skin is no more—or less—anathema to basic civil rights than is discrimination against groups because of their religion, creed, sex, or sexual orientation. When discrimination is at work, it is an instance of those who hold power drawing up petty and arbitrary barriers for the purpose of denying equal participation to those who, if allowed to compete freely within the system, would threaten the status of the power holders.

More Americans participating fully in our society, more Americans allowed to compete for top policy-making roles in government, business, and industry, would make it more difficult for the mediocre men—who have wrecked our economy, involved us in civil wars abroad, and divided us at home—to hold on to their power by limiting the corps of potential competitors.

The Black Scholar 4, no. 1 (September 1972): 30–32.

The device used to limit competition is that of assigning different roles to the different groups within the American society. White males have assigned to themselves such roles as President of the United States, corporate executives, industrialists, doctors, lawyers, and professors at our universities. They have assigned to white women roles such as housewife, secretary, PTA chairman, and schoolteacher. Black women can now be schoolteachers, too, but they are most prominently assigned to domestic roles—maid, cook, waitress, and baby-sitter. Black men are thought to be good porters, bus drivers, and sanitation men.

These are roles which have been engrained into the minds of all of us; and any attempt on the part of the other three groups to rise above our particular role is looked upon with apprehension by the white males who form the establishment.

All too often the potential for full intellectual development and goal realization on the part of minorities and women is suppressed by denying these groups the appropriate job training and educational opportunity necessary to assume a role which white males consider to be their domain.

I do not mean to suggest that there is anything degrading about work as a domestic or in a clerical position or as a teacher or in any other capacity that is honest and satisfying. Hard work at any occupation can be fulfilling and rewarding. But I do object to assigning certain roles to particular groups on the basis of sex and color, when there is no generic reason or suitability. And I resent the efforts of white males to limit competition for the more prestigious and higher-paying occupations.

Blacks, Spanish-speaking Americans, and Indians have long objected to the exclusiveness of the establishment. Today, women are voicing their objections, too; and statistics tell us why. Among all employed women, eighty-two percent are clerical, sales, factory and farm workers or in service occupations. Six percent are medical and health workers, college teachers or other professional and technical workers. Just five percent of American women are managers, officials or proprietors.

If women are, as the Department of Labor has concluded, more reliable and are absent from their jobs less frequently than men, what is the reason for their preponderant employment at the lower level positions and pay scales? Quite simply, it is discrimination.

Women are sick and tired of being told: "See how far you've come? You've come a long way, baby." If that's so, then why is it that of ten thousand civil service employees in jobs paying $26,000 a year or better, only about 150 are women? If it's true, then why are fewer than one percent of federal policy-making positions held by women?

The truth of the matter is that the top policy-making positions within the American establishment remain in the hands of white males who are not responsive to the needs of the poor, minorities, or women. Nor can these men be held in [sic] account for their actions—for their failure to control inflation and unemployment, for their failure to respond to the call of consumers for better products at non-exorbitant costs—because regular citizens have no power to control them or to replace them as long as they deny the great majority of Americans the opportunity to compete freely in our society.

Yet there is hope for oppressed groups if we unite and challenge the forces which now hold the power in our country. This is an effort which requires that these groups—minorities, women, consumers—come together and demand representation in the high councils of the establishment; and it also requires that we forget about role-playing, and seek to allow persons to engage in work which is suited to their intellectual and physical abilities.

It means that blacks must realize that there are other groups who face discrimination, and who, for reasons of their own self-interest, are willing to join forces in breaking down petty and arbitrary barriers against fully productive careers within the mainstream of American life. This is why I have long spoken out in favor of coalition politics; and it is why I have been disturbed that some persons do not understand the wisdom of joint political action.

Black women surely know the value of such action. We face discrimination based on both racism and sexism. And it is important for us to be involved in both black and women's liberation.

Critics of this position suggest that we should first become liberated as a people. I say that there is no need to fight two different battles, but we should fight both at the same time. There is an argument that women's lib is a white woman's thing and that the role to which white women have been assigned should be of no concern to the black woman. Nothing, in my view, could be further from the truth, since the proponents of "black liberation only" envision that black women will someday play the same kind of role that white women now play—which is "American woman."

Cheryl Clark [sic] of the *New York Amsterdam News* has attempted to define just what the American woman is all about. She suggests, ". . . a man comes along and chooses a woman he'll support in exchange for her having and raising kids, keeping house, cooking, shopping, being faithful, tryin' to be half-way attractive, and whatever else."

Such a role does not take into consideration either the needs or the talents of a woman—particularly, the present day black woman. When we consider the fact that twenty-nine percent of black households are headed by a woman, we cannot expect these women to fit into this definition of American woman. When we consider the fact that many other black and white women have to work in order to help their husbands with the bills, we cannot expect them to fit the definition either. When we honestly admit that some women are assertive and aggressive, we cannot expect them to be relegated to being housewife—without their being frustrated in such a capacity. The women's movement seeks to present an alternative to "American woman"—one which I feel is much more conducive to the peculiar nature and needs of the black woman.

Let me strongly take issue with those persons who say that it is time for black women to step back and let black men take the lead. I certainly do not object to black men taking the lead in our struggle for equal rights in America. Yet, I believe that we should not place emphasis on black women stepping back. Rather, we should emphasize the need for black men to step ahead. We cannot afford to have any of our people stepping back. That is not the way to move forward. But it is certainly appropriate and desirable to have black men taking the lead in moving forward.

Neither do I look upon the struggle for equal rights as an all black thing. Every American who believes in liberty and justice for all must join the struggle for equality of rights for blacks and Indians, Puerto Ricans and Chicanos, and women.

Progressive-minded Americans should join in the struggle to end *all* forms of discrimination in America, and to end the narrow instinct of assigning stereotypic roles to particular groups. Human beings cannot so easily be assigned since we are unique in our individual abilities and characters. For this reason, liberation in America must transcend ending discrimination against a particular race. It must entail ending discrimination because of sex, origin, and religion as well.

"Politics Is Every Black Woman's Business"

Delivered before a meeting of the National Council of Negro Women in 1986.

The need born out of the helplessness and powerlessness of black women has once again revived the old adage of "God helps those who help themselves." We recognized that the time had come for the collected, organized political empowerment of black women in this country and decided to put our boat out to sea and gather in the loaves. "Never again" became the watchword!

Our role as black women has never been placed in proper perspective; as a result of historical circumstances, we were able to develop the traits of perseverance, strength, tenacity and determination.

The powerlessness and hopelessness that is all too pervasive in our communities calls for a reawakening, a reenergizing and a rededication to the "activism" of our predecessors who paved many paths for us to follow! Are we guilty about ignoring our brothers and sisters below the first rung of the ladder of success? Have we forgotten the roads over which we have treaded to be here today? Have we ourselves turned away from the struggle? I hope that we are not too absorbed in our own trip across the river to remember either those still neck-deep in the flood or our own proximity to the riverbank.

Transcript in the Shirley Chisholm Papers, MC 1194, Special Collections and University Archives, Rutgers University Libraries.

Are we passing on the principles and ideals to our own children and grandchildren—"planting trees," as Walter Lippman said, "for our children to sit under"—or are they only to inherit a "lust for money, possessions and prestige"? Did the dependency on federal programs during the past 20 years lull us into a state of apathy and indifference? Did we actually believe that we "got over" because life had seemed to be moving along fairly well until President Ronald Reagan came to power in 1980 and commenced to change the total structure and role of the federal government?

We can attempt to excuse our slide into apathy by bemoaning the scarcity of leaders and leadership. True, we do need a Gandhi! But can we wait for the next Dr. King, the next committed idealist to stick his or her head out of the foxhole?

Sisters, we must move again with the inner fires burning within our souls; we must move again for the sake of our children as much as for ourselves. We must beware that we are not creating in the next generation a false sense of security. We must realize that we have left them almost devoid of the basic survival instincts which brought us and our forebears through slavery and sustained us through repressive segregation. The wave created by our progress is now pushing us back out to sea.

There are many who believe that the nation's debt to the black people for the past injustices has been paid and that whites themselves have become victims of reverse discrimination.

The spread of this viewpoint has increased fears among blacks that progress has come to a halt and that hard-won gains are beginning to slip away. The implications of the *Bakke* case in education and the *Weber* case in employment years ago indicate that retrogression has commenced and that the civil rights struggle with its marches and sit-ins has now been feeling the stings of a belated white backlash!

My sisters, where are the fuels of our commitment and righteous anger during the civil rights struggles? These are the fuels that today seem as rare as fifty-cents-a-gallon gasoline!

When it comes right down to it, all we have is each other. And we are no good at all to each other if we remain indifferent to the unfinished or unraveling agenda of the second reconstruction.

As Ma Bethune said: "Yesterday, our ancestors endured the degradation of slavery, yet they retained their dignity. Today, we direct our economic and political strength towards winning a more abundant and secure life. Tomorrow, a new Negro, unburdened by race taboos and shackles, will benefit from more than 350 years of ceaseless striving and struggle. . . . Theirs will be a better world. This I believe with all my heart."

These thoughts are significant because they imply the harnessing of our power which was the basic concept that the founder of this mighty army of black women believed in with all her soul and power.

Can we meet the challenge in 1986? At times, it seems that our spirits are slumbering: it seems that our energies are ebbing: it seems that our eyes have no vision and our ears hear not the call. Our indomitable will and tenacity of purpose must be carried on despite the setbacks that our ethnic group is experiencing under the current administration in Washington.

There is much work that remains on the Agenda . . . an illiterate mother of eight hungry children is unlikely to make the same contribution as an educated woman, a mother of two or three healthy youngsters, who works as a teacher, nurse or in some other vocation.

Our political involvement, sisters, will continue the dreams of Mary Church Terrell and Mary McLeod Bethune in this century— the dream of collective spirits and souls functioning as a giant to become an immovable advocacy force to be dealt with in terms of the issues confronting black women and thus black families.

We have to coalesce and rebel against the forces of suppression, oppression and repression but such an objective means a unity of purpose . . . a germination of the seed of solidarity regardless of economic level which could only result in a stronger, more viable approach to solving many problems.

Sisters, we must become once again a great foundry where human beings are molded into people of pride and integrity. Today, black women are suffering disproportionately in our communities. The physical pain is being endured: the emotional weight may even sometimes be overlooked.

Frederick Douglass said: "A man without force is without essential dignity of humanity. Human nature is so constituted that it cannot honor a helpless man, although it can pity him, and even this cannot be done for long if the signs of power do not arise . . . ."

Let us remember that a great people are not affected by each puff of wind that blows ill. We must fight for belief in ourselves and above all, we must hearken back to the days of darkness when Frederick Douglass, the great abolitionist, even in those times, echoed the famous phrase that has come realistically to haunt black people today in America as they continue the struggle— "Power concedes nothing!"

Malcolm X told us: "Tomorrow belongs to the people who prepare for it today. I tell you: do nothing today and there won't be a tomorrow."

James Baldwin: "Not everything that is faced can be changed, but nothing can be changed until it is faced."

The following lines by the black woman poet, Georgia Douglass Johnson, speak to the emotional pain women also must endure:

The heart of a woman falls back with the night,
And enters some alien cage in its plight,
And tries to forget it has dreamed of the stars
While it breaks, breaks, breaks on the sheltering bars.

Finally, my sisters, it is time for us to gather our strength and bend apart those bars. Then, when the bodies and spirits of all women are truly free, we can be partners in making real the future of our most hopeful dreams!

Future generations of black Americans will either look back with gratitude at our strength and commitment during these final years of the 20th Century, or they will suffer the consequences of our weakness.

6   Women's Rights and Leadership

At present, our country needs women's idealism and determination, perhaps more in politics than anywhere else.

"I'D RATHER BE BLACK THAN FEMALE" (1970)

Chisholm publicly declared she was not only a feminist but an active participant in the feminist movement during the late 1960s. Although such declarations were not politically fortuitous for her, especially as a Black woman, she understood that feminism did not emerge solely from white women's ideological stance against sexism and patriarchy. For Chisholm, feminism was an articulation of her Black womanhood that was grounded in her lived experiences, including the radicalism of her grandmother and others who rejected the status quo. Her feminism was inextricably linked to advocacy around racial justice, equal rights, gender equity, and reproductive justice. While various groups opposed abortion, especially within Black and Brown communities, Chisholm would be a staunch advocate of a woman's right to choose. In particular, she emphasized the devastating impact anti-abortion legislation and rhetoric had on minority and poor women. Whether creating legislation for twenty-four-hour day care centers, advocating for economic protections for domestic workers, or campaigning for more women to be elected to office, she fought tirelessly for women to have a seat at the table, no matter their race or class status.

"Equal Rights for Women"

Congressional floor speech, Washington, D.C., May 21, 1969.

Mr. Speaker, when a young woman graduates from college and starts looking for a job, she is likely to have a frustrating and even demeaning experience ahead of her. If she walks into an office for an interview, the first question she will be asked is, "Do you type?"

There is a calculated system of prejudice that lies unspoken behind that question. Why is it acceptable for women to be secretaries, librarians, and teachers, but totally unacceptable for them to be managers, administrators, doctors, lawyers, and Members of Congress[?]

The unspoken assumption is that women are different. They do not have executive ability, orderly minds, stability, leadership skills, and they are too emotional.

It has been observed before, that society for a long time discriminated against another minority, the blacks, on the same basis—that they were different and inferior. The happy little homemaker and the contented "old darky" on the plantation were both stereotypes produced by prejudice.

As a black person, I am no stranger to race prejudice. But the truth is that in the political world I have been far oftener discriminated against because I am a woman than because I am black.

Prejudice against blacks is becoming unacceptable although it will take years to eliminate it. But it is doomed because, slowly, white America is beginning to admit that it exists. Prejudice against women is still acceptable. There is very little understanding yet of

Congressional Record 115, pt. 10, extensions of remarks (May 21, 1969): 13380–81.

the immorality involved in double pay scales and the classification of most of the better jobs as "for men only."

More than half of the population of the United States is female. But women occupy only 2 percent of the managerial positions. They have not even reached the level of tokenism yet. No women sit on the AFL-CIO council or Supreme Court. There have been only two women who have held Cabinet rank, and at present there are none. Only two women now hold ambassadorial rank in the diplomatic corps. In Congress, we are down to one Senator and 10 Representatives.

Considering that there are about 3½ million more women in the United States than men, this situation is outrageous.

It is true that part of the problem has been that women have not been aggressive in demanding their rights. This was also true of the black population for many years. They submitted to oppression and even cooperated with it. Women have done the same thing. But now there is an awareness of this situation particularly among the younger segment of the population.

As in the field of equal rights for blacks, Spanish-Americans, the Indians, and other groups, laws will not change such deep-seated problems overnight. But they can be used to provide protection for those who are most abused, and to begin the process of evolutionary change by compelling the insensitive majority to reexamine its unconscious attitudes.

It is for this reason that I wish to introduce today a proposal that has been before every Congress for the last 40 years and that sooner or later must become part of the basic law of the land—the equal rights amendment.

Let me note and try to refute two of the commonest arguments that are offered against this amendment. One is that women are already protected under the law and do not need legislation. Existing laws are not adequate to secure equal rights for women. Sufficient proof of this is the concentration of women in lower paying, menial, unrewarding jobs and their incredible scarcity in the upper level jobs. If women are already equal, why is it such an event whenever one happens to be elected to Congress?

It is obvious that discrimination exists. Women do not have the opportunities that men do. And women that do not conform to the system, who try to break with the accepted patterns, are stigmatized as "odd" and "unfeminine." The fact is that a woman who aspires to be chairman of the board, or a Member of the House, does so for exactly the same reasons as any man. Basically, these are that she thinks she can do the job and she wants to try.

A second argument often heard against the equal rights amendment is that it would eliminate legislation that many States and the Federal Government have enacted giving special protection to women and that it would throw the marriage and divorce laws into chaos.

As for the marriage laws, they are due for a sweeping reform, and an excellent beginning would be to wipe the existing ones off the books. Regarding special protection for working women, I cannot understand why it should be needed. Women need no protection that men do not need. What we need are laws to protect working people, to guarantee them fair pay, safe working conditions, protection against sickness and layoffs, and provision for dignified, comfortable retirement. Men and women need these things equally. That one sex needs protection more than the other is a male supremacist myth as ridiculous and unworthy of respect as the white supremacist myths that society is trying to cure itself of at this time.

"Economic Justice for Women"

Delivered at the Broad Street Presbyterian Church in Columbus, Ohio, on January 26, 1970, for a 50th Anniversary of Women's Suffrage celebration organized by Church Women United.

At one time or another we have all used the phrase "economic justice." This afternoon, I would like to turn your attention to economic justice for women. Of course, this is only an illusory phrase, as it is an undeniable fact that economic justice for American women does not exist.

As I look back over the years of my own lifetime, the transformation in the economic, social and political role we women play in American life has been most incredible. But we are still quite a long way from anything like equality of opportunity. We are still in a highly disadvantaged position relative to men. This is revealed by our earnings. On the average, women who are full-time, year-round workers receive only about 60% of what men who are similarly employed earn. The median income for full-time, year-round women workers is $3973, compared to $6848 for men. This is somewhat below the official poverty level decreed for a family of four. This reflects the fact that we are all too often paid less for doing the same work; even more it reflects our concentration in the lower-paid, lesser-skilled occupations, and we are steadily losing ground.

Columnist Clayton Fritchy, in *Women in Office*, noted that "although more women are working, their salaries keep falling behind men's. Some occupations are still closed, by law, to women. In 1940 women held 45% of all professional and technical

Congressional Record 117, pt. 19 (July 12, 1971): 24524–25.

positions against 37% today." Among all employed women—not college women alone—82% are clerical, sales, factory and farm workers or in service occupations. 6% of us are teachers in the grammar and high schools and only 7% of us are medical and health workers, college teachers or other professional and technical workers. Just 5% of us are managers, officials or proprietors.

The factors which have narrowed our opportunities are multiple and complex. There are restrictive hiring practices. There is discrimination in promotions. Many myths, which run entirely counter to the facts, maintain that women make poor supervisors, or that they have substantially higher rates of absenteeism and labor turnover. A recent Department of Labor survey revealed that women are more reliable and are absent less frequently than the male population of our labor force. The myth about the unreliability of women is somewhat like the one about women being bad drivers. That one has been disproven lately also by the insurance companies—women pay lower rates.

The claim is often made, and without the slightest justification, that even women with more than adequate training and knowledge lack the ability to assume higher level positions in the industry. As the late President Kennedy declared in December 1961, in the opening words of his executive order establishing a commission on the status of women, "These continuing prejudices and outmoded customs act as barriers to the full realization of women's basic rights, which should be respected and fostered as part of our nation's commitment to human dignity, freedom and democracy." When President Nixon's first nomination for the Supreme Court was rejected, it appalled and disturbed me greatly that he did not even consider nominating a woman. Our women have too long been overlooked for positions of importance in policy-making and decision areas.

The under-utilization of American women is one of the most senseless wastes of this century. It is a waste our country can no longer afford. David Deith, a financial reporter, wrote that the Swedish national income could be 25% higher if women's labor potential were fully utilized. The standard of living in France would rise 35% if women were as professionally active as men. To my knowledge no comparable studies have been made in the U.S. on women, but Federal Reserve Board member Andrew Brimmer once estimated that racial bias costs our nation 20 billion dollars a year and there are five times more women in America than there are blacks.

Meeting the challenge presented by a dynamic, expanding economy in the '70's and beyond will require that American business employ all the financial, material and human resources at its command. We are expected to maintain and improve a high standard of living for a rapidly growing population. We are called upon to meet greater demands for American goods abroad.

The greatest domestic problems of today—poverty in our urban ghettos, inadequate housing, substandard housing, the lack of meaningful rewarding jobs for thousands of our citizens—are all challenges that the business sector is being asked to take up. At the same time, we must maintain a growing economy in which all can participate.

In mobilizing our resources for the task, we must make sure that none are overlooked; particularly we must train, develop and use effectively the knowledge and skills of all people. It is not enough that we talk of the nation's manpower needs; we are going to need "womanpower" as well.

Statistically, the simple, inevitable fact is that America will have to draw upon the whole of her human resources and offer vastly wider opportunities, without discrimination in race or sex, if we are to accomplish these objectives.

Male prejudice against female achievement is usually in a subtle, often unconscious form. Men who would recoil in horror at the thought of being called anti-feminist, who view themselves as impartial, feel no inconsistency in saying the "little woman's" place is in the kitchen, with the kids, etc., etc. When these men are accused of prejudice, they reply that they are being sensitive to the "female character."

When I decided to run for Congress, I knew I would encounter both anti-black and anti-feminist sentiments. What surprised me was the much greater virulence of the sex discrimination. It seems that while many Americans still harbor racist emotions, they are no longer based on so-called racial characteristics. Paternalism has to a great extent disappeared from racial bias. But I was constantly bombarded by both men and women exclaiming that I should return to teaching, a woman's vocation, and leave politics to the men.

Like every other form of discrimination, anti-feminism is destructive both to those who perpetrate it and to its victims. Male school teachers, for example, are well aware of this. They have had to fight against both men and women who cast aspersions on their maleness because of their vocation. No one knows how many men have declined careers in teaching jobs they would have enjoyed because of the "female" character of that profession. When one group of society is as oppressed as American women are, no one can be free. Males, with their anti-feminism, maim both themselves and their women.

Like black people, women have had it with this bias. We are no longer content to trade off our minds and abilities in exchange for having doors opened for us by gallant men. While most men laugh jeeringly at the fledgling "women's liberation groups" springing up across the nation, they should know that countless women—including their cohorts, their wives, their daughters—silently applaud such groups' existence. We—American women—are beginning to respond to our oppression. While most of us are not yet revolutionaries, we are getting in tune with the cry of the liberation groups. Women are not inherently passive or peaceful. We're not inherently anything, but human. And like every other oppressed people rising today, we're out for freedom—by any means necessary.

Such is the predicament of all American women; the problem is multiplied for those of us who operate also under racial prejudice. So far most of the feminine revolution has been directed at the problems of professional women whose skills are not recognized or rewarded. However, this very fact that professional ladies have spokesmen who will protest their condition gives them hope of alleviating their suffering. I turn now to the specific dilemma of the black woman.

The feminine revolution has been headed mostly by middle class white professional women aimed toward the higher-level jobs. More of our attention should be directed toward those women who comprise the menial working force of our country, particularly, the black woman, who usually has to find employment as a maid, housekeeper, day worker, cafeteria helper, etc. These women are in dead-end jobs, jobs inherently degrading and humiliating, jobs which barely provide a subsistence existence. Today young women are revolting against this kind of subservient employment. They refuse to take a job which robs them of their self-respect and dignity in exchange for a few dollars. They want the opportunity to prove their worth, to show both whites and black men that they are women, black women, and they are proud.

Most of these black women lack the academic training to compete for professional and white collar jobs. Our society must begin to give them training. But in the meantime, there are definite steps which can be taken now to utilize the talents of black women and to provide them with an income above the poverty line, steps which will eliminate the discrimination on the basis of race and sex.

Some of you may be thinking, "How can she say that this discrimination is so virulent? Isn't she the first black female member of Congress? That proves the bias isn't really so great." On the contrary, my battle was long, incredibly hard and continual. Because I pushed, I encountered the strongest prejudice of less competent males, both black and white. That I won is a tribute to the women in my neighborhood who are finally saying "no" to the system. They are fed up. And as each day goes by and the awareness of women to our plight grows, there will be more and more women who will say "no."

We live in revolutionary times. The shackles that various groups have worn for centuries are being cast off. This is evidenced by the "developing" nations of the world, which we consider, for the most part, under-developed. Countries such as India, Ceylon and Israel, have women for presidents, prime ministers and in other decision-making positions. American women must stand and fight—be militant even—for rights which are ours. Not necessarily on soapboxes should we voice our sentiments, but in the community and at the polls. We must demand and get day care centers, better job training, more opportunities to enter fields and professions of our choosing and stop accepting what is handed to us.

"I'd Rather Be Black Than Female"

An article originally published in McCall's *magazine, August 1970.*

Being the first black woman elected to Congress has made me some kind of phenomenon. There are nine other blacks in Congress; there are ten other women. I was the first to overcome both handicaps at once. Of the two handicaps, being black is much less of a drawback than being female.

If I said that being black is a greater handicap than being a woman, probably no one would question me. Why? Because "we all know" there is prejudice against black people in America. That there is prejudice against women is an idea that still strikes nearly all men—and, I am afraid, most women—as bizarre.

Prejudice against blacks was invisible to most white Americans for many years. When blacks finally started to "mention" it, with sit-ins, boycotts, and freedom rides, Americans were incredulous. "Who, us?" they asked in injured tones. "We're prejudiced?" It was the start of a long, painful reeducation for white America. It will take years for whites—including those who think of themselves as liberals—to discover and eliminate the racist attitudes they all actually have.

How much harder will it be to eliminate the prejudice against women? I am sure it will be a longer struggle. Part of the problem is that women in America are much more brainwashed and content with their roles as second-class citizens than blacks ever were.

Let me explain. I have been active in politics for more than twenty years. For all but the last six, I have done the work—all the

Shirley Chisholm Papers, MC 1194, Special Collections and University Archives, Rutgers University Libraries.

tedious details that make the difference between victory and defeat on election day—while men reaped the rewards, which is almost invariably the lot of women in politics.

It is still women—about three million volunteers—who do most of this work in the American political world. The best any of them can hope for is the honor of being district or county vice-chairman, a kind of separate-but-equal position with which a woman is rewarded for years of faithful envelope stuffing and card-party organizing. In such a job, she gets a number of free trips to state and sometimes national meetings and conventions, where her role is supposed to be to vote the way her male chairman votes.

When I tried to break out of that role in 1963 and run for the New York State Assembly seat from Brooklyn's Bedford-Stuyvesant, the resistance was bitter. From the start of that campaign, I faced undisguised hostility because of my sex.

But it was four years later, when I ran for Congress, that the question of my sex became a major issue. Among members of my own party, closed meetings were held to discuss ways of stopping me.

My opponent, the famous civil rights leader James Farmer, tried to project a black, masculine image; he toured the neighborhood with sound trucks filled with young men wearing Afro haircuts, dashikis, and beards. While the television crews ignored me, they were not aware of a very important statistic, which both I and my campaign manager Wesley MacD. Holder knew. In my district there are 2.5 women for every man registered to vote. And those women are organized—in PTAs, church societies, card clubs, and other social and service groups. I went to them and asked for their help. Mr. Farmer still doesn't quite know what hit him.

When a bright young woman graduate starts looking for a job, why is the first question always: "Can you type?" A history of prejudice lies behind that question. Why are women thought of as secretaries, not administrators? Librarians and teachers, but not doctors and lawyers? Because they are thought of as different and inferior. The happy homemaker and the contented darky are both stereotypes produced by prejudice.

Women have not even reached the level of tokenism that blacks are reaching. No women sit on the Supreme Court. Only two have held Cabinet rank, and none do at present. Only two women hold ambassadorial rank. But women predominate in the lower-paying, menial, unrewarding, dead-end jobs, and when they do reach better positions, they are invariably paid less than a man gets for the same job.

If that is not prejudice, what would you call it?

A few years ago, I was talking with a political leader about a promising young woman as a candidate. "Why invest time and effort to build the girl up?" he asked me. "You know she'll only drop out of the game to have a couple of kids just about the time we're ready to run her for mayor."

Plenty of people have said similar things about me. Plenty of others have advised me, every time I tried to take another upward step, that I should go back to teaching, a woman's vocation, and leave politics to the men. I love teaching, and I am ready to go back to it as soon as I am convinced that this country no longer needs a woman's contribution.

When there are no children going to bed hungry in this rich nation, I may be ready to go back to teaching. When there is a good school for every child, I may be ready. When we do not spend our wealth on hardware to murder people, when we no longer tolerate prejudice against minorities, and when the laws against unfair housing and unfair employment practices are enforced instead of evaded, then there may be nothing more for me to do in politics.

But until that happens—and we all know it will not be this year or next—what we need is more women in politics, because we have a very special contribution to make. I hope that the example of my success will convince other women to get into politics—and not just to stuff envelopes, but to run for office.

It is women who can bring empathy, tolerance, insight, patience, and persistence to government—the qualities we naturally have or have had to develop because of our suppression by men. The women of a nation mold its morals, its religion, and its politics by the lives they live. At present, our country needs women's idealism and determination, perhaps more in politics than anywhere else.

"Facing the Abortion Question"

An excerpt from Unbought and Unbossed, *originally published in 1970.*

In August of 1969 I started to get phone calls from NARAL, the National Association for the Repeal of Abortion Laws, a new organization based in New York City that was looking for a national president. In the New York State Assembly I had supported abortion reform bills introduced by Assemblyman Albert Blumenthal, and this had apparently led NARAL to believe I would sympathize with its goal: complete repeal of all laws restricting abortion. As a matter of fact, when I was in the Assembly I had not been in favor of repealing all abortion laws, a step that would leave the question of

Excerpted from Shirley Chisholm, *Unbought and Unbossed*, 40th anniversary ed. (1970; repr., Washington, D.C.: Take Root Media, 2010).

having or not having the operation entirely up to a woman and her doctor. The bills I had tried to help pass in Albany would only have made it somewhat easier for women to get therapeutic abortions in New York State, by providing additional legal grounds and simplifying the procedure for getting approval. But since that time I had been compelled to do some heavy thinking on the subject, mainly because of the experiences of several young women I knew. All had suffered permanent injuries at the hands of illegal abortionists. Some will never have children as a result. One will have to go to a hospital periodically for treatment for the rest of her life.

It had begun to seem to me that the question was not whether the law should allow abortions. Experience shows that pregnant women who feel they have compelling reasons for not having a baby, or another baby, will break the law and, even worse, risk injury and death if they must to get one. Abortions will not be stopped. It may even be that the number performed is not being greatly reduced by laws making an abortion a "criminal operation." If that is true, the question becomes simply that of what kind of abortions society wants women to have—clean, competent ones performed by licensed physicians or septic, dangerous ones done by incompetent practitioners.

So when NARAL asked me to lead its campaign, I gave it serious thought. For me to take the lead in abortion repeal would be an even more serious step than for a white politician to do so, because there is a deep and angry suspicion among many blacks that even birth control clinics are a plot by the white power structure to keep down the numbers of blacks, and this opinion is even more strongly held by some in regard to legalizing abortions. But I do not know any black or Puerto Rican women who feel that way. To label family planning and legal abortion programs "genocide" is male rhetoric, for male ears. It falls flat to female listeners, and to thoughtful male ones. Women know, and so do many men, that two or three children who are wanted, prepared for, reared amid love and stability, and educated to the limit of their ability will mean more for the future of the black and brown races from which they come than any number of neglected, hungry, ill-housed and ill-clothed youngsters. Pride in one's race, as well as simple humanity, supports this view. Poor women of every race feel as I do, I believe. There is objective evidence of it in a study by Dr. Charles F. Westhoff of the Princeton Office of Population Research. He questioned 5,600 married persons and found that 22 percent of their children were unwanted. But among persons who earn less than $4,000 a year, 42 percent of the children were unwanted. The poor are more anxious about family planning than any other group.

Why then do the poor keep on having large families? It is not because they are stupid or immoral. One must understand how many resources their poverty has deprived them of, and that chief among these is medical care and advice. The poor do not go to doctors or clinics except when they absolutely must; their medical ignorance is very great, even when compared to the low level of medical knowledge most persons have. This includes, naturally, information about contraceptives and how to get them. In some of the largest cities, clinics are now attacking this problem; they are nowhere near to solving it. In smaller cities and in most of the countryside, hardly anything is being done.

Another point is this: not only do the poor have large families, but also large families tend to be poor. More than one fourth of all the families with four children live in poverty, according to the federal government's excessively narrow definition; by humane standards of poverty, the number would be much larger. The figures range from 9 percent of one-child families that have incomes below the official poverty line, up to 42 percent of the families with six children or more. Sinking into poverty, large families tend to stay there because of the educational and social handicaps that being poor imposes. It is the fear of such a future for their children that drives many women, of every color and social stratum, except perhaps the highest, to seek abortions when contraception has failed.

Botched abortions are the largest single cause of death of pregnant women in the United States, particularly among nonwhite women. In 1964, the president of the New York County Medical Society, Dr. Carl Goldmark, estimated that 80 percent of the deaths of gravid women in Manhattan were from this cause.

Another study by Edwin M. Gold, covering 1960 through 1962, gave lower percentages but supplied evidence that women from minority groups suffer most. Gold said abortion was the cause of death in 25 percent of the white cases, 49 percent of the black ones, and 65 percent of the Puerto Rican ones.

Even when a poor woman needs an abortion for the most impeccable medical reasons, acceptable under most states' laws, she is not likely to succeed in getting one. The public hospitals to which she must go are far more reluctant to approve abortions than are private, voluntary hospitals. It's in the records: private hospitals in New York City perform 3.9 abortions for every 1000 babies they deliver, public hospitals only 1 per 1000. Another relevant figure is that 90 percent of the therapeutic abortions in the city are performed on white women. Such statistics convinced me that my instinctive feeling was right: a black woman legislator, far from avoiding the abortion question, was compelled to face it and deal with it.

But my time did not permit me to be an active president of NARAL, so I asked to be made an honorary president. My appearances on television in September 1969, when the association's formation was announced, touched off one of the heaviest flows of mail to my Washington office that I have experienced. What surprised me was that it was overwhelmingly in favor of repeal. Most of the letters that disagreed with me were from Catholics, and most of them were temperate and reasoned. We sent those writers a reply that said in part, "No one should be forced to have an abortion or to use birth control methods which for religious or personal reasons they oppose. But neither should others who have different views be forced to abide by what they do not and cannot believe in." Some of the mail was from desperate women who thought I could help them. "I am forty-five years old," one wrote, "and have raised a family already. Now I find that I am pregnant and I need help. Please send me all the information." A girl wrote that she was pregnant and did not dare tell her mother and stepfather: "Please send me the name of a doctor or hospital that would help. You said if my doctor wouldn't do it to write to you. Where can I turn?" We sent the writers of these letters a list of the names and addresses of the chapters of the Clergy Consultation Service on Abortion and suggested that they find a local family planning or birth control clinic.

The reaction of a number of my fellow members of Congress seemed to me a little strange. Several said to me, "This abortion business . . . my God, what are you doing? That's not politically wise." It was the same old story; they were not thinking in terms of right or wrong, they were considering only whether taking a side of the issue would help them stay in office—or in this case, whether taking a stand would help me get reelected. They concluded that it would not help me, so it was a bad position for me to take. My advisers were, of course, all men. So I decided to shake them up a little with a feminist line of counterattack. "Who told you I shouldn't do this?" I asked them. "Women are dying every day, did you know that? They're being butchered and maimed. No matter what men think, abortion is a fact of life. Women will have them; they always have and always will. Are they going to have good ones or bad ones? Will the good ones be reserved for the rich while poor women have to go to quacks? Why don't we talk about real problems instead of phony ones?"

One member asked the question that was on the minds of all the others: "How many Catholics do you have in your district?" "Look," I told him, "I can't worry about that. That's not the problem." Persons who do not deal with politicians are often baffled by the peculiarly simple workings of their minds. Scientists and scholars in particular are bewildered by the political approach. When a member of Congress makes a statement, the scholar's first thought is "Is what he said true? Is he right or wrong?" The falseness or validity of an officeholder's statement is almost never discussed in Washington, or anyplace where politics sets the tone of discourse. The question political people ask is seldom "Is he right?" but "Why did he say that?" Or they ask, "Where does he expect that to get him?" or "Who put him up to that?"

But returning to abortion, the problem that faced me was what action I should take in my role as a legislator, if any; naturally, I intended to be as active as possible as an advocate and publicist for the cause, but was there any chance of getting a meaningful bill through Congress? Some NARAL officials wanted me to introduce an abortion repeal bill as a gesture. This is very common; probably a majority of the bills introduced in all legislative bodies are put in for the sake of effect, to give their sponsor something to talk about on the stump. That was never my style in Albany, and I have not adopted it in Washington. When I introduce legislation, I try to draft it carefully and then look for meaningful support from people who have the power to help move the bill.

So I looked for House members, in both parties and of all shades of conservatism and liberalism, who might get together on abortion repeal regardless of party. I wrote letters to a number of the more influential House members. It would have been easy to get three or four, or even ten or twelve, liberal Democrats to join me in introducing a bill, but nothing would have happened. A majority of House members would have said, "Oh, that bunch again," and dismissed us. But just a few conservative Republican co-sponsors, or conservative Democratic ones, would change all that. The approach I took was eminently sound, but it didn't work. A few members replied that they would support my bill if it ever got to the floor, but could not come out for it publicly before then or work for it. I did not doubt their sincerity, but it was a safe thing to say because the chances of a bill's reaching the floor seemed slim. Several others answered with longish letters admiring my bold position and expressing sympathy, but not agreement. "I am not ready to assume such a position," one letter said. Another said, in almost these words, "This kind of trouble I don't need." So I put my roughly drafted bill in a drawer and decided to wait. There is no point in introducing it until congressmen can be persuaded to vote for it, and only one thing will persuade them. If a congressman feels he is in danger of losing his job, he will change his mind—and then try to make it look as though he had been leading the way. The approach to Congress has to be through the arousal and organization of public opinion.

The question will remain "Is abortion *right*?" and it is a question that each of us must answer for himself. My beliefs and my experience have led me to conclude that the wisest public policy is to place the responsibility for that decision on the individual. The rightness or wrongness of an abortion depends on the individual case, and it seems to me clearly wrong to pass laws regulating all cases. But there is more to it than that. First, it is my view, and I think the majority's view, that abortion should always remain a last resort, never a primary method of limiting families. Contraceptive devices are the first choice: *devices*, because of their established safety compared to the controversial oral contraceptives. The weight of responsible medical opinion, by which I mean the opinions of qualified persons who have never been in the pay of the drug industry, seems to be that the question of the Pill's safety is not proven and that there are clear warnings that much more study is needed. So Pill research should continue, and meanwhile the emphasis—particularly in a publicly supported family planning program—should be on proven safe and effective methods. Beyond that, still from the standpoint of public policy, there must be far more stress on providing a full range of family planning services to persons of all economic levels. At present, the full gamut of services, from expert medical advice to, as a last resort, safe "legal" abortions, is available for the rich. Any woman who has the money and the sophistication about how things are done in our society can get an abortion within the law. If she is from a social stratum where such advice is available, she will be sent to a sympathetic psychiatrist and he will be well paid to believe her when she says she is ready to kill herself if she doesn't get rid of her pregnancy. But unless a woman has the $700 to $1,000 minimum it takes to travel this route, her only safe course in most states is to have the child.

This means that, whether it was so intended, public policy as expressed in American abortion laws (excepting the handful of states where the repeal effort has succeeded) is to maximize illegitimacy. Illegitimate children have always been born and for the foreseeable future they will continue to be. Their handicap is not some legal blot on their ancestry; few intelligent persons give any thought to that today. The trouble is that illegitimate children are usually the most unwanted of the unwanted. Society has forced a woman to have a child in order to punish her. Our laws were based on the Puritan reaction of "You've had your pleasure—now pay for it." But who pays? First, it is the helpless woman, who may be a girl in her early teens forced to assume the responsibility of an adult; young, confused, partially educated, she is likely to be condemned to society's trash heap as a result. But the child is often a worse loser. If his mother keeps him, she may marry or not (unmarried mothers are even less likely to marry than widows or divorcees). If she does not, she will have to neglect him and work at undesirable jobs to feed him, more often than not. His home-life will almost certainly be abnormal; he may survive it and even thrive, depending on his mother's personal qualities, but the odds have to be against him.

Of course, there should be no unwanted children. Whether they are legitimate or illegitimate is not of the first importance. But we will not even approach the ideal of having every child wanted, planned for, and cherished, until our methods of contraception are fully reliable and completely safe, and readily available to everyone. Until then, unwanted pregnancies will happen, in marriage and out of it. What is our public policy to be toward them? There are very few more important questions for society to face; this question is one that government has always avoided because it did not dare intrude on the sanctity of the home and marriage. But the catastrophic perils that follow in the train of over-population were not well known in the past and those perils were not imminent, so the question could be ducked. It cannot be any longer.

For all Americans, and especially for the poor, we must put an end to compulsory pregnancy. The well-off have only one problem when an unwanted pregnancy occurs; they must decide what they want to do and what they believe is right. For the poor, there is no such freedom. They started with too little knowledge about contraception, often with none except street lore and other misinformation. When trapped by pregnancy, they have only two choices, both bad—a cheap abortion or an unwanted child to plunge them deeper into poverty. Remember the statistics that show which choice is often taken: 49 percent of the deaths of pregnant black women and 65 percent of those of Puerto Rican women . . . due to criminal, amateur abortions.

Which is more like genocide, I have asked some of my black brothers—this, the way things are, or the conditions I am fighting for in which the full range of family planning services is freely available to women of all classes and colors, starting with effective contraception and extending to safe, legal termination of undesired pregnancies, at a price they can afford?

"Race, Revolution, and Women"

An article originally published in The Black Scholar, *December 1971.*

Everywhere we turn today we are confronted with a revolution of some kind. Slogans that range from "You've come a long way,

The Black Scholar 3, no. 4 (December 1971): 17–21.

baby" to "All power to the people" have become jaded chants that dribble from the mouths of jaded TV announcers. There is an almost paranoid fear eating at the guts of all Americans. Black-White, Male-Female, Young-Old represent schisms between us. Racial Polarization, the Generation Gap and Virginia Slims are all brand names for products that may become lethal.

The Doomsday Criers are amongst us chanting their wares and bemoaning their fate. Vietnam and the Middle East are no longer powder kegs; they are instead sputtering fuses. The campuses and the ghettos are eruptions of revolutionary acne.

The President circles the globe seemingly handing out *carte-blanche* military commitment credit cards and scientists in Houston dissect dusty rocks in search of other life-forms while humans starve to death—physically, mentally and spiritually—at home and abroad.

The author of *Soul On Ice*, Eldridge Cleaver, has become a soul on the run—an unwilling refugee from his heritage and his mission—a latter-day man without a country.

The King is dead and so are the Kennedy Princes of Politics—victims all of hot lead spit out by paranoia, collective guilt and their destructive hand-maidens—hate and fear. Deaths purchased, some say, by modern-day robber barons immersed in the cement coffin of the status quo.

And here gather we, in this quiet retreat, to debate the possibility that there may be no future. Tomorrow we leave for our homes and our separate battlefields. What is it that we must find here that will sustain and strengthen us in the days, weeks and years ahead?

Communion, understanding, and agape certainly are on the list but there is one other I might point out—Commitment.

Most women in America have never had the opportunity to fully measure the extent of their own personal commitment to ending poverty, to ending racial discrimination, and to ending social and political injustice.

Many of us are old enough to remember the Second World War. In that war, women in many foreign countries learned first-hand what was necessary to maintain life under the most adverse conditions. While they were begging, stealing, fighting and even killing for bits and morsels of food to feed themselves and their families, we continued to enjoy a high standard of living, good jobs and a night's sleep uninterrupted by rifle and artillery fire.

I am not saying that any one of us escaped unscathed by the war and its surrounding horror, but I am saying that the flames in which our steel was forged [were] not hot enough, cruel enough, or close enough to produce an exceptionally high quality steel.

Today we are perched on the precipice of internal holocaust that may well be only the trigger for the world-wide one. And perched there, many of us continue to give the easiest things to give—the most detachable extensions of ourselves—money and sympathy.

There are revolutions going on. It is true that some of them are false, designed to build the ego, cleverly camouflaged in order to sell a product that in the final analysis is harmful to the purchaser's health.

Some of them are revolts by people who are refusing to accept age-worn patterns of doing things and who are therefore carving new ways that are more satisfactory to their needs.

And finally some of them are revolutions in deadly earnest designed to strike off the shackles of oppressed people throughout the world.

Both the so-called Black Revolution and the Woman's Liberation Movements fall into the last two categories. Black people are in deadly earnest about freedom from oppression and women are refusing to accept traditional and stereotyped roles.

Because I am both black and a woman, I will make some comments and observations about both.

First, the Black Revolution is not solely black. I say that what Black people in America are doing, is participating in a world-wide rebellion that encompasses all aspects of human life.

When we talk about the Black Revolution, therefore, we immediately attempt to limit the goals of the black man, attempt to strip black revolutionaries of the right to be idealistic, attempt to strip the black man of the right to feel that what he wants is not just freedom for himself, but a totally new, totally free world.

When we separate the so-called Black Revolution in America from the other revolutions—in literature, in the church, in the arts, in education and throughout the world—we attempt to maintain our own peculiar form of slavery. One of the most noted and most quoted black revolutionaries in this country was Malcolm X. While Malcolm was on a trip through the Holy Land he sent back a letter that read in part:

> You may be shocked by these words coming from me, but I have always been a man who tries to face facts and to accept the reality of life as new experiences and knowledge unfold it. The experiences of this might have taught me much and each hour in the Holy Land opens my eyes even more. . . . I have eaten from the same plate with people whose eyes are the bluest of blue, whose hair was the blondest of blond, and whose skin was the whitest of white . . . and I felt the same sincerity in the words and the deeds of these

"white" Muslims that I felt among the African Muslims of Nigeria, Sudan and Ghana.

As Eldridge Cleaver so aptly pointed out, there were many blacks who were outraged and felt that Malcolm had betrayed them with that statement. It may very well have been Malcolm's signature on his own death warrant, but the point that I want you to bear in mind is that it is exactly that type of personal courage and integrity that marks the true revolutionary.

Malcolm X was certainly aware that as an established black leader who had consistently, constantly and continually assailed the "white devil" here at home, he was jeopardizing his position. But I think that Malcolm also knew, instinctively, what a Roman slave Epictetus had in mind when he said: "No man is free until he is master of his own mind."

White women must realize that black people in America are not yet free and know that they are not yet free. That is true also for a great number of dark-skinned people throughout the world. But I do not find it astonishing that there are so many people who are aware that they are not yet free. What I do find astonishing is that so many of the non-homogenous groupings that we call "white western" think of themselves as free. The master does not escape slavery simply because he thinks of himself as free as the master. Neither do the brother and sister of the master escape slavery when they stand idly by and watch their brother enslave their brother. The master is inseparably bound to the slaves and so is white America inseparably bound to black America.

A few months ago while testifying before the Office of Federal Contract Compliance, I noted that anti-feminism, like every form of discrimination, is destructive both to those who perpetrate it and its victims; that males, with their anti-feminism, maim both themselves and their women. Bear in mind that that is also true in terms of black and white race relations.

No one in America has escaped the wounds imposed by racism and anti-feminism. In *Soul On Ice* Eldridge Cleaver pointed out in great detail how the stereotypes were supposed to work. Whether his insight is correct or not, it bears closer examination.

Speaking of the white woman in the passage "The Primeval Mitosis," Cleaver describes her stereotype thusly, ". . . she is required to possess and project an image that is in sharp contrast to his (the white man), so that the effeminate image of her man can still, by virtue of the sharp contrast in the degrees of femininity, be perceived as masculine. Therefore she becomes 'ultra-feminine.'"

Isn't this an essential part of what the Women's Liberation Movements are all about? Women, especially in the upper classes, have been expected to be nothing more than dangling, decorative ornaments—non-thinking and virtually non-functional.

In other places in the passage, Cleaver describes the other stereotypes that white western society has accepted in the place of reality. He states the black male is expected to supply the society with its source of brute power through his role as the "supermasculine menial"—all body and no brain.

The white male has assigned himself the role of the "omnipotent administrator[,]" all brain and no body, because that could be seen as the clearly superior role. The black female was assigned the role of "subfeminine" or Amazon.

What the roles and the strange interplay between them have meant to America, Cleaver goes on to point out quite well. There is only one thing that I want to point out. Because of the bizarre aspects of the roles and the strange influence that non-traditional contact between them has on the general society, blacks and whites, males and females must operate almost independently of each other in order to escape from the quicksands of psychological slavery. Each—black male and black female—white female and white male[—]must escape first from his or her own historical traps before they can be truly effective in helping others to free themselves.

The goal must clearly be freedom—integration is not yet feasible as a goal. It is not feasible because integration depends on mutual concepts of freedom and equality.

Cleaver stripped from some of our eyes for all time, the wool that we tried so desperately to hold over them.

Black women and white women have been, for the most part, the opposite sides of the same coin, as have been black men and white men. Our society has always required that those coins come up head and head or tails and tails for all kinds of spurious reasoning. But no matter what the reasoning, it is part of the reason why white women are not now and never have been truly accepted working in the ghetto.

One of the questions that I am most often asked by white women these days is "What can we do?"

In many ways it is a strange question—strange because the phrase: "to help you people" is only implied. It is strange because of the implied assumption that they are free to help and strange because of the implied assumption that they are in a position to help.

I have responded to that question in many ways, pointing out the political arena, education and many other things. But I have always left only the implication of the real answer, the one thing that they not only might do—the only thing that they must do.

Today I must state it. Free yourselves! And in order to do that you must first free yourselves of the assumption that you are now free.

I have pointed out time and time again that the harshest discrimination that I have encountered in the political arena is anti-feminism—from both males and brainwashed "Uncle Tom" females.

When I first announced for the United States Congress last year, both males and females advised me, as they had when I ran for the New York Assembly, to go back to teaching, a woman's vocation, and leave politics to men.

I did not go back then and I will not go back as long as there exists a need to change the politics of this country. Like the colleagues that I had in Albany, many of my fellow members in the House treat me with a deference that is patronizing.

On May 20 of this year I introduced legislation concerning the equal employment opportunities of women. At that time I pointed out that there were three and one-half million more women than men in America but that women held only two percent of the managerial positions; that no women sit on the AFL-CIO Council or the Supreme Court; that only two women had ever held Cabinet rank and that there were at that time only two women of ambassadorial rank in the diplomatic corps. In the Congress there were only ten representatives and only one senator. I stated then as I do now that this situation is outrageous.

I would like to quote an excerpt from the speech that I made on the Floor that day:

It is true that part of the problem has been that women have not been aggressive in demanding their rights. This was also true of the black population for many years. They submitted to oppression and even cooperated with it. Women have done the same thing. But now there is an awareness of this situation, particularly among the younger segment of the population.

As in the field of equal rights for blacks, Spanish-Americans, Indians and other groups, laws will not change such deep-seated problems overnight. They can be used to provide protection for those who are most abused, and begin the process of evolutionary change by compelling the insensitive majority to re-examine its unconscious attitudes.

Women in this country must become revolutionaries. We must refuse to accept the old—the traditional roles and stereotypes.

Because of the present situation the tactics for black women must be slightly different than the tactics for white women but the goal can be the same.

The tactics of revolution used by the white liberal community must be, as they will be, slightly different than the tactics used by the black ghetto community but the goal can be the same.

The goal, though, must be more than political freedom. It must be more than economic freedom. It must be total freedom to build a world-wide society predicated on the positive values of all human life.

It must be freedom from the waste and ravages of all natural resources including human resources.

Women must do more than sacrifice husbands and sons in the present Social Revolution. They must also sacrifice themselves. And for many women, black and white, those who will call first for that sacrifice will be their own sons—their own husbands.

We must start in our own homes, our own schools and our own churches. This does not mean talk about integrated schools, churches or marriage when the kind of integration one is talking about is black with white.

We must work for—fight for—the integration of male and female—human and human. Franz [*sic*] Fanon pointed out in *Black Skins—White Masks* that the anti-Semitic was eventually the anti-Negro. I want to point out that both are eventually the Anti-Feminist. Furthermore I want to point out that all discrimination is eventually the same thing—anti-humanism.

Our task will not be easy. It will be hard—but it must be done. Perhaps the greatest power for social change, for a successful Social Revolution, lies in our hands. But it is not an unlimited power nor is it an invincible power. The use of power will always cause a reaction, therefore we must use our power well and we must use it wisely. Godspeed our success.

"The Black Woman in Contemporary America"

A lecture delivered at a conference at the Institute for Afro-American Culture at the University of Missouri-Kansas City, June 17, 1974.

Ladies and gentlemen, and brothers and sisters all—I'm very glad to be here this evening. I'm very glad that I've had the opportunity to be the first lecturer with respect to the topic of the black woman in contemporary America. This has become a most talked-about topic and has caused a great deal of provocation and misunderstandings and misinterpretations. And I come to you this evening to speak on this topic not as any scholar, not as any academician, but as a person that has been out here for the past twenty years, try-

Transcript in the Shirley Chisholm Papers, MC 1194, Special Collections and University Archives, Rutgers University Libraries.

ing to make my way as a black and a woman, and meeting all kinds of obstacles.

The black woman's role has not been placed in its proper perspective, particularly in terms of the current economic and political upheaval in America today. Since time immemorial the black man's emasculation resulted in the need of the black woman to assert herself in order to maintain some semblance of a family unit. And as a result of this historical circumstance, the black woman has developed perseverance; the black woman has developed strength; the black woman has developed tenacity of purpose and other attributes which today quite often are being looked upon negatively. She continues to be labeled a matriarch. And this is indeed a played-upon white sociological interpretation of the black woman's role that has been developed and perpetrated by Daniel Moynihan and other sociologists.

Black women by virtue of the role they have played in our society have much to offer toward the liberation of their people. We know that our men are coming forward, but the black race needs the collective talents and the collective abilities of black men and black women who have vital skills to supplement each other.

It is quite perturbing to divert ourselves on the dividing issue of the alleged fighting that absorbs the energies of black men and black women. Such statements as "The black woman has to step back while her black man steps forward" and "The black woman has kept back the black man" are grossly, historically incorrect and serve as a scapegoating technique to prevent us from coming together as human beings—some of whom are black men and some are black women.

The consuming interest of this type of dialogue abets the enemy in terms of taking our eyes off the ball, so that our collective talents can never redound in a beneficial manner to our ethnic group. The black woman who is educated and has ability cannot be expected to put said talent on the shelf when she can utilize these gifts side-by-side with her man. One does not learn, nor does one assist in the struggle, by standing on the sidelines, constantly complaining and criticizing. One learns by participating in the situation—listening, observing and then acting.

It is quite understandable why black women in the majority are not interested in walking and picketing a cocktail lounge which historically has refused to open its doors a certain two hours a day when men who have just returned from Wall Street gather in said lounge to exchange bits of business transactions that occurred on the market. This is a middle-class white woman's issue. This is not a priority of minority women. Another issue that black women are not overly concerned about is the "M-S" versus the "M-R-S" label. For many of us this is just the use of another label which does not basically change the fundamental inherent racial attitudes found in both men and women in this society. This is just another label, and black women are not preoccupied with any more label syndromes. Black women are desperately concerned with the issue of survival in a society in which the Caucasian group has never really practiced the espousal of equalitarian principles in America.

An aspect of the women's liberation movement that will and does interest many black women is the potential liberation, is the potential nationalization of daycare centers in this country. Black women can accept and understand this agenda item in the women's movement. It is important that black women utilize their brainpower and focus on issues in any movement that will redound to the benefit of their people because we can serve as a vocal and a catalytic pressure group within the so-called humanistic movements, many of whom do not really comprehend the black man and the black woman.

An increasing number of black women are beginning to feel that it is important first to become free as women, in order to contribute more fully to the task of black liberation. Some feel that black men (like all men, or most men) have placed women in the stereotypes of domestics whose duty it is to stay in the background—cook, clean, have babies, and leave all of the glory to men. Black women point to the civil rights movement as an example of a subtle type of male oppression, where with few exceptions black women have not had active roles in the forefront of the fight. Some like Coretta King, Kathleen Cleaver, and Betty Shabazz have come only to their positions in the shadows of their husbands. Yet, because of the oppression of black women, they are strongest in the fight for liberation. They have led the struggle to fight against white male supremacy, dating from slavery times. And in view of these many facts it is not surprising that black women played a crucial role in the total fight for freedom in this nation. Ida Wells kept her newspaper free by walking the streets of Memphis, Tennessee, in the 1890s with two pistols on her hips. And within recent years, this militant condition of black women, who have been stifled because of racism and sexism, has been carried on by Mary McLeod Bethune, Mary Church Terrell, Daisy Bates, and Diane Nash.

The black woman lives in a society that discriminates against her on two counts. The black woman cannot be discussed in the same context as her Caucasian counterpart because of the twin jeopardy of race and sex which operates against her, and the psychological and political consequences which attend them. Black women are crushed by cultural restraints and abused by the legitimate power structure. To date, neither the black movement nor women's liberation succinctly addresses itself to the dilemma confronting the black who is female. And as a consequence of ignoring or being unable to handle the problems facing black women, black women themselves are now becoming socially and politically active.

Undoubtedly black women are cultivating new attitudes, most of which will have political repercussions in the future. They are attempting to change their conditions. The maturation of the civil rights movement by the mid '60s enabled many black women to develop interest in the American political process. From their experiences they learned that the real sources of power lay at the root of the political system. For example, black sororities and pressure groups like the National Council of Negro Women are adept at the methods of participatory politics—particularly in regard to voting and organizing. With the arrival of the '70s, young black women are demanding recognition like the other segments of society who also desire their humanity and their individual talents to be noticed. The tradition of the black woman and the Afro-American subculture and her current interest in the political process indicate the emergence of a new political entity.

Historically she has been discouraged from participating in politics. Thus she is trapped between the walls of the dominant white culture and her own subculture, both of which encourage deference to men. Both races of women have traditionally been limited to performing such tasks as opening envelopes, hanging up posters and giving teas. [laughter and clapping] And the minimal involvement of black women exists because they have been systematically excluded from the political process and they are members of the politically dysfunctional black lower class. Thus, unlike white women, who escape the psychological and sociological handicaps of racism, the black woman's political involvement has been a most marginal role.

But within the last six years, the Afro-American subculture has undergone tremendous social and political transformation and these changes have altered the nature of the black community. They are beginning to realize their capacities not only as blacks, but also as women. They are beginning to understand that their cultural well-being and their social well-being would only be affirmed in connection with the total black struggle. The dominant role black women played in the civil rights movement began to allow them to grasp the significance of political power in America. So obviously black women who helped to spearhead the civil rights movement would also now, at this juncture, join and direct the vanguard which would shape and mold a new kind of political participation.

This has been acutely felt in urban areas, which have been rocked by sporadic rebellions. Nothing better illustrates the need for black women to organize politically than their unusual proximity to the most crucial issues affecting black people today. They have struggled in a wide range of protest movements to eliminate the poverty and injustice that permeate the lives of black people. In New York City, for example, welfare mothers and mothers of schoolchildren have ably demonstrated the commitment of black women to the elimination of the problems that threaten the well-being of the black family. Black women must view the problems of cities such as New York not as urban problems, but as the components of a crisis without whose elimination our family lives will neither survive nor prosper. Deprived of a stable family environment because of poverty and racial injustice, disproportionate numbers of our people must live on minimal welfare allowances that help to perpetuate the breakdown of family life. In the face of the increasing poverty besetting black communities, black women have a responsibility. Black women have a duty to bequeath a legacy to their children. Black women have a duty to move from the periphery of organized political activity into its main arena.

I say this on the basis of many experiences. I travel throughout this country and I've come in contact with thousands of my black sisters in all kinds of conditions in this nation. And I've said to them over and over again: it is not a question of competition against black men or brown men or red men or white men in America. It is a question of the recognition that since we have a tremendous responsibility in terms of our own families, to the best of our ability, we have to give everything that is within ourselves to give in terms of helping to make that future a better future for our little boys and our little girls—and not leave it to anybody.

[Frances] Beal describes the black woman as a slave of a slave. Let me quote:

By reducing the black man in America to such abject oppression, the black woman had no protector and she was used—and is still being used—in some cases as the scapegoat for the evils that this horrendous system has perpetrated on black men. Her physical image has been maliciously maligned. She has been sexually molested and abused by the white colonizer. She has suffered the worst kind of economic exploitation, having been forced to serve as the white woman's maid and wet-nurse for white offspring, while her own children were more often starving and neglected. It is the depth of degradation to be socially manipulated, physically raped and used to undermine your own household—and then to be powerless to reverse this syndrome.

However, Susan Johnson notes a bit of optimism. Because Susan, a brilliant young black woman, has said that the recent strides made by the black woman in the political process are a result of the intricacies of her personality. And that is to say that as a political animal, she functions independently of her double jeopardy. Because confronted with a matrifocal past and present, she is often accused of stealing the black male's position in any situation beyond that of housewife and mother. And if that were not enough to burden the black woman, she realizes that her political mobility then threatens the doctrine of white supremacy and male superiority so deeply embedded in the American culture. So choosing not to be a victim of self-paralysis, the black woman has been able to function in the political spectrum. And more often than not, it is the subconsciousness of the racist mind that perceives her as less harmful than the black man and thus permits her to acquire the necessary leverage for political mobility. This subtle component of racism could prove to be essential to the key question of how the black woman has managed some major advances in the American political process.

It is very interesting to note that everyone—with the exception of the black woman herself—has been interpreting the black woman. It is very interesting to note that the time has come that black women can and must no longer be passive, complacent recipients of whatever the definitions of the sociologists, the psychologists and the psychiatrists will give to us. Black women have been maligned, misunderstood, misinterpreted—who knows better than Shirley Chisholm?

And I stand here tonight to tell to you, my sisters, that if you have the courage of your convictions, you must stand up and be counted! I hope that the day will come in America when this business of male-versus-female does not become such an overriding issue, so that the talents and abilities that the almighty God has given to people can be utilized for the benefit of humanity.

One has to recognize that there are stupid white women and stupid white men, stupid black women and stupid black men, brilliant white women and brilliant white men, and brilliant black women and brilliant black men. Why do we get so hung-up in America on this question of sex? Of course, in terms of the black race, we understand the historical circumstances. We understand, also, some of the subtle maneuverings and machinations behind the scenes in order to prevent black women and black men from coming together as a race of unconquerable men and women.

And I just want to say to you tonight, if I say nothing else: I would never have been able to make it in America if I had paid attention to all of the doomsday-criers about me. And I want to say in conclusion that as you have this conference here for the next two weeks, put the cards out on the table and do not be afraid to discuss issues that perhaps you have been sweeping under the rug because of what people might say about you. You must remember that once we are able to face the truth, the truth shall set all of us free.

In conclusion, I just want to say to you, black and white, north and east, south and west, men and women: the time has come in America when we should no longer be the passive, complacent recipients of whatever the morals or the politics of a nation may decree for us in this nation. Forget traditions! Forget conventionalisms! Forget what the world will say whether you're in your place or out of your place! Stand up and be counted! Do your thing, looking only to God—whoever your God is—and to your consciences for approval.

I thank you.

Address to the Conference of Black and Latin Women in Art and Politics

Delivered at the City College of New York, November 10, 1977, before a conference organized by the Black and Latin Women's Organization of City College New York.

The misinterpreted, the maligned, the insulted black woman who must bear the brunt and the burden of everything that's negative in this society. And that has been the kind of traditional thing: the Matriarch, the Sapphire and all of the negative connotations that are placed on the black woman. And if it were not for the perseverance and the strength and the dominance of the black woman's character, many things could not have happened in this society today. Let me take you back very briefly into history and bring you up to the present—and I shan't be long, because I speak very rapidly.

We know that, basically, the emasculation of the black male in our society was and is rooted in the historical circumstances of this racist nation. That black women are not responsible for what has happened in black males in this society. But, as usual, in order to find a scapegoat we always look for those elements in the society which are the helpless and the powerless elements that cannot hit back at times. Black sisters: You are not responsible!

The fact of the matter is, because of the emasculation of our men we have had to develop the perseverance; the tolerance, yes; and the assertiveness, yes; and the dominance, if you will, in order to be able to hold together some kind of semblance of a family unit

Transcribed from Pacifica Radio recording, https://archive.org/details /pacifica_radio_archives-IZ1405.

when our men were torn from us as a result of the institution of slavery! Now, if it were not for the strength of the black woman, the black family as we know it today—and I say it publicly!—the black family as we know it today would not be together at all. And that is not to say that we are blaming our black men at all, because we understand what has happened in this society. But I am just a little bit sick and tired of people placing upon the black sisters in America that kind of responsibility and the brunt of that kind of burden.

As a black woman who faces a double jeopardy in this society, the jeopardy of being black and a female at the same time, it has not been easy. I have risen to the top only because of my determination and only because of the development of tremendous self-confidence in myself and my own faith in God! And many of you have heard me say this before, that my creed is as I walk this planet called Earth, "I look to no man walking this earth for approval"— and I use the term "man" generically. I look to no man walking this earth for approval of what I do or what I feel; I only look to my God and my conscience for approval. If I did not do that, I could not persevere. I could not be where I am today. Because throughout my entire adult life, the presence of the numerous doomsday criers about me—telling me what I should do, what I should not do, what I should say, what I should not say—"Who do you think you are?"

Black sisters and Hispanic sisters, let me tell you something: Nobody is going to give anything to us because we are black and/or Hispanic or because we are at the bottom of the economic ladder of this society. We are going to have to recognize that we have the potential within ourselves to mesh together as a unit and to move forward together in this society and get over this pettiness as to whether or not you are Hispanic or whether or not you are black, because the same forces are keeping back both of us in this society!

A mature individual is an individual that has the ability to sublimate a lot of pettiness and foolishness and to use our energies in order to consolidate whatever gains we have made so that we don't retrogress much further—because right now we are retrogressing in this society. We don't have to love each other. It would be far better if we loved each other. It would be far better if every Hispanic woman loved every black woman and if every black woman loved every Hispanic woman. It would be far better! But the most important thing is that for the Hispanic woman and for the black woman, the same forces in this society are keeping us down to the bottom of the heap—and when are we going to wake up and understand that?

And even though we are increasing quantitatively in the city of New York, in the next four or five years, even though we might be sixty or seventy percent of the population, we are not going to have any power, we are not going to have any clout, because we all want to do our own little thing in our own little niche, not realizing that the consolidation of power on the part of Hispanic and black people can bring us to the top in this city.

We hear a great deal of talk about the Women's Movement. I've heard a lot of black sisters and Hispanic sisters say, "Oh, I don't have time for them. They don't understand us." The challenge is for us to come within these groups and begin to give the groups some sense of direction in which they need to go. Whether or not you can accept the Women's Movement, the Women's Movement is going to go ahead, with or without you! But the fact of the matter is that within the Women's Movement there are certain aspects that are important to us as minority women and we have to help push those aspects ahead. What are those aspects I'm talking about?

I'm talking about the necessity for day care centers in this country. And that is a basic plank in most of the Women's Movement groups in this country today. And you need to get on the inside and to work on the committees and the different groups that will push day care in this country. Because you know that the statistics indicate that sixty percent of the minority women in this country head the families, and that in order for you to be a productive citizen, in order for you to get the opportunity to acquire the requisite skills to function in an automated and technological society you need day care to take care of your end for your youngsters. So you can't stay on the outside and knock them over the head! You have to come on the inside.

We as minority women, I daresay for the most part, we're not interested in whether they call (I know I'm not!) whether they call me Miss, Mrs. or "*Mizz*" Chisholm. It's just another label. Or the fact that sometimes in the Women's Movement, sometimes we have groups asking us or feeling that we should picket a place that only admits white males. A few years ago, a couple of my friends in the Women's Movement got very angry with me because I refused to walk a picket line down the Wall Street area so the women could enter during the course of the day after their business on Wall Street. And I told them, "No!" Because that's not *it*! That's not it. They have to understand that the minority woman in America today is not interested in all these things. We're interested, and we have to be interested, in *survival*. So because we have to be interested in and concerned with survival, we are interested in white women in the Women's Movement, for example—if they really have a concern for their minority sisters—getting on the day care issue, getting on the minimum wage, making sure that the opportunities are open so that minority women can begin to elevate themselves. Not by word, but by deed! *This* is where it's at!

But at the same time, sisters, you just cannot stand up on the outside and complain. You've got to get on the inside and teach them and show them, because a lot of them don't know. They really don't understand. And sometimes we—and I'm going to tell you—we are very stubborn. We get very rigid in our thoughts. Because not only are we sometimes stubborn towards our white sisters who might not really know, we are also sometimes stubborn towards our own black males. Well, let me get into that a little bit!

You know, they have tried sometimes to keep us divided by saying that the black woman is a "matriarch." By saying the black woman should stay home and "push her man"—and all of these phrases that we hear. And in many instances, we realize that if the black woman stayed home to "push her man" she wouldn't be able to take care of her family or the responsibilities that she has in this society. Now, whether you like to hear it or not, it's as simple as that; it is a fact of life that black women have to deal with. Now having said that much, the next thing is this: no particular group, black women and/or black men, white women and/or white men, has any kind of superior brain power over the other group. There's stupid men and stupid black women. There are bright black men and there are bright black women. And what we really need instead of getting engaged in a lot of meaningless rhetoric and hitting out at each other, we need to see if we can come together and utilize the collective brain power of black men and black women who have it to give and supplement each other in the struggle! *That's* what we need to do!

But I'm trying to tell you today that you have to become involved. And you have to become involved with more than your little circle of friends, or the little niche you talk on the phone with or the people with whom you always related to. You've got to spread out, broaden! You have to grow! You have to develop! You have to understand! You have to be tolerant!

I had the opportunity in 1971, '72 to run around this country saying that I wanted to be president of this country. I knew that I was going to be laughed at! So what's new? But how dare Shirley Chisholm—a black and a female—run around the country saying that she wants to be the captain of the ship of state? How dare I?! That's not tradition! Traditionally, only white males are supposed to do this kind of thing. But I ran. I ran only because there were people in twenty-five states that raised monies—not because I thought I was *cute*! But because people said, "You have something going and we need to get this country moving in another kind of direction." I knew it took guts, courage, audacity, nerves, stamina, intelligence and everything else to do it!—and I knew the moment I got out there to do it that everybody would be saying something!

But I did it! I did it because in spite of what anybody may say or anybody might feel, *I look to nobody on this earth to tell whether or not I should do it!*

I'm a catalyst for change, brothers and sisters: I'm going to be controversial 'til the day I die! Because I'm a catalyst for change, and I believe in stirring up people and making people think and making people realize that they have to move.

The time has come when we in this room can be no longer the passive, complacent arm-chair recipients of whatever the morals or the politics of this nation is going to decree for us as a people who are trying to get our own out here, in the scheme of things. But we have got to make it happen! We've got to help to make it happen! And you can only begin to help to make it happen by becoming excited and stimulated and involved!

After twenty-one years in this business—for ten years a speech-writer—and one of the reasons that I think that I wanted to get in this business, because (without sounding modest in the least), I was giving my brainpower to a lot of dumb folks who were running for office and winning—on *my* brains! And that was one of the reasons why I felt, "Well, therefore, if I had an opportunity to really get out there and let the people feel me and know me . . ." Because I knew if I depended on white males or black males I wasn't going anyplace fast! I knew that because of the feeling towards women, and particularly a black woman, in the political arena. Because even today, even though I am somewhat successful, I am still ignored by a lot of black males and white males. But that doesn't bother me! Because as I said to you earlier: I look to no man walking this earth for approval of what I am going to do or what I am about!

So, my brothers and sisters, take a lesson from a woman who was born right here in New York City; a woman who came from a very, very poor family; a woman who never dreamt that today she would be the senior woman in the House of Representatives—the only one now: I know that you can do it! All you gotta do: get your head together. Think. Don't let anybody put anything over on you. Don't follow the pack—because you want to follow the pack even if the pack might be wrong, but your conscience tells you it's not the right thing to do—*don't do it!* And you will be surprised: You will get the strength and the stamina to march on!

"The Viability of Black Women in Politics"

In this speech, delivered February 25, 1984, Chisholm establishes the case for Black women's political development that she would use when cofounding the National Congress of Black Women later that year.

Good evening. I am very pleased to be able to share my thoughts with you on the viability of black women in politics. I suppose my own history makes me somewhat of an expert on this topic. Surprisingly, I have rarely been asked to discuss black women as politicians. I am happy for that opportunity tonight. I believe that this situation is a reflection of the lack of focus on increasing the numbers of black female politicians. A variety of factors account for this lack of focus.

When you look at the statistical data, it is obvious that black women still occupy the bottom rung of the economic ladder in disproportionate numbers. What follows, of course, is that their participation in the decision-making process is less than it needs to be, and the ability of this group to make its voices heard about such problems as day care, health care and children's problems has been decimated. Of course, we have come a long way from the days of Ida B. Wells as a crusader against lynching and a leading suffragette. But let us not forget that the election of Shirley Chisholm, Cardiss Collins and Barbara Jordan occurred within the last decade. The presence of Fannie Lou Hamer and Pat Harris at the Democratic National Conventions in leadership roles is all *very* recent history, and the presence of Gloria Toote, a nomination

Transcript in the Shirley Chisholm Papers, MC 1194, Special Collections and University Archives, Rutgers University Libraries.

speaker for President Reagan at the Republican Convention, is definitely a recent phenomenon.

The black woman, if I may draw a caricature, continues to bear a burden unlike any other in society. She suffers from a twin jeopardy: she has inherited a psychological and political disadvantage which has become a double-edged sword inflicted and sometimes self-inflicted on black women at every level of society. In short, black women are crushed by cultural restraints and abused by legitimate political power which has been, and continues to be, vested in leaders from the white male world.

The black woman's role has not been placed in its proper perspective, particularly in terms of the current economic upheaval in America today. Let's face it. The thrust of the Civil Rights struggle focused on acknowledging and acting upon the fact that the black *man* was a full human being. While black women were certainly expected to prepare the chicken dinners and sweet potato pies for the strategy meetings and the civil rights marches, rarely were we expected or even asked to participate in the planning of these events. In fact, the one woman who did emerge as a civil rights leader, Ella Baker, did so by describing herself as a facilitator rather than a "leader." Without her efforts, it is doubtful that S.N.C.C. would have emerged as such a viable unit within the Civil Rights Movement. The failure of the Civil Rights Movement and even the Women's Liberation struggle to address our concerns has resulted in a heightened consciousness that black women must seize political power in their own right.

Too often black women have been content to place their own political aspirations on the back-burner. Sometimes, they have felt that entering politics would hurt their marriage and/or family. On other occasions, they have stepped aside for a black male candidate not because he had better qualifications but merely because of his gender. Having the support of a spouse and one's children is important to any politician. Considerations, in this area, must be worked out by anyone in politics. In some situations, these family considerations may lead to a decision not to run for office. However, black women should no longer abdicate their right to political office merely because of a gender difference. Talent, intelligence and political acumen should judge a politician's ability—not whether or not they shave every morning.

When I first started in politics some 30 years ago, women were doing the traditional jobs in politics: envelope-stuffing, answering phones at the campaign headquarters and making the food for political meetings. When an Assembly seat was created for blacks in Brooklyn in the mid-'60's, many male community leaders thought they should be the "anointed one." My position was simply that "they were wrong." I had paid my political dues by working in the political club system in Brooklyn for years, in some cases much longer than my male rivals, and I intended to reap the benefits of this work. In the end I was successful in my bid for an Assembly seat in the New York State Legislature for largely three reasons: I was persistent; most of the workers in the political clubs in Brooklyn were women; and I had the support of a good political organizer, Mr. Wesley Mc. Holder.

Let me describe this formula for political success as a model for other future black women politicians. While most historians will properly describe me as a fighter for women's rights, they will erroneously conclude that my success was exclusively due to the support of women. In fact, my political career would probably have not been successful without one man, Wesley Holder, who was my political mentor and strategist. Not only was "Mac," as he's affectionately known, a brilliant political strategist, he believed in two political principles which guided us to many successful elections. First, blacks had to exercise political power like any other ethnic group in this society in order to be respected. This meant that we had to demand the same political "perks" as white politicians and the political machine had to believe that we could not be taken for granted. So a little independent flexing of the muscle was also part of his agenda. Second, Mac believed that black women were easier to elect than black men. This view fascinates everyone in politics that I've ever met. At first glance, one would assume that the influence of the church in the black community, if nothing else, would reverse this opinion. But we should not forget that it's the women in the church who raise more money on Women's Day than the men do on Men's Day. It's our church sisters who do the hard work of organizing and participating in successful church events. While many still don't want us in the pulpit, increasingly the ministerial brethren have realized that women can be very helpful to the work of the church by serving on the trustee board.

These same women actively support their alumni associations, their social clubs and in the case of New York, their political clubs. Mac used his already organized cadre of women as the base of our political organization. Using organized women's groups to support your candidacy can be the key to a successful campaign. Having a political advisor or advisors whom you can trust is also important. Political candidates have so many responsibilities that it is impossible for them to analyze every political decision thoroughly. Political advisors can be useful in offering objective viewpoints and a "clarity of vision" which the candidate herself may not have. So the second step to building a political organization of support is the development of key political strategists who truly have your interest at heart and can provide you with good political advice.

Despite good political advice and a strong political organization you cannot get anywhere unless you as a candidate want to win. The persistence I spoke of earlier must come from you. As a candidate, black women cannot be put off by the fact that a black man, white man or white woman wants the office. If you feel you are qualified and want to run, then get organized and take it to them: most black women candidates are better qualified than their opponents anyway. Otherwise, they would not have reached the point of vying for political office.

A longer issue than the tension between women and men as candidates is the question of money. The one advantage black politicians, male or female, have over their white counterparts is the fact that black politicians do not have to spend as much money to get elected. Black voters are not won over by T.V. or radio commercials. They want to see their candidates at community events up close and personal. Their campaign literature also does not have to be as elaborate or sophisticated, which cuts down on costs. This general rule is true, however, only for predominantly black populated districts. For example, in my congressional races, I spent a half million dollars. Women generally compensate for a lack of funds by superior political organization. For example, Marcy Kaptur, a white freshman congresswoman from Ohio, defeated an incumbent Republican congressman who had received several million dollars from the Republican National Committee. Marcy raised only a few hundred thousand dollars but she has a superior political organization. Her fundraising was all done through small events such as coffee-klatches, pancake breakfasts, etc. Black women will probably have to depend on this method of fundraising but this should not inhibit their ability to be successful.

The viability of black women in politics in the '80's will be determined by their political organization. A total involvement in the system is required for black women to succeed. Voter registration, lobbying and influencing decisions *and* getting into decision-making positions are all important elements of establishing political power. The issues cry out for the attention of black women. Job opportunities for low-income women, day care, adolescent pregnancy, and health care await the perspective of black women politicians. For example, the congresswomen in the caucus for women's issues have developed a bill to address the economic inequalities faced by American women, the Economic Equity Act. The benefits of this legislation, unfortunately, are not directed toward the needs of the poor and minority women. The authors of this legislation represent middle-class suburban areas. Despite their commitment to women's rights, the Equity Act reflects the needs of *their constituencies*. While Katie Hall of Gary and Cardiss Collins of Chicago are members of the caucus, they cannot be expected to shift the focus of the act without some support. Black women once represented a strong voice within the caucus when Yvonne Burke, Barbara Jordan and myself were in Congress. Along with Cardiss, we comprised almost 25% of the Democratic women members of the caucus. At that time, the caucus' views were more representative of poor and minority women. The "next-in-line" in terms of political aspirants, in all three areas, were black men. This occurred because women had not moved into the political positions necessary to catapult them into Congress when we left. This situation can only be remedied by women getting elected to their state legislatures, city councils and school boards. Appointed positions also can bring black women into the political arena. Appointees like Pat Harris, as Secretary of H.U.D. and later H.H.S., Mary F. Berry, as the Assistant Secretary for Education, and Eleanor Holmes Norton, as Chair of EEOC, became important policy-makers in the Carter Administration.

Black women must search for creative ways to join the political system. History has always demanded a great deal from us as a people and as women. While we have been falsely labeled as matriarchs and "sapphires," we have developed certain survival characteristics—perseverance, strength, tenacity, and endurance—which have enabled us to rise to the occasion under the most difficult of circumstances. With determination and courage, these qualities will help black women also succeed in politics.

Thank you.

7 *Youth and Student Revolution*

If those in power will not respond to their simple demands for justice, their violent young hands will be laid upon the structure of the social and political system, and they will try to tear it down.

"YOUTH AND AMERICA'S FUTURE," in *Unbought and Unbossed* (1970)

The electricity of the student and peace movement in the 1970s ushered in a new activist and voting constituency in America. Chisholm saw the youth as a valuable constituency that was central to a radical political democracy and future of America. She viewed college campuses as a main site to advocate for human rights and, she dared to say, "political revolution." More than any other group, young people helped energize Chisholm politically and lobbied her to chart a path to run for the presidency. Her tour of campuses across the country allowed her to introduce her vision for social change. In the decade after her retirement as an elected official, she continued to lecture on politics and social change, determined to empower a younger generation of activists and political leaders. As a result of her engagement with American youth, her work inspired a generation of politically engaged figures that would include the likes of U.S. Representative Barbara Lee, the Reverend Al Sharpton, and U.S. Representative Hakeem Jeffries.

"Progress through Understanding"

A commencement address delivered at Howard University, June 6, 1969,
and entered into the Congressional Record *on June 16 of that year.*

Mr. Speaker, on June 6 I was privileged to speak at the commencement exercises at Howard University. I found this a special challenge because Howard has been for many years in the vanguard of the black movement. She remains so today, in spite of the disturbances which wrecked her campus among so many others this year. While I strongly support the movement of which Howard's black students are a part, I am deeply concerned about the corrosive misunderstanding and hostility which has consequently arisen between black and white, between young and old. Realizing how difficult it will be for people with such different world views as these groups, I feel it essential that we approach one another with mutual respect and a willingness to listen honestly.

To underscore my feelings, I wish to include the text of my speech in the *Congressional Record*:

PROGRESS THROUGH UNDERSTANDING

This is a proud moment for me. I am here to speak to you, not so much because of what I am expected to say, but because I am simultaneously the Representative of two oppressed groups. I am Black, and I am a woman, and I am the first person who in spite of this double handicap has been elected to the Congress of the United States. For that reason, my appearance is sort of a historic

Congressional Record 115, pt. 12, extensions of remarks (June 16, 1969): 15972–73.

occasion. It is difficult to take part in a historic occasion. Every eye is fixed upon one. Every slip will be noticed and criticized with scant mercy.

I have searched my heart to discover what I should say to you today. To make the task more difficult, I am aware that there are two audiences here, and perhaps I should make different speeches to each of them. There are the old and the young, the fairly-satisfied and the fiercely-unfulfilled, the dwellers in the present and the citizens of the future. They seem to have so little in common that they often cannot talk to each other. What can I say to both of them? The gap between the older and young generations is one of the most baffling and disturbing facts of our time. Why has it opened? Can it be bridged? Whose fault is it? These questions perturb and preoccupy many of us, particularly those of us who are educators.

Here at Howard University, I think it is particularly imperative that these questions be answered. In some of what I am going to say, I may depart from the etiquette that should govern a guest's behavior and criticize my host. Believe me, I do so out of concern and respect, because I think it is vital to raise some very basic issues here and now. More than any other institution, perhaps, Howard is faced with choices that probably will mean its life or death. They will also be vital to larger institutions of which Howard is a vital part—the federal city Washington, and our nation as a whole.

It is perhaps the most difficult thing in the world to be at once Black and American. Some have given up trying to live with the contradictions involved. They have rejected the society by which they feel themselves rejected. They talk of revenge and martyrdom, and scorn their elders who chose the course of working for limited, possible gains.

Those elders, although some of them admire and some share the moral indignation of the young, recoil from the behavior that it leads to. Violence, confrontation and rebellion are self-defeating, they believe. They will end in repression and failure.

Probably we all know this dialog, and many of us have taken part in it. For Black Americans, the tensions between the generations have taken on particular acuteness and have especially serious implications. For us, a choice between subservience and alienation is not an academic or philosophical question, as it is with many other Americans. Here at Howard, the extreme attitudes and the range of shades of feeling between the two have all had their spokesmen. The dialog has been, in one way or another, going on for several years. Its outcome is still in doubt. It cannot remain in doubt much longer.

Everywhere today, one sees the same pressure for reformation of our existing institutions. Everywhere one sees the good standing in the way of the better. In our churches the division is between the defenders of the spiritual and moral truths that have sustained hundreds of generations, and those who say that truths are worthless if they are not put to work to serve men in the streets of our time and speak to them in terms they can understand and relate to their real lives. Our cities are approaching paralysis, unable to meet today's problems with yesterday's methods of organization and finance. Many unions, formed to proclaim and defend the brotherhood of working men, have turned out to be jealous defenders of the status quo and obstacles to the progress of men and women who want only their birthright—a meaningful, decent-paying job.

The list could be multiplied, by examination of all our institutions and analysis of what it is in each one that forms its own particular version of the problem. But in each case the challenge is basically the same. The old methods will not solve the new problems. Traditional institutions are unable to meet contemporary needs. They must reform or die.

This is certainly true of the United States Congress, as I am learning and as many new members have had to learn before me. The dead hand of tradition is heavier there than anywhere else one looks. This institution, the House of Representatives and Senate, was designed to be the capstone of our system of representative democracy. Today, whom does it represent? The war industries are well represented, the manufacturers of aircraft and weapons systems. The oil industry is represented. While working people go without to pay their income taxes, it gets a 27 1/2 percent forgiveness on its share of the cost of government. For what? For using up an irreplaceable national resource. Why should anyone be allowed to profit, let alone receive special consideration on his tax bill, for doing such a thing?

It is because oil states are Southern states from which the same members are returned to Congress from safe, one-party districts year after year until they become the most senior and powerful names on the Hill.

Examples could be multiplied, but this is enough to illustrate why special interests dominate the Congress and the public interest comes second.

We are waging a tragic, unjust, wasteful and illegal war in which we have no national interest at stake. As the casualty lists mounted and as the character of that war became clear, pressure grew to end it. The last administration was driven from office by that pressure—a lesson that the new administration does not show the slightest sign of having studied. And in Congress, what has been the effect of this outpouring of public opinion against the war? A handful of members—21, of whom I am one—have taken the only practical course. We have declared that until that war is ended and our national wealth and energy turned to fighting the war here at home against poverty, racism and ignorance, we will vote for no more military spending bills. But the response of most House members has been to continue their support of the war policy and military waste. Others have started, in traditional Congressional style, to work both sides of the street. They are talking against the war, but they keep on voting for it.

What kind of human being can know the useless, tragic waste of this war, and the staggering list of unmet human needs in our own cities and countryside, and vote for the war? But apart from that, what kind of representative government do we have when the Congress can continue to do this? It would not be possible if the institution were not frozen—petrified—into obsolete methods, by which I mean chiefly its seniority system. A safe district and a sound heart are all one needs to become powerful in Congress. It would be funny if it were not so dangerous.

I omitted schools from my list of institutions that are faced with the challenge—to change or die—because I wanted to deal with them at more length, and particularly with the institutions of higher learning like Howard that have in the past been the sources of the leaders of the black race. Howard's past is a proud one. Its list of distinguished graduates includes many truly great men; it and its retiring president have been pioneers in the creation of the great body of civil-rights law; diplomats, scientists, judges, public officials, physicians, teachers who have made enduring marks on their society, have been graduated from this school.

Now, Howard is two years into its second century. Like our nation itself, I think it is on trial for its life. The greatness of its past is no guarantee of its future. In fact, if it remains the prisoner of its past success, it will be sure to fail.

The United States will soon begin its third century. The first two have been marked by prosperity, peace and freedom on a scale new in man's history. But from its founding, this nation concealed a fatal flaw. Its design was intended to establish and preserve freedom. The design was drawn by men who owned slaves. With few exceptions, they did not even feel the inconsistency of their words and their deeds. Ninety years later, the new nation was nearly torn in two as it tried to repair the flaw in its founding. The nation survived, but the wrongs were not righted. They still are not righted, and they will not be righted in our time at the rate things are going.

What is the relevance of this to Howard University, or of Howard to the greater society? This question was asked by earlier generations here, and they answered it in their own way. The eminence of this university is evidence that those answers were not wrong. But were they right enough[?] Are they right for our time[?] I think it is hardly necessary to say that they are not.

Students have made known in no uncertain terms what they think must be the role of this university in the future, in this community and in the nation. They are saying—as they are saying on other campuses for other reasons—"You are not with it." They are saying, "We cannot stay aloof from the problems that cry out for solution. If the future is not going to be better than the past, we do not care whether we have a future."

To the older generation, that sounds like a repudiation of them and of all they have done and endured. But I think it is not. I think it is more of an appeal, a passionate appeal for understanding, alliance and cooperative effort. The fierce clarity of the moral vision of the young is beautiful, and it is true. But it is often not matched by practical wisdom to make that vision real, to make the world flesh. If I have to choose between the vision and the wisdom, between rebellion and submission, I must choose the vision and the rebellion. But I do not think it has come to that yet. The time is nearly here, but it is not yet.

What can we do? What can we all do together? There is the answer. We must get together. We must understand and love each other, and we must build a community. Black teachers and scholars have lived in their own special kind of ivory tower. They must come down from it. A black university has no room at this time for mere "academicians." It needs scholars, but they must be men of action, who are able to apply their knowledge of the world around them in which their brothers and sisters suffer, starve and die. They must hear what their community is saying, and go into it and work.

There are unique, irreplaceable roles that a black university can play—and this must become truly a black university if it is to play them. It can assume its rightful position of leadership in the field of urban studies. Here, in the heart of one of the nation's largest cities, it can apply scholarship, research and the skills of the trained mind to defining the problems of the cities and discovering solutions to them.

For instance, it could have pioneered in the fields of legal protection of the poor, and in welfare rights law. This great work is being done, but it is being done largely by others. It should have been done here.

Howard can lead in the recovery and recreation of black culture, history, art and tradition. It should be a center for the study of non-white cultures, a source of vitality, energy and self-respect for young men and women who are insisting on restoring their rightful heritage, which has been denied them.

These are the kinds of things that are meant by the overworked word "relevance." One is weary of some words, and relevance is one of those.

I want to say some things directly to the younger audience here, because most of this has been an exhortation to the older audience. I want to say five things, and I think I will say them in the form of a letter.

Dear Graduates, You will continue to find it difficult, as you have found it, to tolerate what you think of as the apathy and backwardness of some of your older folks. But try to understand, and learn from them what they still have to teach, as you continue your own independent growth.

You know that you must continue to fight the system that has been denying you the opportunity to be a total man or woman. But fight intelligently. Fight so that you get results and achieve something. You can't tear down everything and build everything new at once. Be practical. You can learn this from the men and women who have, in their own best consciences, fought the same fight before you, as they can learn many vital things from you.

You will have to guard against becoming like some of the older folks when you get out into the community. They have been absorbed by the society as it is and adjusted to things as they are until they would not really think of changing them. Now that you have graduated, don't cop out. Don't let yourselves be, in the current jargon, co-opted.

Remember, too, that you are not the end. It will not be long before you are an older generation. You must be conscious of your crucial importance as models and images for younger blacks. Your actions and your appearance must command respect, and imitation, and you must stay true to yourselves and your honor and pride in being the first generation of your race in our nation with the prospect of reaching full maturity and individuality as men and women, complete human beings.

And finally, I hope many of you will run for office. Wherever I go, I meet students who come up to me and ask, "How can I get into office?" The answer is to work for it. Get into public life, make your voice heard on public issues, study, prepare, keep trying. We need you perhaps most of all in the political field. Some Americans perhaps can afford the luxury of electing politicians who do not truly represent them—although I think they really cannot. But black Americans have been under-represented throughout history, and are pitifully under-represented now. Strictly on a population basis, there should be five or six times as many black Members of Congress as there are in this session. I hope it will be a very short time before that inequity is put right, and I hope that some of you listening to me today will be the ones to do it.

Our task at this moment in history is a great one, and if we are to perform it we must first understand what it is. We must neither withdraw from our society and nation, nor be absorbed by it. We must, for our own sakes and for everyone's sake, find a better way. To adopt what two sociologists, Christopher Jencks and David Riesman, concluded on the problem, we must find forms of education that will help black people cope with the white world without becoming either completely alienated from it or subservient to it. And we must, in a larger context, build new institutions or reform our old ones so that there are avenues of upward mobility and achievement that will allow black citizens to maintain creative tension between themselves and the white world, instead of becoming wholly adapted to it.

If we fail, this nation will be poorer for it, and if we succeed, it will be richer indeed.

"Lowering the Voting Age to 18"

Congressional floor speech, Washington, D.C., July 29, 1969.

Mr. Speaker, our young Americans will one day inherit the management and maintenance of our political system. In order for our system of government to work at its best it must produce the greatest good for the greatest number of people while it continues to protect the basic rights and liberties of each individual.

At a time when there is a great amount of talk and interest throughout the country about the rights and welfare of minority groups and at a time when we have just finished celebrating the basic holiday of our democracy—July 4—I would like to enter a plea for what is estimated to be either the first or second largest minority group in our country. That minority group is the youth between the ages of 16 and 21.

The U.S. Bureau of Census in July 1968 estimated the size of that age group at 21,679,000—close to 10 percent of the population of the country. The size of that figure alone would seem to warrant their occasional refusal to participate in the war in Vietnam and other salient activities and aspects of our society on the basis that they have no direct representation.

The reason that I quote the statistics for the age bracket between 16 and 21 is very simple. If we wait 2 years to pass a bill lowering the voting age, approximately 200,000 youths will have joined the ranks of that underrepresented minority group.

In the war the average age of those who fight and die are under 21. In fact, in Brooklyn, where my home district is, there was a recently reported case of a young marine who, at only 15, acquired the distinction of being our youngest fatality in Vietnam.

Congressional Record 115, pt. 16, extensions of remarks (July 29, 1969): 21301.

Many youths are not politically involved and have a deep concern for the complex social problems that now plague the country. At present there are about 5,000 VISTA volunteers on active duty in this country and there have been more than 16,000 since inception. The overwhelming majority have been youths between 18 and 21.

In the past election many young men and women were actively involved in political campaigns, but there were also many who were not. Those who were not were youths who have been discouraged from participating in the political system for various reasons. One of these reasons was to be found in the response of the general electorate in the last election involving the late Robert Kennedy, Senator Eugene McCarthy and the recent primary mayoralty election in New York City.

At the age of 18 young Americans must bear arms if called upon, and are considered adults in civil and criminal courts of law. The age of 18 is and has been considered the age of maturity in America.

Opinion polls have shown that 64 percent of the American voting public favors a lowering of the voting age to 18.

Young people, because of the educational emphasis in the high schools on politics and our particular life-style, are generally more aware politically than their parents.

They are well-steeped in the belief that the right to vote is the fundamental requirement for citizen participation in our democracy. They are as aware as we are that this country came into being because American colonists would not stand for taxation without representation. They are aware of the close parallels between their present situation and the position of earlier Americans. They are also aware of the close parallels between their situation and the struggle of black Americans for political freedom in this country because many of them are black.

We cannot, in good faith, continue to deny these young adults the rights and privileges of adulthood while calling upon them to exercise their restraint and responsibilities.

House Joint Resolution 18 follows:

H.J. Res. 18

Joint resolution proposing an amendment to the Constitution of the United States to provide that the right to vote shall not be denied on the account of age to persons who are eighteen years of age or older.

Resolved by the Senate and House of Representatives of the United States of America in Congress assembled (two-thirds of each House concurring therein). That the following article is proposed as an amendment to the Constitution of the United States, to be valid if ratified by the legislatures of three-fourths of the several States within seven years from the date of its submission to the States by the Congress:

"Article—

"Section 1. No citizen of the United States who is eighteen years of age or older shall be denied the right to vote by reason of age.

"Sec. 2. The Congress shall have power to enforce this article by appropriate legislation."

"Youth and America's Future"

An excerpt from Unbought and Unbossed, *originally published in 1970.*

One question bothers me a lot: Who's listening to me? Some of the time, I feel dishearteningly small and futile. It's as if I'm facing a

Excerpted from Shirley Chisholm, *Unbought and Unbossed*, 40th anniversary ed. (1970; repr., Washington, D.C.: Take Root Media, 2010).

seamless brick wall, as if most people are deaf to what I try to say. It seems so clear to me what's wrong with the whole system. Why isn't it clear to most others? The majority of Americans do not want to hear the truth about how their country is ruled and for whom. They do not want to know why their children are rejecting them. They do not dare to have to rethink their whole lives. There is a vacuum of leadership, created partly by the bullets of deranged assassins. But whatever made it, all we see now is the same tired old men who keep trucking down front to give us the same old songs and dances.

There are no new leaders coming along. Where are they? What has happened suddenly? On the national level, on the state level, who commands respect, who is believed by a wide enough cross section of the population to qualify as a leader? I don't see myself as becoming that kind of a leader. My role, I think, is more that of a catalyst. By verbalizing what is wrong, by trying to strip off the masks that make people comfortable in the midst of chaos, perhaps I can help get things moving.

It may be that no one can have any effect on most adults in this society. It may be that the only hope is with the younger generation. If I can relate to them, give them some kind of focus, make them believe that this country can still become the America that it should have been, I could be content. The young may be slandered as "kooks" and "societal misfits" by frightened, demagogic old men, but that will not scare them. They are going to force change. For a while they may be beaten down, but time is on their side, and the spirit of this generation will not be killed. That's why I prefer to go around to campuses and talk with the kids rather than attend political meetings. Politicians tell me I'm wasting my time and energy.

"They don't vote," I'm told. Well, I'm not looking for votes. If I were, I would get the same kind of reception that a lot of political figures get when they encounter younger people, and I would deserve it.

There are many things I don't agree with some young zealots about. The main one, I suppose, is that I have not given up—and will not give up until I am compelled to—my belief that the basic design of this country is right. What is essential is to make it work, not to sweep it away and substitute—what? Something far worse, perhaps.

Most young people are not yet revolutionary, but politicians and police and other persons in power almost seem to be conspiring to turn them into revolutionaries. Like me, I think, most of them are no more revolutionary than the founders of this country. Their goals are the same—to insure individual liberty and equality of opportunity, and forever to thwart the tyrannous tendencies of government, which inevitably arise from the arrogance and isolation of men who are securely in power. All they want, if it were not too unfashionable for them to say so, is for the American dream to come true, at least in its less materialistic aspects. They want to heal the gaping breach between this country's promises and its performance, a breach that goes back to its founding on a Constitution that denied that black persons and women were full citizens. "Liberty and justice for all" were beautiful words, but the ugly fact was that liberty and justice were only for white males. How incredible that it is nearly two hundred years since then, and we have still to fight the same old enemies! How is it possible for a man to repeat the pledge of allegiance that contains these words, and then call his fellow citizens "societal misfits" when they are simply asking for liberty and justice?

Such schizophrenia goes far back. "All forms of commerce between master and slave are tyranny," intoned Thomas Jefferson, who is rumored to have had several children by black women on his estate. If the story is true, the great democrat was a great hypocrite. Even if it is not true, it has verisimilitude. It could be a perfect metaphor for the way our country was founded and grew, with lofty and pure words on its lips and the basest bigotry hidden in its heart.

The main thing I have in common with the kids is that we are tired of being lied to. What we want is for people to mean what they say. I think they recognize at least that I'm for real. They know most adults are selling something they can't deliver.

Nowhere near enough young persons are involved in politics. Too many have been discouraged from participating, for various reasons. Some retired into inactivity after 1968, the year when Robert Kennedy and Martin Luther King were killed, Eugene McCarthy was ignored by the men who controlled the Democratic convention, the Chicago police attacked them in the streets, and finally, Richard Nixon was elected President. It was a discouraging year for youth, a year when their hopes were trampled into the mud one after another. Not much since then has given young people any hint that the forces of reaction are not firmly in control.

One reason for youthful distaste for politics has been the fact that the eighteen to twenty-one-year-old population was for years our largest disenfranchised group. At eighteen, young persons were legally adults in most states, and could be prosecuted as grownups; they were enjoined to bear arms if called, and die if unlucky. They could see clearly that they were being given all of the duties and none of the privileges of citizenship. Congress has moved to correct this long-standing injustice; it remains to be seen how quickly and in how great numbers young people avail themselves of the ballot. It is my belief that in two or three years, at most, from the time Congress acted in the spring of 1970, the under-twenty-one voting bloc will be a major factor in political calculations, and a major force for progress.

The most tragic error into which older people can fall is one that is common among educators and politicians. It is to use youth as scapegoats for the sins of their elders. Is the nation wasting its young men and its honor in an unjust war? Never mind—direct your frustration at the long-haired young people who are shouting in the streets that the war must end. Curse them as hippies and immoral, dirty fanatics; after all, we older Americans could not have been wrong about anything important, because our hearts are all in the right place and God is always on our side, so anyone who opposes us must be insane, and probably in the pay of the godless Communists.

Youth is in the process of being classed with the dark-skinned minorities as the object of popular scorn and hatred. It is as if Americans have to have a "nigger," a target for its hidden frustrations and guilt. Without someone to blame, like the Communists abroad and the young and black at home, middle America would be forced to consider whether all the problems of our time were in any way its own fault. That is the one thing it could never stand to do. Hence, it finds scapegoats. Few adults, I am afraid, will ever break free of the crippling attitudes that have been programmed into their personalities—racism, self-righteousness, lack of concern for the losers of the world, and an excessive regard for property. One reason, as I have noted, is that they do not know they are like this, and that they proclaim ideals that are the reverse of many of their actions. Such hypocrisy, even if it is unconscious, is the real barrier between them and their children.

Individually and collectively, Americans can no longer get away with proclaiming their democratic faith and jealously guarding their special privileges. We cannot hope any longer to be believed when we claim to be defending freedom, after so many years of being seen to care nothing about the freedom of citizens of Latin American, Asian, European, and Caribbean nations where we prop up dictatorial regimes. The rest of the world sees through the sham, when we pour billions in "foreign aid," which is really military assistance, into underdeveloped countries where the citizens continue to starve—as do millions of our own.

If it is not too late for America to be saved, the young will save it—and the blacks, the Indians, the Spanish-surnamed, the young women, and the other victims of American society. They, if any, will become the conscience that the Country has lacked. They will try to force it to practice what it has preached. Such sentiments have become such a cliché of oratory that I am afraid they have lost all force. They must be taken seriously. I have traveled, I have spoken to, I have looked at too many young persons, black and white, not to take these ideas seriously. I have looked in their faces and seen something I had never seen before, even in the faces of white students, suburban children in their early teens. They are ready to die for their convictions. Their parents do not know what they think. They could never believe that their children have reached such a point. But these young people—so young, so strangely attractive—have resolved that the United States must become the society it has always claimed to be, and that they will make it so. If those in power will not respond to their simple demands for justice, their violent young hands will be laid upon the structure of the social and political system, and they will try to tear it down. There is no rhetoric in what I am saying; it is a simple fact. If it happens, it will mean that our streets would be forever stained with the blood of our best young sons and daughters.

Whenever I speak to student groups, the first question they ask me is "Can't you do something about the war?" The next one usually is "How can you stand to be part of this system?" They mean, "How can you stay in Congress and keep talking about progress, about reconciliation, after all that this society has done to you and your people?" It is the hardest question I could be asked, and the answer is the most important one I can offer. I try to explain to them: "You can be part of the system without being wedded to it," I say. "You can take part in it without believing that everything it does is right. I don't measure America by its achievement, but by its potential. There are still many things that we haven't tried—that I haven't tried—to change the way our present system operates. I haven't exhausted the opportunities for action in the course I'm pursuing. If I ever do, I cannot at this point imagine what to do next. You want me to talk to you about revolution, but I can't do that. I know what it would bring. My people are twelve percent of the population, at most fifteen percent. I am pragmatic about it: revolution would be suicide."

What is the alternative? What can we offer these beautiful, angry, serious, and committed young people? How are we all to be saved? The alternative, of course, is reform—renewal, revitalization of the institutions of this potentially great nation. This is our only hope. If my story has any importance, apart from its curiosity value—the fascination of being a "first" at anything is a durable one—it is, I hope, that I have persisted in seeking this path toward a better world. My significance, I want to believe, is not that I am the first black woman elected to the U.S. Congress, but that I won public office without selling out to anyone. When I wrote my campaign slogan, "Unbossed and Unbought," it was an expression of what I believe I was and what I want to be—what I want all candidates for public office to be. We need men and women who have far greater abilities and far broader appeal than I will ever have, but who have my kind of independence—who will dare to declare that they are free of the old ways that have led us wrong, and who owe nothing to the traditional concentrations of capital and power that have subverted this nation's ideals.

Such leaders must be found. But they will not be found as much as they will be created, by an electorate that has become ready to demand that it control its own destiny. There must be a new coalition of all Americans—black, white, red, yellow and brown, rich and poor—who are no longer willing to allow their rights as human beings to be infringed upon by anyone else, for any reason. We must join together to insist that this nation deliver on the promise it made, nearly 200 years ago, that every man be allowed to be a man. I feel an incredible urgency that we must do it now, if time has not run out, it is surely ominously short.

8 Poetry

*The black students kept to their own tables at the cafeteria. We talked. No
one said "rap" then, but that's what we did.*

REFLECTING ON HER COLLEGE DAYS IN *UNBOUGHT AND
UNBOSSED* (1970)

Across three decades of public speaking, the power of Chisholm's oratory
was known to excite hearts and minds in classrooms, churches, college
auditoriums, campaign rallies, and political conventions throughout
the nation. It comes as no surprise, then, that she was a poet in her private
life. At times witty, pensive, and inspiring, she used verse as a way to
make sense of her place in the social and political struggles that whirled
around her. Although she made a conscious choice to keep most of
her poems private, there were a handful that she published in newspapers,
shared with students at high school recitals, and performed at Black
poetry productions in Brooklyn. Chisholm's poem "Land of Our Birth"
shows us hints of the deep emotional life that flowed underneath her public fight for social justice. In a contemporary framing of hip-hop, Chisholm
had bars.

"Land of Our Birth"

This poem was first introduced to the public when Chisholm recited it in the documentary New York Illustrated: The Irrepressible Shirley Chisholm, *which was aired October 11, 1969. It also appeared in some newspapers later that year.*

Land of our birth
Tell us in words simple and plain
The reason for all of our torture and pain
Are we not part of this nation strong?
What have we done that is so wrong?

Land of our birth,
Tell us by deeds, sincere and true
The reason we are not really part of the crew
Did we not sacrifice, and hope not in vain,
To be assured that there would be equal gain?

Land of our birth
Tell us in song, hearty and loud
Amidst the singing, jostling crowd
That we are all citizens of your realm
And that you are captain at the helm

Transcribed from *The Irrepressible Shirley Chisholm*, NBC News Special, 1969, videorecording, www.youtube.com/watch?v=ERGWEG4LcpI.

Land of our birth,
The time has come for action fast
We can no longer live in the past!
This mighty land of powerful and free
Must now demonstrate a real democracy

Acknowledgments

The idea for this book began during the pandemic when I was asked to write an introduction to one of Chisholm's previously authored books. I found myself scouring a number of Chisholm's speeches and position papers, and it struck me that although she gave numerous speeches and had significant writings, much of the material had not been used by scholars. While I had written extensively about Chisholm's breadth as a politician and political strategist, I found it necessary to delve into what makes her a significant public intellectual. Inextricably linked to framing her intellectualism was highlighting Chisholm's writings and speeches on issues that are not associated with her, like police brutality, foreign affairs, and colonialism.

I owe a debt of gratitude to the second half of the Shirley Chisholm Project, and that is Torrese Arquee, whose support and assistance at SCP and on this book has been immeasurable.

Work on Black women requires a significant amount of stamina, encouragement, and support. I have been extremely fortunate for the mentorship and scholarship of former professors who have been instrumental to both my professional and academic journey—Darlene Clark Hine (whose support is immeasurable), Sonia Sanchez, Bettye Collier Thomas, Robin D.G. Kelley, Martha Biondi, and the late Richard Iton.

I began my work on Chisholm at Columbia University's Institute for Research and African American Studies, and I have been mentored and nurtured by some of the best scholars in the world. Special thanks to the late Manning Marable and Steven Gregory. For over fifteen years Farah Griffin has been and continues to be an amazing mentor, and I am forever indebted for that mentorship as well as her research on the Black feminist intellectual tradition that was extremely helpful for this work. Other IRAAS family include Samuel Roberts, Shawn Mendoza, and Sharon Harris; special thanks for your encouragement this year.

Thank you, Barbara Winslow, for your support, scholarship, and faith in me as director of the Shirley Chisholm Project at Brooklyn College. I thank my colleagues at Brooklyn College in the Africana Studies Department, especially Prudence Cumberbatch, George Cunningham, and Dale Byam, along with the entire faculty and staff, in addition to my other Brooklyn colleagues affiliated with the Women's and Gender Studies Program, especially Irva Adams.

I appreciate the University of California Press and its staff for their work on the project—special thanks to Nora Becker. I am forever indebted to the support of my editor Niels Hooper, who believed in the manuscript from the beginning pitch and was steadfast until its completion.

I am especially grateful to the blind reviewers who took the time to read the introductions and provided immensely helpful comments that made for a stronger manuscript. I would like to thank the archivists at the Rutgers University Special Collections and Brooklyn College Special Collections, in particular Marianne LaBatto.

During the writing of this book I also started with my work as a historical consultant on the feature film *Shirley*, which continues to increase interest in Chisholm. I am thankful to have worked with producers John Ridley and Regina King and staff on this amazing project. I would like to thank Regina King, who has taken on the Herculean task as producer and the lead role of *Shirley*, for her commitment to Chisholm and her legacy. I am indebted to her overwhelming support of me in this project.

No one creates and writes in isolation, nor do we achieve anything by ourselves. I have a phenomenal village of family and friends and appreciate them all: Melba Hyman, Yvonne Pugh, Zariah Dawson, Zhavon Malone, Jean Wiggins, Dr. Julius Garvey, Alice Malbrough, Valerie Thomas, Cleveland Parks, Julia O'Neil, Julia Parks-O'Neil, Rene Anderson, Kevin Anderson, Madelon Hendricks, Maureen Aguirre, Ricardo Aguirre, Shauna Brown, Keith Smith, Shakira Coppeny, Umindi Francis, La Tasha Levy, Maxine Matthews, Carla Brown, Deborah Peaks Coleman, Alecia Mason, Minnie McDonald, Monique Mc Donald-Harris, Kaye Morgan, Carlene Lang, and Patricia Lattimore. Thank you to my First Baptist Church of Crown Heights family, my amazing Sorors of

Delta Sigma Theta Sorority, Inc., and the Sister Scholars of the Delta Research and Education Foundation.

I am extremely fortunate to have an entire village of family and friends who have been a support system for myself and the public and scholarly work on Chisholm that spans over a decade. While my father, Leonard Fraser, passed many years before this book, his influence and spirit still loom over everything that I write and create. The last year of completing this book has been one of the most trying times of my life, with the death of the two most important women in my life: my lovely sister Ruwanda Fraser and my beloved mother Shirley Fraser. I am grateful that my mother saw the book cover and forever thankful for her encouragement and support of me and this work. In the midst of sorrow, I completed this work with the joyful birth of my amazing son Amari Malbrough, who makes everything worthwhile. I am also thankful for my lovely niece Nia Fraser, who is an inspiration. Last, I am forever grateful for the love and support of my husband, Russell Malbrough, for this book and my many endeavors.

Selected Bibliography

This bibliography, rather than covering every aspect of Shirley Chisholm's life, identifies works that are integral in exploring her political and intellectual legacy and her place in a Black feminist intellectual tradition.

Bambara, Toni Cade. *The Black Woman: An Anthology*. New York: New American Library, 1970.

Bay, Mia, Farrah J. Griffin, Martha Jones, and Barbara Savage. *Toward an Intellectual History of Black Women*. Chapel Hill: University of North Carolina Press, 2015.

Beal, Frances M. *Black Women's Manifesto; Double Jeopardy: To Be Black and Female*. New York: Third World Women's Alliance, 1969.

Biondi, Martha. *To Stand and Fight: The Struggle for Civil Rights in Postwar New York City*. Cambridge, MA: Harvard University Press, 2003.

Bogues, Anthony. *Black Heretics, Black Prophets: Black Radical Political Intellectuals*. New York: Routledge, 2003.

Brown, Tammy L. "'A New Era in American Politics': Shirley Chisholm and the Discourse of Identity." *Callaloo* 31, no. 4 (2008): 1013–25.

Chisholm, Shirley. *The Good Fight*. New York: Harper and Row, 1973.

———. "Race, Revolution, and Women." *Black Scholar* 3, no. 4 (1971): 17–21.

———. *Unbought and Unbossed*. Boston: Houghton Mifflin, 1970.

Clarke, Cheryl. *"After Mecca": Women Poets and the Black Arts Movement*. New Brunswick, NJ: Rutgers University Press, 2004.

Collins, Patricia Hill. *Black Feminist Thought: Knowledge, Consciousness, and the Politics of Empowerment*. Boston: Unwin, Hyman 1990.

Cruse, Harold. *The Crisis of the Negro Intellectual: From Its Origins to the Present*. New York: William Morrow, 1967.

Fraser, Zinga A. "Dreaming of Democracy: Shirley Chisholm's Political Life." In *The Right to Be Elected: 100 Years since Women's Suffrage*, Boston Review/Forum, edited by Jennifer M. Piscopo and Shauna L. James, 94–104. Chicago: Haymarket Books, 2020.

Gallagher, Julia A. *Black Women and Politics in New York City*. Urbana: University of Illinois Press, 2012.

Giddings, Paula. *Where and When I Enter: The Impact of Black Women on Race and Sex in America*. New York: Bantam Books, 1985.

Guy-Sheftall, Beverly. *Words of Fire: An Anthology of African-American Feminist Thought*. New York: New Press, 1995.

Haskins, James. *Fighting Shirley Chisholm*. New York: Dial Press, 1975.

Hine, Darlene Clark. *Hine Sight: Black Women and the Reconstruction of American History*. Bloomington: Indiana University Press, 1994.

Hunter, Tera. "The Forgotten Legacy of Shirley Chisholm: Race versus Gender in the 2008 Democratic Primaries." In *Obama, Clinton, Palin: Making History in Election 2008*, edited by Liette Gidlow, 66–85. Urbana: University of Illinois Press, 2008.

McClain, Paula D., Niambi Carter, and Michael C. Brady. "Gender and Black Presidential Politics: From Chisholm to Moseley-Braun." *Journal of Women, Politics, and Policy* 27, nos. 1–2 (2005): 51–68.

Ransby, Barbara. *Ella Baker and the Black Freedom Movement: A Radical Democratic Vision*. Chapel Hill: University of North Carolina Press, 2003.

Taylor, Ula. "The Historical Evolution of Black Feminist Theory and Praxis." *Journal of Black Studies* 29, no. 2 (November 1998): 234–53.

Thomas, Bettye Collier. *Jesus, Jobs, and Justice: African American Women and Religion*. New York: Alfred Knopf, 2011.

White, Deborah Gray. "Mining the Forgotten: Manuscript Sources for Black Women's History." *Journal of American History* 1, no. 74 (June 1987): 237–42.

Williams, Hattie V. *Bury My Heart in a Free Land: Black Women Intellectuals in Modern U.S. History*. Santa Barbara, CA: Bloomsbury, 2017.

Winslow, Barbara. *Shirley Chisholm: Catalyst for Change*, New York: Westview Press, 2014.

Index

and student aid at, 58–59; white
faculty at, 60–61
Black communities: Black colleges'
role in, 12–14, 244–45; Black
studies as transformative for, 30
Black cultural nationalism, 16
Black feminist intellectual tradition,
5, 18–26
Black history, 11–12, 30. *See also* Black
studies
Black Jack (Missouri), 132
Black liberation, 25, 176, 215–17
Black Lives Matter movement, 2–3
Black men: abortion views of,
197–98; Black women as
competitors of, 22, 215, 220–21;
electability of, vs. Black women,
233; emasculation of, 210, 215,
223–24; as focus of civil rights
movement, 231; importance of
college degrees to, 56; sexism of,
22, 25; stereotypes of, 210, 227;
traditional occupations of, 174
Black nationalism, 16, 25
Black Power movement, 15, 16, 19, 23
Black refugees, 141–50
Black Revolution, 208–9
Black Scholar, The (journal), 16; "The
Politics of Coalition" in, 173–78;
"Race, Revolution, and Women"
in, 205–14; "The White Press" in,
136–41
Black Skins—White Masks (Fanon),
214
"Black Struggle in History for
Excellence in Education" (1984
lecture), 55–65
Black studies: at Brooklyn College, 7,
30; current opposition to, 3–4; in

elementary and secondary
education, 4; student protests in
origins of, 50–51; teaching methods
of, 52–53; as transformative for
Black communities, 30; women's
studies in relation to, 49–55
"Black Studies and Women's
Studies" conference (1983), 49–55
Black Woman, The (Bambara), 21
"Black Woman in Contemporary
America, The" (1974 lecture),
21–22, 214–22
Black women: and abortion, 24, 183,
197–99, 205; in Black liberation, 25,
176, 215–17; as competitors of Black
men, 22, 215, 220–21; culture of
dissemblance in, 22–23; double
jeopardy of, 21–22, 25, 176, 217–18,
224; economic justice for, 191–92;
electability of, vs. Black men, 233;
in family life, 219–20, 224; feminist
intellectual tradition of, 5, 18–26; as
freedom fighters, 25–26; and
Hispanic women, 223–29;
intellectualism of, 15–20; as leaders
of civil rights movement, 20–21,
177, 217–19, 231; maternal mortality
rates for, 24–25, 199, 205; as
matriarchs, 215, 223, 227, 236;
origins of strength of, 178, 215,
223–24, 236; political organization
and involvement of, 178–82,
218–22, 233–35; as politicians,
viability of, 230–36; as revolutionaries, tactics of, 213–14; role in
contemporary America, 214–22;
stereotypes of, 210, 217, 227;
traditional occupations of, 174, 191;
in women's movement, 22, 176

cities: model, 130, 152; urban blight in, 125; urban renewal in, 130–32. *See also* housing

City College of New York, "Address to the Conference of Black and Latin Women in Art and Politics" at, 223–29

civil disobedience, 115

civil rights, Nixon's lack of enforcement of, 103, 110–12

Civil Rights Commission, U.S., 61, 110, 114, 133

civil rights movement: Black women as leaders in, 20–21, 177, 217–19, 231; feminists emerging from, 51; focus on Black men in, 231; retrogression in, 179–80; sexism in, 217; women's liberation in relation to, 176

Civil War, American, 74–77

Clarke, Cheryl, 20, 176

class bias, in women's studies, 50

class divide, 13, 17–18

class mobility, 44, 45

Clay, William L., Sr., 153*fig.*

Cleaver, Eldridge, 206, 209, 210–11

Cleaver, Kathleen, 25, 217

Clergy Consultation Service on Abortion, 200

"Closing Remarks" (1983 speech), 49–55

coalition politics, 159, 173–78, 256

Coast Guard, U.S., 148–49

Cold War, 66, 81, 94

colleges and universities: advice to students graduating from, 245–46; affirmative action in, 179; as audience for Chisholm's

speeches, 10–13, 250–51; challenges facing Black students at, 55–65; financial aid at, 58–59; importance of degrees from, 55–56; integration of, 59–62; majority-white, Black students and faculty at, 58–60, 63; poor preparation in public schools for, 56–57; revolutions on, 237; student movement at, 50–51, 237. *See also* Black colleges

Collins, Cardiss, 158*fig.*, 230, 235

Collins, George W., 153*fig.*

Collins, Patricia Hill, 16, 18

colonialism, in Barbados, 6

colonization of Black people, 12–13, 71–81; capitalism in, 12–13, 74–75; and Cold War hypocrisy, 66; education in, 13–14, 74–81; vs. other colonized groups, 71–74, 76; slavery in, 72–75

color tax, 121

Columbia University, 6

Combahee River Collective, 20

Commerce Department, U.S., 67–68

commitment, 206–7

communism: foreign aid and, 83, 84, 94; refugees from, 145–46

communities: Black colleges' role in, 12–14, 244–45; Black studies as transformative for, 30; control of schools by, 16–17, 35–41

Comprehensive Drug Abuse Prevention and Control Act of 1970, 106

Concord Baptist Church (Brooklyn), 167

Cone, James, 8–9

Congress, U.S.: bills as gestures in, 201–2; Black and women members of, 23, 185, 193, 212; culture of dissemblance in, 23; elections of 1968 for, 7, 194; seniority system of, 242; special interests in, 241; Vietnam War and, 241–42. *See also* House of Representatives; Senate; *specific laws and members*

Congressional Black Caucus, 23, 153*fig.*

congressional floor speeches by Chisholm: "The Attica Prison Uprising" (1971), 99–100; "Equal Rights for Women" (1969), 184–86, 212–13; "Lowering the Voting Age to 18" (1969), 247–49; "On Busing Desegregation" (1971), 10, 115, 118–20; "On Captive Nations Week" (1970), 66, 81–82; "People and Peace, Not Profits and War" (1969), 67–71; "Racism and Polarization" (1971), 116–18

Congressional Record, 137, 238

conservatives, Southern, on education of Black Americans, 76–77

Constitution, U.S.: equal rights amendment to, 185–86; voting age amendment to, 249

constitutions, state, 76

contraceptives, 24, 189, 192, 198, 203

Conyers, John, Jr., 153*fig.*

Coolidge, Calvin, 71

Cooper, Anna Julia, 15

Cornell University, 51

corporate social responsibility, 2–3

corruption, police, 102, 110, 114

counterculture, 37–38

court system: recommendations for reform of, 113–14; reform under Nixon, 102, 107–9; refugees in, 148

crime: in ghettos, 102, 124; organized, 109; rates under Nixon, 101–3; white collar, 108–9

Crime Commission, 107

criminal justice, 98–114; Nixon's policies on, 98, 101–13; presidential campaign position paper on, 98, 101–14; recommendations for reform of, 113–14. *See also* policing; prisons

Cuban refugees, 143–45

cultural implantation, 13, 76–77

cultural nationalism, Black, 16, 25

cultural transmission, 76–77

culture: in colonization, 72–74, 76–78; of dissemblance, 22–23

Cyprus, 150

Davis, Angela, 112

Dawkins, Ben C., 165

day (child) care: cost effectiveness of federal spending on, 44–49; as issue in women's movement, 216, 226

"Day Care Dilemma, The" (1976 article), 44–49

Day Care Services Act, 45, 47–49

de facto segregation, 165

Defense Department, U.S., 68–69

defense spending, 67–71, 130–31, 163

Deith, David, 189

de jure segregation, 165

Dellums, Ronald V., 153*fig.*

democracy: foreign aid in support of, 84–85; hypocrisy around talk of, 115, 251

Democratic National Conventions, 155*fig.*, 156*fig.*, 230

Dennison, George, 42

deportation, of refugees, 144

deprivation, cycle of, 161

desegregation. *See* integration

developing countries: foreign aid to, 83–88; women political leaders in, 192

Development Assistance Committee, 85

dictatorships, foreign aid to, 84–85

Diggs, Charles C., Jr., 153*fig.*

discrimination. *See* racism; sexism

dissemblance, culture of, 22–23

dissent, political, under Nixon, 112–14

divorce laws, 186

Dixon, Julian, 147

Dominican Republic, 84

double jeopardy, of Black women, 21–22, 25, 176, 217–18, 224

"Double Jeopardy: To Be Black and Female" (Beal), 21–22

Douglass, Frederick, 181

dropping out, 32–33

Drug Abuse and Education Act of 1969, 105

Drug Abuse Prevention and Control Act of 1970, 106

drug use and abuse: in counterculture, 38; Nixon's policies on, 98, 102, 105–6; programs addressing, 105–6; in public schools, 56–57; war on drugs and, 98

Du Bois, W. E. B., 13, 79

Dunbar High School (Washington, D.C.), 64

Eastern Europe, 81, 146

economic aid. *See* foreign aid

Economic Equity Act, 235

economic justice, 187–92

"Economic Justice for Women" (1970 speech), 187–92

Economic Opportunity Act of 1964, 106, 160

economic refugees, 142–43

economy, U.S.: in Civil War, 75; economic justice for women in, 187–92; education and power in, 77, 80–81; inflation in, 68, 126–27, 166, 175; recession of 1970s in, 45, 169

education, higher. *See* colleges

education, public school, 30–65; accountability in, 17, 39–40; alleviation of injustice as purpose of, 30; Black studies classes in, 4; challenges facing Black children in, 56–57; of Chisholm, 6–7, 30; Chisholm's career in, 7, 30–31, 195; after Civil War, 75–81; class size in, 34; in colonization of Black people, 13–14, 74–81; community control of, 16–17, 35–41; cultural implantation in, 13, 76–77; dropping out of, 32–33; funding for, 31, 38, 67–68, 127, 128; harm caused in, 42–43; Head Start program in, 67, 163; integration in, 40–41; intellectual vs. emotional aspects of, 32; racism in, 30; relevance of, 31, 36, 39–42; residential segregation in, 123;

Federal Housing Administration (FHA), 136

federal spending: at Black colleges, 58–61; on day care programs, 44–49; on defense, 67–71, 130–31, 163; on drug programs, 106; on education, 31, 38, 67–68; on foreign aid, 83–88; on housing, 126, 128–32, 135; on prisons, 107; on Vietnam War, 68–70, 169

"Female Studies" (Tobias), 51

feminism: anti-feminism, 190, 209–10, 212, 214; Black intellectual tradition in, 5, 18–26; Chisholm's participation in, 22–23, 183; and civil rights movement, 51; minority women's experience missing in, 50; white, 22, 24. *See also* women's movement

FHA. *See* Federal Housing Administration

Finch, Robert, 68

"first asylum" cases, 142–44

"First Street School, The" (Dennison), 42

Fisk University, 62, 64

floor speeches. *See* congressional floor speeches

Florida, 3, 143, 145, 146

Floyd, George, 2

food aid, to Africa, 147–48

Ford, Gerald, 44–49, 158*fig.*

foreign aid, 83–88; to Africa, 93–97, 147–48; to Latin America, 85–86; to Middle East, 92; objectives of, 83; as percentage of gross national product, 85; presidential campaign position paper on restructuring of, 83–88

Foreign Aid Bill of 1971, 83

foreign policy, refugee policy in, 142, 149–50

France, 189

Franklin, John Hope, 30

Frazier, E. Franklin, 13, 73

freedmen, 73, 74

freedom: foreign aid in support of, 84–85; as goal of women's movement, 213–14; hypocrisy around talk of, 66, 70, 115, 251–52; integration and, 211; oppressed people's demands for, 12, 208; teachers' need for, 36–37; white misunderstandings of, 209–12

freedom fighters, Black women, 25–26

Fritchy, Clayton, 187–88

funding. *See* federal spending

Galamison, Milton, 8

Garvey, Marcus, 6

gender differences: in absenteeism rates, 175, 188; in income, 187; in traditional occupations, 173–75; in views on abortion, 197–98

gender discrimination. *See* sexism

gender roles, traditional, 173–77

gender stereotypes, 184, 195, 208, 210, 217, 227

General Accounting Office, U.S., 69

generation gap, 239–40

Geneva Conference on African Refugees (1981), 147–48

genocide, vs. abortion, 24, 197–98, 205

Geo (magazine), 143

68; education policy in, 31;
Judiciary Subcommittee on Civil
Rights, 111; number of women in,
185, 212. *See also specific laws and
members*

housing, 120–36; APHA standards
for, 133–34; average costs of, 123;
blockbusting in, 109, 122;
exclusionary zoning in, 125,
127–28, 132; mortgages in, 121, 123,
125, 126–27; presidential campaign
position paper on, 120–36;
property taxes on, 125–28, 135;
recommended next steps on,
134–36; rental, 121–24; residential
segregation in, 121–24, 128, 132–33;
suburban, 125, 127, 128; ways of
reducing costs of, 126–29; white,
problems with, 124–27. *See also*
ghettos

Housing Act of 1949, 120, 134
Housing and Urban Development
(HUD), U.S. Department of, 130,
132–33, 236
Housing and Urban Development
Act of 1968, 129
Howard University, "Progress
Through Understanding" speech
at, 12, 238–46
HUD. *See* Housing and Urban
Development
humanism: anti-humanism, 115, 214;
radical, 19, 25, 115
humanitarianism, in refugee policy,
144, 146
human rights, 237
Hunter-Gault, Charlayne, 25
hypocrisy, 66, 70, 115, 251–54

identity politics, 159
"I'd Rather Be Black Than Female"
(1970 article), 183, 193–96
"I Have a Dream" (King), 14
immigrants: as colonized people,
71–72, 74, 76; racial composition
of, 143; vs. refugees, 142–43
imperialism, in Barbados, 6
income: college degrees in relation
to, 56; gender gap in, 187
India, 192
Indiana Reformatory, 106
industrial education, 79
inferiority myth, 32
inflation, 68, 126–27, 166, 175
innovation, in education, 36
Institute for Afro-American Culture,
"The Black Woman in Contemporary America" speech at, 21–22,
214–22
Institute for Afro-American Studies,
55
institutional reform, need for,
240–46, 255–56
integration: freedom and, 211; in
higher education, 59–62; in public
schools, 40–41, 164–66. *See also*
busing
intellectual tradition, Black feminist,
5, 18–26
Inter-American Development Bank,
87
interdiction, 148–49
interdisciplinary scholarship, 51, 53
interest rates, mortgage, 125, 126–27
International Development
Association, 87
International Monetary Fund, 96

military, U.S.: drug abuse in, 105; federal spending on, 67–71, 130–31, 163; in foreign aid, 84–87; surveillance by, 112

Mills College, 11

minorities. *See* marginalized people; *specific groups*

missile defense system, 67–68

missionary schools, 77–78

Mississippi, 111–12

Mitchell, John, 132

Mitchell, Parren J., 153*fig.*

model cities, 130, 152

moderates, Southern, on education of Black Americans, 76–79

Mondale, Walter, 47–48

Morrison, Toni, 15

mortgages: average costs of, 123; interest rates on, 125, 126–27; racism in, 121

Moynihan, Daniel, 215

Mozambique, 94, 96

Mrs. label, 216, 226

Ms. label, 216, 226

Museum of the City of New York, 2

Muslims: in Arab–Israeli conflict, 88–92, 150; white, 208–9

NAACP, 117

Namibia, 94

NARAL, 23, 196–97, 200, 201

Nash, Diane, 217

National Association for the Advancement of Colored People. *See* NAACP

National Association for the Repeal of Abortion Laws. *See* NARAL

National Association of Educational Broadcasters, 140

National Conference of Christians and Jews (NCCJ), 117–18

National Congress of Black Women, 23, 230

National Council of Negro Women, 218; "Politics Is Every Black Woman's Business" speech at, 178–82

National Institute on Drug Abuse, 105–6

nationalism, Black, 16, 25

National Organization of Women (NOW), 23

National Science Teaching Association, "Necessity for a New Thrust in Education Today" speech at, 30–44

National Urban League (NUL), 117

National Women's Political Caucus, 23–24

Native Americans, as American captives, 82

native people, colonization of, 71–74, 76

NATO, 85, 96

NCCJ. *See* National Conference of Christians and Jews

"Necessity for a New Thrust in Education Today" (1973 speech), 30–44

neglect, benign, 93, 147

Negro Heritage Week, 55

"neighborhood schools," 165

Netflix, 1

New American Review (journal), 42

news industry: hiring practices of, 137–41; Nixon's harassment of, 103; posthumous coverage of Chisholm in, 1; sexism and racism in, 136–41

New York Amsterdam News (newspaper), 16, 176
New York City: Black and Hispanic population of, 225; political organization of Black women in, 219; white supremacy in politics of, 66. *See also* Brooklyn
New York Illustrated: The Irrepressible Shirley Chisholm (documentary), 258–59
New York Post (newspaper), 141
New York State, prisons in, 98, 99–100, 104, 106–7
New York State Assembly: abortion reform bills in, 196–97; Chisholm's first election to, 7, 194, 232; context of Chisholm's time in, 23; education policy in, 31
New York State Joint Legislative Committee on Crime, 107, 109
New York Times (newspaper), 1, 138
Nicaraguan refugees, 144
"9 Haiku" (Sanchez), 25–26
Nix, Robert N. C., Sr., 153*fig.*
Nixon, Richard: Africa policy of, 93–95; busing under, 111, 133, 165–66; Chisholm's presidential campaign announcement on, 168–72; criminal justice policies of, 98, 101–13; day care programs under, 46–47; defense spending under, 67, 70, 130–31, 163; foreign aid under, 85, 93; housing policy of, 121, 126, 130–33; and Middle East crisis, 91–92; OEO under, 163; in presidential elections, 133, 139, 252; school integration under, 164–66; Supreme Court nomina-

tions by, 103, 164, 166, 188; Vietnam War policy of, 163, 166–67, 241; voting rights under, 111–12, 164
No Knock tactics, 110
nonviolence, 117
Norton, Eleanor Holmes, 236
NOW. *See* National Organization of Women
nuclear families, 46
NUL. *See* National Urban League

Office of Economic Opportunity (OEO), 111, 162–63
Office of Federal Contract Compliance, 209–10
oil industry, 241
"On Busing Desegregation" (1971 speech), 10, 115, 118–20
"On Captive Nations Week" (1970 speech), 66, 81–82
open housing, 121, 132, 134
opportunity, lack of, role in poverty, 160
oppressed people: demands for freedom by, 12, 208; revolutions by, 207–14. *See also* marginalized people; *specific groups*
oral contraceptives, 203
oral tradition, Black, 8–9
oratorical style of Chisholm, 8–11, 257
Organization of African Unity, 94
organized crime, 109

pacifism, 69
Pakistan, 92
Palestinians, 90–92
pardons, presidential, 109

Powell, Adam Clayton, 8
Prairie View A&M Texas Southern
University, 62
Pratt, John H., 61
pregnancy: maternal mortality rates
in, 24-25, 199, 201, 205; unwanted,
204-5. *See also* abortion
"Presidential Campaign Announcement" (1972 speech), 159,
167-73
presidential campaign of Chisholm,
154-56*figs.*; announcement of, 159,
167-73; consistency of positions
in, 10; marginalized people as
focus of, 159; motivations for, 228;
public conflicts with Black
political elites in, 23; young
people's role in, 237
presidential campaign position
papers of Chisholm: on Africa,
93-97; on criminal justice, 98,
101-14; on foreign aid, 83-88; on
housing, 120-36; on Middle East,
88-92
presidential elections: of 1960, 139;
of 1968, 133, 248, 252; of 1972, 133;
of 2020, 2; of 2024, 2; Southern
Strategy in, 110-12, 166. *See also*
presidential campaign of
Chisholm
presidential pardons, 109
President's Committee on Urban
Housing, 129
President's Foreign Intelligence
Advisory Board, 143
press. *See* news industry
Pride, Inc., 69
principals, school, 35-36, 39

prisons: conditions in, 99-100,
106-7, 113; drug offenders in, 105;
federal spending on, 107; mass
incarceration in, 98; under Nixon,
102, 106-7; recommendations for,
113-14; riots in, 98, 99-100, 104,
106; sentencing in, 108, 109, 114
private police, 101
professional success, importance of
college degrees in, 55-56
"Progress Through Understanding"
(1969 speech), 12, 238-46
property taxes, 125-28, 135
public housing, 129, 130
public television, 140-41
public transportation, 124
Puerto Ricans: and abortion, 197,
205; as American captives, 82; in
community control of schools,
40-41
Purnell, Brian, 7

"Race, Revolution, and Women"
(1971 article), 205-14
racial segregation. *See* integration;
segregation
racial stereotypes, 184, 195, 210
racism, 115-50; as anti-humanism,
115; in double jeopardy of Black
women, 21-22, 25, 176, 217-18, 224;
in educational system, 30; in
employment, 174-78; future of,
184; harm to racists caused by,
210; invisibility of, 115, 119, 193;
Kerner Commission on, 70; in
news industry, 136-41; and
polarization, 116-18; in politics,
184, 190; in poverty, 161; in

education, 59–62; in public schools, 40–41, 164–66; residential, 121–24, 128, 132–33. *See also* integration
self-actualization, 32
self-determination, 6, 14, 84, 85
self-help organizations, 162–63
self-respect, 32
Senate, U.S.: on day care centers, 47; Labor and Public Welfare Committee, 106; number of women in, 185, 212; surveillance of members of, 112. *See also specific laws and members*
seniority system of Congress, 242
sentencing, 108, 109, 114
Seventeenth Assembly District, 7
sexism: as anti-humanism, 115; of Black men, 22, 25; in civil rights movement, 217; in double jeopardy of Black women, 21–22, 25, 176, 217–18, 224; in educational system, 30; in employment, 174–78, 184; in housing, 136; invisibility of, 193; in news industry, 136–41; in politics, 184, 190, 212; vs. racism, difficulty of navigating, 21–22, 193–96
sexual assault, 102
Shabazz, Betty, 25, 217
Sharpton, Al, 237
Shirley (film), 1
Shirley Chisholm Project, 5
Simon, Paul, 62
Simpson-Mazzoli Bill, 148
single-parent families, 46
Skinner, B. F., 43
slavery: end of, 74–75; freedom of white people in, 209; slaves as

colonized people, 72–75; status of Black women in, 220
slum clearance, 134–35. *See also* ghettos
Smith, Barbara, 19, 54
SNCC. *See* Student Nonviolent Coordinating Committee
social class. *See* class; middle class
social clubs, 7
social justice: in Civil War, 75; criminal justice in relation to, 112–13
social movements, women's role in building, 19. *See also specific movements*
social responsibility, corporate, 2–3
Social Security Act, 45, 48
social welfare programs, cost effectiveness of, 44–49
society, traditional gender roles in, 173–77
Soul on Ice (Cleaver), 206, 210–11
South, the: colonization of Black people in, 75–81; education of Black people in, 76–81; home rule in, 75–76; school integration in, 164–66
South Africa, 94, 96, 150
South Carolina, 61, 62, 165–66
South Carolina State University, 62
Southern Christian Leadership Conference (SCLC), 117
Southern Regional Education Board, 63
Southern Strategy, 110–12, 166
South Korea, 145
South Vietnam, 145
Soviet Union, 81, 91–92
space program, 131
Spain, 85, 87

Founded in 1893,
UNIVERSITY OF CALIFORNIA PRESS
publishes bold, progressive books and journals
on topics in the arts, humanities, social sciences,
and natural sciences—with a focus on social
justice issues—that inspire thought and action
among readers worldwide.

The UC PRESS FOUNDATION
raises funds to uphold the press's vital role
as an independent, nonprofit publisher, and
receives philanthropic support from a wide
range of individuals and institutions—and from
committed readers like you. To learn more, visit
ucpress.edu/supportus.